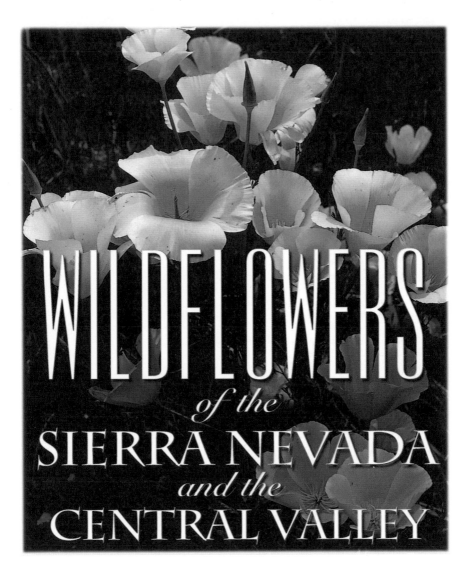

WILDFLOWERS

of the

SIERRA NEVADA

and the

CENTRAL VALLEY

Laird R. Blackwell

LONE
PINE

D0028364

© 1999 by Lone Pine Publishing
First printed in 1999   10 9 8 7 6 5 4 3 2
Printed in Canada
All rights reserved. No part of this work covered by the copyrights hereon may be reproduced or used in any form or by any means—graphic, electronic or mechanical—without the prior written permission of the publisher, except for reviewers, who may quote brief passages. Any request for photocopying, recording, taping or storage on information retrieval systems of any part of this work shall be directed in writing to the publisher.

The Publisher: Lone Pine Publishing

206, 10426 – 81 Ave.	202A, 1110 Seymour St.	1901 Raymond Ave. SW, Suite C
Edmonton, AB T6E 1X5	Vancouver, BC V6B 3N3	Renton, WA 98055
Canada	Canada	USA

Website: http://www.lonepinepublishing.com

Canadian Cataloguing in Publication Data

Blackwell, Laird R. (Laird Richard), 1945–
    Wildflowers of the Sierra Nevada and the Central Valley

    Includes bibliographical references and index.
    ISBN 1-55105-226-1

    1. Wildflowers—California—Central Valley (Valley)—
Identification. I. Title.
QK149.B52 1998   582.13'09794'5   C98-910682-9

Editorial Director: Nancy Foulds
Project Editor: Erin McCloskey
Technical Review: Joseph L. Medeiros
Production Manager: David Dodge
Layout & Production: Chris Taylor
Book Design: Rob Wiedemann, Michelle Bynoe, Chris Taylor
Cover Design: Rob Wiedemann
Illustrations: Linda Kershaw, p. 42. Joseph L. Medeiros, p. 288. Used by permission.
Photography: Laird R. Blackwell
Cartography: Volker Bodegom
Scanning & Film: Creative Edge
Code: 04

The publisher acknowledges the support of the Department of Canadian Heritage.

Contents

Dedication

For Melinda, my partner and soulmate in love and adventure.

Acknowledgments

Thanks to my colleagues and students at Sierra Nevada College who have inspired and supported me over the years in my teaching and writing.

Thanks to my mother who got me interested in wildflowers in the first place, and to my fellow mountain creatures who share my love for the wilds.

Special gratitude to the people of Lone Pine Publishing who have been such supportive, gracious, and wise partners in the production of these wildflower books. Special thanks to Nancy Foulds and Erin McCloskey for their careful and professional editing. I can't imagine better publishers to work with.

And heart-felt gratitude to Joe Medeiros, professor of Botany at Sierra College, for his careful reading and critiquing of this book. I didn't take all his suggestions, though, so don't blame him!

QUICK KEY TO FLOWERS

CENTRAL VALLEY–FOOTHILLS   (0–2500') — grouped by elevation
3 or 6 petals: *White*

color and number of petals (flowers may appear under more than one elevation and/or petal color)

flower name and page number

Fremont's camas
p. 49

color represents flower family in this book

CENTRAL VALLEY–FOOTHILLS   (0–2500')

3 or 6 petals: *White*

| Fremont's camas p. 49 | Globe lily p. 50 | White fritillary p. 52 | Hyacinth brodiaea p. 66 | Glassy onion p. 70 |

Yellow/Orange

| Paper onion p. 70 | Common muilla p. 71 | Matilija poppy p. 98 | Dwarf hespero-chiron p. 131 | Gold nuggets p. 51 |

Red/Pink

| Yellow pussy ears p. 51 | Pretty face p. 73 | Cream cups p. 97 | Glassy onion p. 70 | Twining snake lily p. 72 |

Blue/Purple

| Tolmie's pussy ears p. 50 | Camas lily p. 53 | Ithuriel's spear p. 65 | Blue dick p. 67 | Wild hyacinth p. 68 |

5

4 petals: *White*

Harvest brodiaea
p. 69

Lacepod
p. 81

Shiny peppergrass
p. 82

Shepherd's purse
p. 82

Wild radish
p. 83

Yellow/Orange

Milkmaids
p. 85

Watercress
p. 87

Field mustard
p. 83

Tropidocarpum
p. 84

Western wallflower
p. 90

Red/Pink   ***Blue/Purple***

California poppy
p. 95

Caespitose poppy
p. 95

Frying pans
p. 96

Wild radish
p. 83

Shieldleaf
p. 89

5 petals: *White*

Chinese houses
p. 145

American brooklime
p. 164

Mouse-ear chick-
weed p. 103

Meadow chickweed
p. 103

California sandwort
p. 104

Common catchfly
p. 105

Foothill saxifrage
p. 112

Fringed woodland
star p. 113

Smooth woodland
star p. 113

Foothill phacelia
p. 125

Caterpillar phacelia p. 126

Varied-leaf phacelia p. 127

Varied-leaf nemophila p. 128

Dwarf hespero-chiron p. 131

Valley tassels p. 149

Cream sacs p. 149

Douglas pogogyne p. 173

Skullcap p. 177

Needle navarettia p. 189

Mustang clover p. 192

Globe gilia p. 193

Whorled lupine p. 216

Bowl clover p. 227

Aquatic buttercup p. 237

Waterfall buttercup p. 238

Yellow/Orange

Western rue-anemone p. 239

Miner's lettuce p. 253

Dwarf cliff sedum p. 136

Pacific sedum p. 137

Live-forever p. 138

Butter-and-eggs p. 147

Yellow-and-white monkeyflower p. 153

Bush monkeyflower p. 153

Floriferous monkey-flower p. 156

Common monkey-flower p. 159

Grand collomia
p. 194

Hill lotus
p. 218

Scotch broom
p. 223

Torrey's lotus
p. 224

Western buttercup
p. 237

Red/Pink

Wild carnation
p. 102

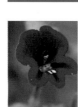

California Indian
pink p. 106

Pansy monkey-
flower p. 146

Purple owl's clover
p. 148

Douglas monkey-
flower p. 151

Small-flowered mon-
keyflower p. 151

Kellogg's monkey-
flower p. 152

Bolander's monkey-
flower p. 152

Indian warrior
p. 154

Applegate's
paintbrush p. 155

Giant red
paintbrush p. 155

Clasping henbit
p. 172

Whitestem
hedgenettle p. 175

Horse-mint
p. 178

Bird's eye gilia
p. 188

Slender phlox
p. 190

Showy phlox
p. 191

Mustang clover
p. 192

Tiny trumpet
p. 195

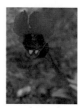

Staining collomia
p. 195

Whisker brush
p. 196

Baby stars
p. 196

Canchalagua
p. 204

Tangier pea
p. 219

Spring vetch
p. 220

Balloon clover
p. 221

Bearded clover
p. 222

Tomcat clover
p. 222

Redbud
p. 223

Harlequin lupine
p. 225

Blue/Purple

Western rue-
anemone p. 239

Red larkspur
p. 240

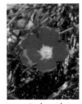

Red maid
p. 254

Baby blue-eyes
p. 123

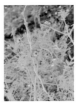

Blue fiesta flower
p. 124

Mariposa phacelia
p. 125

Chinese houses
p. 145

Foothill penstemon
p. 150

Chia
p. 174

Self-heal
p. 176

Toothed downingia
p. 182

Fringed downingia
p. 182

Folded downingia
p. 183

2-horned downingia
p. 183

Bird's eye gilia
p. 188

Globe gilia
p. 193

Canchalagua
p. 204

Douglas lupine
p. 213

Valley lupine
p. 214

Miniature lupine
p. 214

Succulent lupine
p. 215

Spider lupine
p. 216

Bush lupine
p. 217

Beautiful lupine
p. 217

Winter vetch
p. 220

Varying number of petals: *White*

Yellow/Orange

Royal larkspur
p. 235

Slender larkspur
p. 240

Wooly marbles
p. 266

Pearly everlasting
p. 270

Sacramento Valley
buttercup p. 236

Tidy tips
p. 263

Goldfield
p. 264

Common tarweed
p. 265

Blennosperma
p. 266

Brass buttons
p. 267

Red/Pink

Blue/Purple

Common senecio
p. 268

Pineapple weed
p. 268

Bitterroot
p. 255

California thistle
p. 267

Sierra lessingia
p. 269

LOW MONTANE–HIGH MONTANE–ALPINE (2500–13,000')

3 or 6 petals: *White*

Plain leaf fawn lily
p. 54

Washington lily
p. 57

Corn lily
p. 59

Sand corm
p. 60

Death camas
p. 60

Lesser star tulip
p. 61

Leichtlin's mariposa
lily p. 61

Hyacinth brodiaea
p. 66

Paper onion
p. 70

Common muilla
p. 71

Yellow/Orange

Red sierra onion
p. 77

Prickly poppy
p. 99

Dwarf hespero-
chiron p. 131

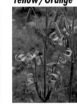
Leopard lily
p. 56

Tiger lily
p. 57

Red/Pink

Purple fritillary
p. 58

Davidson's fritillary
p. 58

Pretty face
p. 73

Scarlet fritillary
p. 55

Swamp onion
p. 74

Blue/Purple

Sierra onion
p. 74

Three-bracted onion
p. 75

Flat-stemmed onion
p. 76

Camas lily
p. 53

Ithuriel's spear
p. 65

11

4 petals: *White*

| Harvest brodiaea p. 69 | Shiny peppergrass p. 82 | Shepherd's purse p. 82 | Brewer's bittercress p. 86 | Watercress p. 87 |

Yellow/Orange

| Deer's tongue p. 208 | Pussypaws p. 259 | Tahoe yellow cress p. 87 | American winter-cress p. 88 | Mountain tansy mustard p. 88 |

Red/Pink

Western wallflower p. 90 | Lemmon's draba p. 91 | California poppy p. 95 | Rosy sedum p. 141 | Northern gentian p. 207

Blue/Purple

| Pussypaws p. 259 | Shieldleaf p. 89 | American brooklime p. 164 | Alpine veronica p. 164 | Torrey's blue-eyed mary p. 168 |

5 petals: *White*

| Sierra gentian p. 205 | Hiker's gentian p. 206 | Mouse ear chickweed p. 103 | Meadow chickweed p. 103 | California sandwort p. 104 |

Mountain chickweed
p. 107

Douglas catchfly
p. 108

King's sandwort
p. 109

Foothill saxifrage
p. 112

Fringed woodland
star p. 113

Smooth woodland
star p. 113

Rock star
p. 114

Brewer's mitrewort
p. 115

Pink alumroot
p. 116

Fringed grass-of-
Parnassus p. 117

Smooth grass-of-
Parnassus p. 117

Brook saxifrage
p. 118

Bog saxifrage
p. 118

Tolmie's saxifrage
p. 119

Sierra saxifrage
p. 119

Varied-leaf phacelia
p. 127

Varied-leaf
nemophila p. 128

Mitten-leaf
nemophila p. 129

California hespero-
chiron p. 131

Dwarf hespero-
chiron p. 131

Timberline phacelia
p. 133

Hot-rock penstemon
p. 163

Alpine paintbrush
p. 166

Skullcap
p. 177

Pennyroyal
p. 179

Mustang clover
p. 192

Globe gilia
p. 193

Ballhead gilia
p. 198

Spreading phlox
p. 199

Coville's phlox
p. 199

Granite gilia
p. 200

Alpine gentian
p. 209

Long-stalked clover
p. 226

Shasta clover
p. 226

Carpet clover
p. 227

Bowl clover
p. 227

White lupine
p. 229

Whitney's locoweed
p. 231

Aquatic buttercup
p. 237

Waterfall buttercup
p. 238

Western rue-
anemone p. 239

Alpine columbine
p. 248

Miner's lettuce
p. 253

Toad lily
p. 258

Narrow-leaved
montia p. 258

Yellow/Orange

Lemmon's catchfly
p. 108

Pacific sedum
p. 137

Sierra stonecrop
p. 139

Narrow-leaf
stonecrop p. 140

Yellow-and-white
monkeyflower p. 153

Bush monkeyflower
p. 153

Primrose monkey-
flower p. 156

Floriferous monkey-
flower p. 156

Mountain monkey-
flower p. 159

Common monkey-
flower p. 159

Hairy owl's-clover
p. 165

Grand collomia
p. 194

Hill lotus
p. 218

Torrey's lotus
p. 224

Yellow lupine
p. 229

Pink/Red

Western buttercup
p. 237

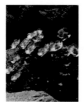
Alpine buttercup
p. 249

Wild carnation
p. 102

California Indian
pink p. 106

Rock star
p. 114

Pink alumroot
p. 116

Small-flowered
monkeyflower p. 151

Bolander's monkey-
flower p. 152

Indian warrior
p. 154

Applegate's
paintbrush p. 155

Giant red
paintbrush p. 155

Scarlet monkey-
flower p. 157

Lewis monkeyflower
p. 158

Scarlet penstemon
p. 160

Mountain pride
p. 161

15

Copeland's owl's-clover p. 165

Lemmon's paintbrush p. 166

Little elephantheads p. 167

Bull elephant's head p. 167

Whitestem hedge-nettle p. 175

Horse-mint p. 178

Pennyroyal p. 179

Slender phlox p. 190

Showy phlox p. 191

Mustang clover p. 192

Bridge's gilia p. 193

Tiny trumpet p. 195

Staining collomia p. 195

Whisker brush p. 196

Baby stars p. 196

Scarlet gilia p. 198

Spreading phlox p. 199

Coville's phlox p. 199

Spring vetch p. 220

Harlequin lupine p. 225

Long stalked clover p. 226

Shasta clover p. 226

Crimson columbine p. 247

Red maids p. 254

Narrow-leaved montia p. 258

Blue/Purple

Mariposa phacelia
p. 125

Low phacelia
p. 127

California waterleaf
p. 130

Star lavender
p. 130

Ballhead phacelia
p. 132

Showy penstemon
p. 161

Meadow penstemon
p. 162

Gay penstemon
p. 162

Torrey's blue-eyed
mary p. 168

Alpine penstemon
p. 169

Self-heal
p. 176

Bacigalupi's
downingia p. 184

Porterella
p. 185

Globe gilia
p. 193

Low polemonium
p. 197

Great polemonium
p. 197

Sky pilot
p. 201

Showy polemonium
p. 201

Explorer's gentian
p. 209

Bush lupine
p. 217

Beautiful lupine
p. 217

Broad-leaf lupine
p. 228

Torrey's lupine
p. 228

Brewer's lupine
p. 230

Slender larkspur
p. 240

17

QUICK KEY

Varying number of petals: *White*

Monkshood
p. 243

Glaucous larkspur
p. 244

Marsh marigold
p. 242

Drummond's
anemone p. 245

Fendler's meadow-
rue p. 246

Three-leaf lewisia
p. 256

Nevada lewisia
p. 257

Pussypaws
p. 259

Wooly marbles
p. 266

Pearly everlasting
p. 270

Yellow/Orange

Rosy pussytoes
p. 270

Coulter's daisy
p. 274

Drummond's thistle
p. 276

Yarrow
p. 277

Sacramento Valley
buttercup p. 236

Water-plantain
buttercup p. 241

Fendler's
meadowrue p. 246

Common senecio
p. 268

Mule ears
p. 271

Balsamroot
p. 271

Biglow's
sneezeweed p. 273

California
coneflower p. 273

Heartleaf arnica
p. 275

Soft arnica
p. 275

Orange mountain
dandelion p. 278

18

Red/Pink

| Shaggy hawkweed p. 278 | Silky raillardella p. 280 | Alpine gold p. 281 | Bitterroot p. 255 | Pussypaws p. 259 |

Blue/Purple

| California thistle p. 267 | Anderson's thistle p. 276 | Western eupatorium p. 279 | Sierra lessingia p. 269 | Leafy-headed aster p. 272 |

| Wandering daisy p. 274 | Dwarf alpine daisy p. 281 |

Introduction

California is world renowned for its wildflowers: with environments ranging from ocean beach, prairie grassland, and oak savanna to coniferous forest, alpine tundra, and cold and hot desert, California boasts over 5000 species of native plants and another 1000 or so 'aliens' that have been introduced. If you exclude the deserts and just consider the 'California Floristic Province' (those areas of California and small areas of southwestern Oregon, northern Baja, and western Nevada that extend west of the crest of the north-south running Sierra Nevada-Cascade ranges), there are still almost 5000 species of vascular plants (including over 4100 species of natives). This is considerably more than the number of species in the entire central and northeast United States and adjoining parts of Canada—an area 10 times larger!

alpine columbine

The flora of the California Floristic Province (CA-FP) is also remarkable for its high percentage of endemics: almost 50% of the CA-FP natives grow nowhere else in the world! This is an extremely high percentage for a continental area, but with its highly specialized environments and forbidding high mountain and desert eastern border, the CA-FP is very like an island—in space and in time. It's exciting to know that many flowers of this island occur only here—you have to come to high mountain ridges in the Sierra to experience that gorgeous creamy-white alpine columbine; you have to find a drying vernal pool in the Central Valley or bordering foothills to encounter that charming blue downingia.

toothed downingia

Despite the great numbers of endemics, still about 50% of the native species of this island apparently can (or could) 'swim,' for they are found here and also at great distances from California—in the Rockies and across to eastern America, in northern Europe, Africa, and South America. It is exciting, and somehow comforting, to find an old Sierra friend, like the delicate blue alpine veronica, nestled in a meadow in the Swiss Alps!

alpine veronica

We are truly blessed with the California flora, with its great diversity of species and large numbers of endemics, and also with its stunning floral displays: hillsides ablaze with solid masses of color; mountain meadows thick with grasses and floral jewels; rock ledges and boulder fields strewn with bright lichen and brighter plants; cold, windswept alpine ridges matted with prostrate miniature gardens.

In so many places, you find great masses of flowers, symphonies of colors, hours of delight. But probably the most spectacular of all the CA-FP floral displays are the spring gardens of the Central Valley grasslands and adjoining foothills: although urbanization, agriculture, and grazing over the last century or so have greatly diminished what used to be solid wildflowers for as far as the eye could see, a few remnants of this incredible floral 'sea' still remain—enough to thrill us with the glory of what's left (and a fierce determination to preserve it) and to fill us with nostalgic fantasies of the past.

hillside of flowers

One of the great gifts of living in or near the Sierra is being able to follow the amazing wildflower blooming as it moves up the slopes and through the seasons. In February, March, and April, when winter snow still lies (and flies) thick and heavy up in the high mountains and you feel a craving for color and new life, you can with a few hours travel be born again with the lush greens and intense flower colors of the rolling foothills and Central Valley 'prairie.'

In July and August, when the lowlands have long since forgotten any color but scorched brown, you can climb up to the mild, blue-sky summer days of the upper mountains and revel again in all the wildflower color and vibrant life.

alpine miniature garden

Although autumn and winter are spectacular and enjoyable in their own rights and have their own essential parts to play in the cycles of life, we can—with a little knowledge, planning, and travel—enjoy the colors and vitality of spring and summer for at least seven months of the year! So come along with me and follow the flowers from sea level in the Central Valley to the tops of the peaks of the high Sierra, from the first glimmerings of spring in February and March in the Valley to the last gasps of summer in September in the high mountains.

Central Valley floral display

foothill flowers   high mountain wildflower meadow

21

Organization of the Book and Areas Covered

Five elevational zones are used in this book. There are numerous ways to conceptualize and delineate the major environments for plants in California: geographic subdivisions, life zones, vegetative types or forms, plant communities, etc. I have focused here on elevations, since I encourage you to observe the blooming of the flowers as it progresses up the Sierra western slope like a slow tide with the passing months. The five elevational zones (with their relationship to some other methods of delineation) are:

CENTRAL VALLEY: 0–300'
'California Prairie' in Barbour and Major (1977)

FOOTHILLS: 300–2500'
'Blue Oak-Digger Pine Forest' in Barbour and Major (1977)

LOW MONTANE: 2500–6500'
combines 'Sierran Yellow Pine'
     and 'Sierra Montane Forest' in Barbour and Major (1977)
Yellow Pine Belt
Transitional Life Zone

MID TO HIGH MONTANE: 6500–10,500'
'Upper Montane-Subalpine Forests' in Barbour and Major (1977)
combines Red Fir Belt and Subalpine Belt
combines Canadian and Hudsonian Life Zones

ALPINE: 10,500–13,000'*
'Alpine' in Barbour and Major (1977)
Alpine Belt
Arctic-Alpine Life Zone

*Although there are several California peaks over 14,000', Mt. Dana at 13,053' is the highest peak in the area covered by this book.

The elevational ranges of the zones are, of course, approximate and can vary by 1000' or more depending on whether you are in the northern or southern areas. This book covers only the central and northern Sierra from Yosemite to the northern boundary of the Sierra where the Cascades begin with Mt. Lassen. The part of the Sierra south of Yosemite is not included.

On the east-west dimension, the book covers most of the California Floristic Province from the Central Valley (the Sacramento Valley and the northern part of the San Joaquin Valley) east into the foothills and on up to the top of the Sierra (and to the adjoining Carson Range in the Tahoe area). The coastal ranges and the Pacific beaches to the west of the Central Valley are not covered.

This map shows the approximate locations covered in this book of the five elevational zones.

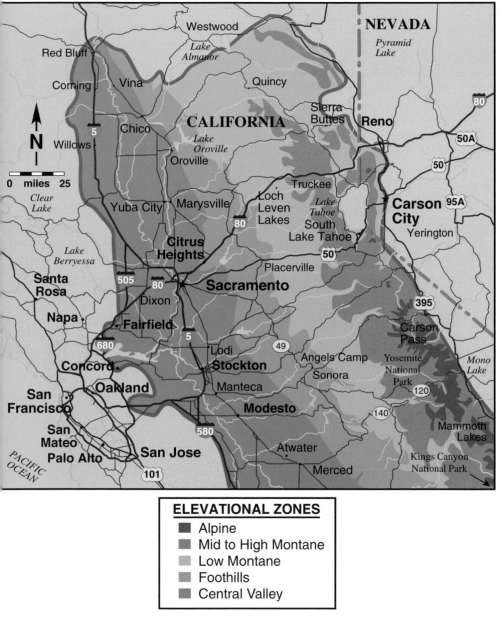

ELEVATIONAL ZONES
- Alpine
- Mid to High Montane
- Low Montane
- Foothills
- Central Valley

Each elevational zone is discussed with photos that show characteristics and typical floral displays. Also, several special areas (with particularly great flower displays) in each zone are described in more detail.

23

The species accounts are divided into sections by families (17 of the most interesting and most likely to be encountered). It has been my experience over 20 years of teaching wildflower field courses that by far the easiest way to learn to identify and know flowers is by first learning families. If you understand the characteristics that typify a family, you will know what to look for in a flower, which will make identification much easier and will help you understand the flower's structure and function and its 'personality'—how it lives its life and how it is connected to other flowers and other factors in its environment. If you know families, you will have a big head start on knowing any flower anywhere.

For each family, there is first an introduction describing its characteristics, local and global distribution, major genera, etc. Then, on the following pages, flowers of that family are presented with names, descriptions, anecdotes, and photos. Scientific names are those used by the most recent *California Plant Manual* (Jepson, 1993). When these names are recent changes, the older names are also included. The flowers within each family are sequenced by elevational zone, moving up from the Central Valley to the highest peaks. When a flower occurs in more than one elevational zone, all zones in its range are indicated at the top of the page.

Elevational ranges of the zones and locations of plants can vary somewhat depending on latitude and on local conditions. It should therefore be recognized that the numbers given are approximations.

member of the Snapdragon family

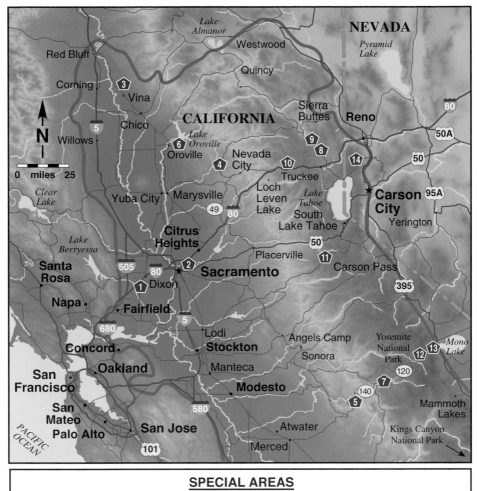

SPECIAL AREAS

Central Valley
1 Jepson Prairie
2 Phoenix Park
3 Vina Preserve

Foothills
4 Independence Trail
5 Hite's Cove Trail
6 Table Mountain

Lower Montane
7 Yosemite Valley
8 Sagehen Creek
9 Kyburz Flat

Mid to High Montane
10 Castle Peak
11 Winnemucca Lake Trail
12 Tuolumne Meadows

Alpine
13 Tioga Crest and Mt. Dana
14 Mt. Rose

How to Use this Book

There are several ways you might use this book to identify and to get to know a flower you come across.

1) Use the 'quick and easy' pictorial guide at the beginning of the book (within each elevational zone flowers are sequenced by number of petals and color). When you think you've found your flower in the index, turn to its photo and description on the indicated page.

2) If you think you know the family and/or the genus of the flower, look at the family-genus index or the scientific name index and turn to the appropriate pages to check the photo and description.

3) Skim through the photographs in the book until you find the flower.

4) Read each flower description (with photo) until you find the flower.

5) Study the introductions to the families in Part II to discover the characteristics of the families and to appreciate the commonalities and the diversity of the flowers within those families. When you think you know your flower's family, leaf through the pages in that section.

6) Study the entire book before you go out in the field.

However you use the book, you can use it for at least seven months of the year as you follow the flowers through elevational zones and seasons:

CENTRAL VALLEY	late February, March, and April
FOOTHILLS	March, April, and May
LOWER MONTANE	April, May, June, and July
MID TO HIGH MONTANE	June, July, and August
ALPINE	July, August, and early September.

Of course, each elevational zone has its own seasons. The months indicated are the times when the most flowers will be in bloom in that zone. Some other flowers may bloom later as that zone moves into its autumn; in a few cases some very 'precocious' flowers may bloom earlier than the indicated times.

CAUTION: When you walk among the flowers, do so carefully and respectfully; do not pick any flowers. Images of fresh, living flowers in your mind are far more satisfying than bouquets of shriveled flowers in your hand.

Elevational Zones

Central Valley (0–300')

'The great Central Plain of California, during the months of March, April, and May, was one smooth, continuous bed of honey bloom, so marvelously rich that, in walking from one end of it to the other, a distance of more than 400 miles, your foot would press about a hundred flowers at every step...all the ground was covered, not with grass and green leaves, but with radiant corollas, about ankle-deep next to the foothills, knee-deep or more five or six miles out...sauntering in any direction, hundreds of these happy sun-plants brushed against my feet at every step, and closed over them as if I were wading in liquid gold.'

John Muir, *The Mountains of California*

Central Valley wildflower garden

Few environments have undergone such radical change as has the Central Valley in the last 100 years. Agriculture, grazing, housing developments, and industrialization have all taken their toll on the great grassland prairies. Now only a few traces remain of what was once a spectacular wildflower 'sea.'

But some of these traces are glorious, reminding us of what once was and strengthening our resolve to preserve what still is. And they need our help, for many remaining areas are rapidly shrinking and disappearing as roads are widened, ground is plowed under, pavement is laid. Most vestiges of the great wildflower prairies are now behind fences. Much is private property, and some are environmental preserves (mostly Nature Conservancy and United States Fish & Wildlife Service [USFWS] national wildlife refuges).

flowers behind fence

Though the fabulous wildflower seas are largely gone, by visiting the preserves and by slowly wandering backcountry Central Valley roads, you can still see many flowers and get some feel for the magnificent displays that once were. You can still find grasslands with solid patches of goldfield*, lupine*, red maid*, Ithuriel's spear*, fiddleneck, and butter-and-eggs*. You can still find creeks bordered by throngs of buttercups*. You can even still find an occasional vernal pool with its amazing, specialized flowers—meadowfoam ringing its edges, and downingia*, clover*, and navarettia* covering its drying floor.

When winter has lingered long enough, when the calendar and your thoughts turn to spring, come to the Central Valley and explore its wildflower wonders and awaken a dormant part of yourself.

* indicates flowers described and illustrated in this book.

meadowfoam (*Limanthes douglasii*)

27

backroad flowers

Central Valley grassland

Central Valley treasures

Where to See the Flowers

Explore narrow country roads that meander through the less developed parts of the Central Valley; most flower fields will be behind livestock fences, but they are still beautiful. Try roads like Routes 140, 20, 32, and 36 as they ascend from Central Valley towns toward the foothills; explore backcountry roads like J9 and J16 between Merced and Sacramento or more major highways like Routes 149 and 99 near Chico.

Visit the Nature Conservancy's Jepson Prairie Preserve outside Dixon and Phoenix Park in Sacramento to see some remarkable flowers of native grasslands and vernal pools: the rare white fritillary*, Cleveland's shooting star, muilla*, hyacinth brodeaia*, elegant brodeaia*, violet, gold nuggets*, and several species of those fascinating *Downingia* (e.g., *cuspidata*, *bicornata*, *ornatissima*, *concolor*). Visit (with a docent) Vina Preserve north of Chico to get an idea of the Central Valley that John Muir wrote about with its flat fields thick with goldfield*, butter-and-eggs*, and meadowfoam.

Starting in late February and early March, the flowers begin to emerge, the colors awaken, the 'tide' of wildflower blooming begins to cover the slopes of the Sierra to culminate in August and even September on the highest peaks. Although by March and April you can visit the awakening flowers in the foothills, it is well worth returning at intervals (of perhaps every two weeks) well into May to your favorite Central Valley treasures, for as the early bloomers fade and go to seed, late bloomers arrive to take their place.

As you look out over a field splotched with goldfield*, tidytip*, and lupine* and dotted with occasional white shooting star and dark blue larkspur*, as you kneel by a drying vernal pool and delight in the meadowfoam, clover*, and downingia*, imagine the glorious displays as far as the eye could see in the days of Muir but be thankful and grateful for what remains— reminders of our past and of our responsibilities to perpetuate and nourish beauty into our future.

Foothills (300–2500')

In late February and early March when the colors of spring are beginning to sprinkle the Central Valley grasslands, a little higher up in the Sierra foothills the muted greens of winter begin to shine with a new vitality. Although there are a few early wildflowers already blooming here (e.g., foothill shooting star, rue-anemone*, foothill saxifrage*), the explosion of spring palettes the foothills are renowned for is still a few weeks away.

Even without all their flowers yet in bloom, these voluptuous, rich green, softly curving hills seem to soothe and lift your soul (especially for people escaping for a day or so from the winter of the higher mountains), but the wild eruption of color soon to arrive like a 'tide' surging up from the Central Valley will blow your mind.

In mid-March and April, the 'tide' of color arrives and foothill blooming reaches its peak—in some places the hills are so vibrant and thick with flowers that you almost need sunglasses to look at them. Poppy*, goldfield*, blue dick*, purple owl's-clover*, fiddleneck, lupine*, cream cups*—the rolling hills are draped with fields of sunshine and rainbows.

rolling green hills

But the spectacular gardens are not limited to these open, sun-drenched fields. Even in the deep shade of those marvelous, gnarly oaks you can find glorious wildflower gardens dense with color—Chinese houses*, Indian pink*, nemophila*, fiesta flower*.

Although some new flowers will come to the foothills in May, the solid masses of color will last only a few weeks, usually from mid-March to mid-April, then they will fade as the 'tide' moves on and up to higher elevations.

poppies

Where to See the Flowers

Take long, leisurely drives on those wonderful backroads winding through the foothills—Route 49 is the most renowned and is perfectly numbered for your search for spring 'gold.' Several west-east routes (e.g., Routes 140, 120, 32, and 36) coming off the main north-south Central Valley thoroughfares (Routes 5 and 99) take you gently up into the foothill flowers and are well worth exploring.

Chinese houses

29

backroad flowers

As you leave the Central Valley and its fences below you, you will still encounter many wildflower displays behind fences (mostly grazing land), but you will also find some open places beckoning you to explore on foot. Two of the most spectacular wildflower trails in California are in the foothills—one clinging to the forested slopes above the south fork of the Yuba River (Independence Trail off Route 49 between Nevada City and North San Juan) and the other perched precariously on a sun-beaten hillside swarming with masses of flowers above the south fork of the Merced River off Route 140 just a few miles west of Yosemite (Hite's Cove Trail).

On Independence Trail (at about 1200'), which in places consists of elaborately constructed bridges clinging to the steep hillside, you will encounter some extremely interesting flowers of primarily shaded slopes: pacific sedum* with its remarkable round-leaf rosettes, showy phlox*, saxifrage, rue-anemone*, and clusters of Indian pink*. Though you won't find solid hillsides of flowers on this trail, you will find a great variety of intriguing plants that change as the season progresses.

Hite's Cove Trail

In a good year Hite's Cove Trail is one of the most glorious floral displays anywhere: the narrow trail winds precariously up and down the south-facing slope above the river in places partly shaded, in places intersected by creeks, but for the most part completely exposed to the blazing sun.

You will walk through solid masses of oranges, purples, whites, and lavenders...hillsides thick with poppy*, bird's eye gilia*, fiddleneck, blue dick*, purple owl's-clover*, Chinese houses*, nemophila*, miniature lupine*, and goldfield* interspersed with Indian pink*, harlequin lupine*, red maid*, woodland star*, baby blue eyes*, wild ginger, live-forever*, and cream cups*, and at stream crossings, waterfall buttercup*, rue-anemone*, monkeyflower*, and saxifrage*. Hite's Cove is a truly remark-able place that everyone should experience at least once, and even better, year after year. I've been visiting it for over 20 years now, and each

Hite's Cove flowers

year is memorable for its own distinct displays and its own color scheme. Some years it's almost solid yellows and oranges, other years it's blues and pinks. (Be sure to sign in at Savage's Trading Post before you start your hike.)

In a few places in our area you can find the 'foothills' plunked down right in the middle of the Central Valley. In Sutter Buttes and especially on Table Mountain outside Oroville, volcanic buttes and mesas rise abruptly from the Central Valley grasslands to 1500'.

Both places are difficult to access but in different ways. You can only enter the rolling slopes of Sutter Buttes with a guide. There *is* a public road that winds up Table Mountain, but most of the mountain is behind private fences. But drive up Table Mountain at the right time in a good year and you will see an amazing display. Above the slopes of Ithuriel's spear*, globe lily*, iris, and glassy onion* you will find the tabletop 'spray painted' with coats of goldfield*, parvisedum*, lupine*, and meadowfoam. And if you're lucky, you will find the incredibly large and showy bitterroot*.

And most amazing are the vernal pools created by the hardpan of volcanic rock. As the winter water slowly evaporates, these pools become 'ponds' of blossoms, miniature color-coded topographic maps of flowers delineating micro-changes (in inches) in ground contours: goldfield*, blennosperma*, white shooting star, clover*, veronica, plantain, violets, monkeyflower*, and several species of those wonderful and endearing downingia*.

Even from the road the display is stunning—flats so bright and solid with color that they must be beacons for birds and insects flying hundreds of feet overhead. Don't miss Table Mountain in late March: it will dazzle your days and brighten your memories for months afterwards!

Sutter Buttes

Table Mountain flowers

31

Low Montane (3000–6500')

As April turns to May, the glorious wildflower displays of the foothills are rapidly drying up. There are, of course, some flowers that are only now beginning to bloom in the foothills (e.g., blazing star, soaplily, clarkia), but the massive fields of color move up to higher elevations, where they are eagerly awaited by us 'wintered-out' mountain dwellers. It's a wonderful gift to be able to travel down to the Central Valley and foothills to see flowers in the middle of a long mountain winter, but there's something even more deeply satisfying and thrilling to experience the wildflower 'tide' surging to meet you at your own home.

As you climb up the western slope of the Sierra out of the foothills and into the lower mountains, the oaks and Douglas-fir gradually diminish to be replaced by dense forests of ponderosa pine, lodgepole pine, and white fir. Some fascinating plants occur in these forests, but the most spectacular wildflower displays at these elevations are probably the large, open meadows often wound through with meandering streams or dotted with ponds or small lakes.

In late April or more commonly in May, these meadows begin to stir with the first signs of spring. Among the first to bloom along the edges of the meadows—still damp from recently melted snow, but quickly drying out—are such dazzlers as Beckwith violet, star lavender *, and dandelion (with its bright and cheery flower). Out in the wetter parts of the meadow an explosion of color is on the way: masses of water-plantain buttercup* sprinkled with patches of marsh marigold*, elephant's head*, shooting star (primrose family), and perhaps Sierra rein orchid*.

camas lily field

But probably the most stunning May display in the low mountains is the 'sea' of deep blue-purple camas lily*, often interwoven with the intriguing and aromatic dirty socks*. If you're lucky or well informed (or both), you will discover wet meadows (very wet meadows) filled with acres of this magnificent flower. Take a picnic (and galoshes!) and enjoy this spring gift; it will lift your spirits and remind you of all the joys of spring and summer to come.

The low montane zone covers a wide elevational range (from 3000–6500') and so will be in bloom (at some elevation) for quite some time. But even at the upper limits of this zone you can find blooming from April/May right on through July. Most early bloomers (like camas lily) will dry up within a couple weeks, but then many other species will emerge in this hospitable environment. In this regard, the low montane elevations are different from the Central Valley and the foothills where the blooming season is relatively short. At these lower elevations, the rains of winter and early spring are usually followed by months of blazing hot, bone-dry weather, so the conditions are too harsh for most flowers after April or early May—most flowers (predominantly annuals) appear at nearly the same time and go through their blooming, pollination, and seeding very quickly (in many cases in only a few weeks).

In contrast, as you move higher out of the foothills and into the low montane elevations, spring and summer aren't so hot and dry—the heavy winter snows of the higher reaches of this zone provide a steady water source, at least for a while, as they slowly melt. These conditions are more conducive for a longer blooming season (both for individual plants and for a sequence of different species in one location). Return repeatedly to these low montane meadows and woods from May through July or August and discover some new wildflower delight each time.

Where to See the Flowers

You will encounter many spectacular meadows as you take some major west-east routes up into the Sierra. Routes 140, 120, 108, 4, 88, 49 (as it turns east toward Yuba Pass), 70, 32, and 36 will all take you up out of the foothill oak woodlands into the pine and fir forests of the low montane. You will pass some beautiful meadows along the roads and can take some trails that lead to wonderful wildflower areas. Route 80, though a bit too fast and too developed for much roadside wildflower viewing, passes by Loch Leven Trail with its dazzling June display of fawn-lily*.

field of onions where earlier there were camas lilies

Yosemite Valley

Route 140, which takes you to some of the best foothill flowers in March and April (see Hite's Cove Trail description, pp. 30–31), also takes you to awesome Yosemite Valley (3500–4000'). A walk here in late April or May can be an overpowering experience: the waterfalls are thundering, the meadows are greening, and the flowers are beginning to erupt—all your senses will be alive and alert to new beginnings and seemingly infinite possibilities. Some early flowers that you may see in Yosemite Valley at this time include a variety of violets of various colors (blue, white, yellow), dogwood, snowplant, bleeding heart, and wild ginger. In June and July look for carpets of pussypaw*, fields of sneeze-weed*, and an occasional harvest brodiaea*, centaurium*, and cow parsnip in the grassy meadows. Into August (and even September) you can find the lavender lessingia* and the yellow-orange goldenrod dominating these meadows. As the violets are harbingers of spring in the Yosemite Valley, so goldenrod is the foreteller of autumn.

In and around the Tahoe Basin (Lake Tahoe, at 6230', is near the top of the low montane zone), there are some large, open meadows that are in magnificent bloom from May through at least July. (Obtain my *Wildflowers of the Tahoe Sierra* to help you explore the wildflowers of the Tahoe area.) Along Sagehen Creek (north of Truckee) just to the west of Route 89 and for a couple miles to the east of Route 89 to Stampede Reservoir, you will find glorious wet meadows of shooting star, bog saxifrage*, rein orchid, elephant's head*, marsh marigold*, Jacob's ladder*, buttercup*, monkeyflower*, and paintbrush*, and certainly one of the most extensive and spectacular masses of camas lily* anywhere in the Sierra.

Kyburz Flat

A few miles north on Route 89 you will come to a dirt road that takes you to Kyburz Flat—a broad, open meadow around a grass-choked pond. In addition to many flowers already mentioned as prevalent along Sagehen Creek, Kyburz Flat boasts extensive vernal pools with wonderful early-season displays of porterella*, woolly marble*, and navarettia*. In the shallows of the pond are masses of flashy yellow pond lily; along its edges are the unusual hesperochiron* and blue curls.

As May and June come to the low montane, so does the wildflower 'tide.' And even as the flowers begin to emerge in the higher elevations in July, these lower montane regions will continue to be resplendent in species, so go back again and again!

Sagehen Meadow

Mid to High Montane (6500–10,500')

In late June (or if winter snows have been particularly heavy, in early July) the wildflower 'tide' begins to arrive in the high mountains. In the shade of woods there are still patches, or even small mounds, of crusty snow, but out in the open the flowers are already beginning to unfold in all their glory. It's such an exhilarating time of year in the Sierra—almost every day is warm and dry and clear with crystal blue skies. You can almost see the plants grow by the hour and the flowers open by the minute!

Some afternoons the skies grow thick for a couple hours with fluffy cumulus clouds— it may rain briefly, or even snow! But there is just enough precipitation to water the plants; the sky clears and the summer sun returns. The air is bright and clean and filled with the promise of things to come. The mountains call and the wildflower 'tide' is again bursting on the land and raising your spirits. Laughter hangs in the air mingling with the fragrances from the flowers. Everything seems to have a life of its own, sweeping you along in its joy.

mountain garden in Tahoe

As you climb up into the upper montane elevations, the forests begin to change, subtly at first, from ponderosa pine to Jeffrey pine and from white fir to red fir. But as you go higher, the changes become more dramatic. The forests begin to look and feel different: more frequent, dense pockets of red fir, small groves of delightfully 'cheeky' mountain hemlock, occasional wispy-needled western white pine, and weathered, twisted juniper standing ancient sentinel. And finally, near timberline, gnarled and embattled whitebark pine mark the upper limit beyond which no trees will grow.

high mountain garden

In late June, and more so in July and August, the flowers fill these mid to high montane elevations. The thick duff in the forests is sprinkled with color from the snowplant, pinedrop and other wintergreens, the orchid coralroot, yellow

whitebark pines and arnica

35

arnica

Castle Peak garden

lousewort, white or pink thimble-berry, and false Solomon's seal. In small openings, columbine*, meadowrue*, larkspur*, twinberry, arnica*, and current canopy the ground, which is thick with straw-berry and blue-eyed Mary*.

Dry hillsides amaze you with their dense gardens of horsemint*, grand collomia*, pennyroyal*, mule ears*, and both showy* and hot-rock* penstemon. But probably the most breath-taking sights are those astounding high mountain wildflower meadows thick with colors and scents, exploding with rainbows and butterflies and bees. Just sit for hours and watch and hear the world being born.

Where to See the Flowers

The high Sierra is filled with large, open meadows. Some are close to roads, but the most spectacular will take a little hiking to reach. The trail up the east side of Castle Peak north of Tahoe takes you in a few miles to several stunning flower fields along seeps and springs. In July and August you can sit among shoulder-high gardens of columbine*, larkspur*, monkshood*, lupine*, daisy*, senecio*, paintbrush*, cow parsnip*, and bush cinquefoil with dense masses of rein orchid, monkeyflower*, veronica*, elephant's head*, shooting star, and willowherb covering the ground underneath. Your gaze constantly shifts from these small plants in the understory to those much bigger plants towering over them, then up to Castle Peak's craggy summit, then out to the mountains way off in the distance.

Continuing up to the summit (at about 9500') takes you into a whole other environment with very different plants, many of which can also be found above timberline (see description of Alpine zone, pp. 38–40).

Equally glorious flower displays occur along the short (3–4 mile) trail from Carson Pass (south of the Tahoe area) to Frog Lake, Winnemucca Lake, and Round Top Lake

36

(8500–9500'). Here you will encounter seep-spring meadows so thick with flowers that you can hardly find the trail: dense gardens of almost all the flowers of Castle Peak plus the beautifully blue and pink bluebell, intricate iris, and the bizarre and stunning deer's tongue*. In the vicinity of the lakes you will find the beautiful heaths—red heather, white heather, bog laurel, and Labrador tea—spectacular masses of Sierra primrose and bright gardens of sedum*, geum, and iris. All the flowers, the deep-blue lakes ringed with rocky cliffs, the rushing snow-melt creeks, the endless azure sky. Prepare to be swept away by the 'tide.' You'll never be the same person again!

garden on Winnemucca Lake trail

Less of a hike and more of a leisurely traipse is huge, open Tuolumne Meadows in the high country of Yosemite. It is accessible by road, though you will probably want to wander out in the meadow away from the crowds. At about 9000', you are getting near the top of the mid to high montane zone. The highest peaks are beckoning, but this enormous meadow has much to keep you happy here as well: dense patches of red-orange Lemmon's paintbrush* and blue penstemon*; florescent purple Sierra gentian* and green-speckled, white alpine gentian* partially hidden in the grass; bright buttercups and daisies; towering deer's tongue*. Everywhere you wander you discover new treasures— plant, animal, and rock—and this is just the starting point for hundreds of miles of mountain hiking.

As John Muir said, 'Come to the mountains and get their good tidings.'

Tuolumne Meadows

37

Alpine (10,500–13,000')

In a usual year (if there is such a thing), by mid- to late July the wildflower 'tide' has passed timberline and has reached the summits of the highest peaks. Although many of the lush meadows of the mid to high montane elevations are still in peak bloom through at least mid-August, the remarkable alpine gardens of the highest ridges are now also calling for your affection. And what gifts these gardens have to offer!

As you follow the flowers up toward timberline, you begin to notice changes. The high elevation trees—western white pine, western juniper, mountain hemlock—are rapidly fading out, leaving only the whitebark pine to struggle for survival. As you near timberline, the whitebark pine becomes dwarfed (in height), though often massive in breadth. You will often find these hardy souls—probably hundreds of years old—dwarfed to gnarled, twisted, stunted guardians of the alpine threshold.

timberline trees

Before you reach these trees, you will probably encounter many robust flowers of wet and dry areas that are at least 1' and sometimes 2' tall—lupine*, fireweed, penstemon*, monkeyflower*, senecio*, arnica*, Jacob's ladder*, corn lily*. But when you pass the last of the whitebark pines, you enter an entirely different world, open and exposed to blinding sun and searing winds.

The air is thin and your breath is short. You feel light and expansive and your spirit soars into infinity. You can see forever: range after range, valleys, lakes, endless sky. It feels like you're being taken back to the very center, to the origins, to the spirit behind all form.

alpine environment

But you can feel the sun and wind on your skin and the pristine air circulating in your lungs. And the flowers! None taller than a few inches, most fiercely and joyfully hugging the ground, contouring every rock and hollow with mats and cushions of dense, tiny leaves.

It is a world of magic and wonder, a perfect ending to the long wildflower 'tide' you have followed since February and March. The plants are small, but the flowers seem strangely huge. Then you realize that most of these dwarfed plants bear low elevation-sized blooms! These alpine gardens, so splendid in their grace and tenacity, are my very favorite, the perfect culmination in the endless cycles of seasons, in the timeless spirals of birth, youth, aging, death, and rebirth.

alpine penstemon

Where to See the Flowers

Much of the high country in Yosemite (the southern limit of the area covered in this book) is near or above timberline. Perhaps the most spectacular alpine areas are those peaks along Yosemite's eastern edge (some extending slightly east of the park): here the Tioga Crest just east of Saddlebag Lake and north of the Tioga Pass Road (Route 120) and Mt. Dana (at 13,053') just south of the Tioga Pass Road provide acres and acres of alpine ridges and flats adorned with some of the alpine flora's most spectacular members. Climbing up the steep slopes from Saddlebag Lake to the Tioga Crest or ascending the flanks of Mt. Dana itself is slow and hot work, but there's so much to see.

dwarfed daisies above timberline

Along the creeks coming down from above you will find some robust plants from lower elevations thriving, but as you reach the talus slopes and dry, rocky flats and ledges near the top, only the hardiest true alpine plants remain. Look for the gorgeous white alpine columbine* , the purple alpine penstemon*, the creamy butterball, the lemon yellow sulphur flower (of the buckwheat family), the bright yellow and sticky alpine gold*, dwarf alpine daisy*, and lupine*.

And then, only very near the summit of Mt. Dana (and near or at the summits of a few other of the highest peaks to the south of Dana) comes the most remarkable alpine gift of all—a piece of the rich blue sky growing out of the rocks. Sky pilot* is an amazing treasure of deep blue or lavender flowerheads. At the top of Mt. Dana it seems that sky and ground blend and that you can reach out and touch it all—all of Yosemite, and much beyond.

alpine gold on the Tioga Crest

Mt. Rose, on the northeast edge of Tahoe, doesn't quite reach 11,000', but the last quarter mile or so of the trail is above timberline. You go through a 'tunnel' of embattled and dwarfed whitebark pine and come out the other end into a strange alpine world of 'painted' rock (various colors of lichen), howling wind, and miniature gardens of flowers clinging to the ground. White to pink to lavender phlox* spreads across wide areas; alpine buttercup* hides under rock ledges; showy polemonium*, alpine gold*, alpine daisy*, cut-leaf daisy, alpine cryptantha, butterball, and sandwort* all interweave like a fine alpine cloth. And right at the top, as you huddle from the wind behind a rock shelter, you will find the delicate yellow

sky pilot

39

sulphur flower (*Eriogonum umbellatum*)

flowers of Lemmon's draba huddling with you.

Mt. Rose is somewhat of an anomaly for an alpine peak because the winds are so strong in winter that very little snow sticks to its summit, though it lies deep and heavy on the shoulders. I skied and scrambled to the summit a cold day in November, struggling through a 6–10' snowpack for most of the way, and was surprised to find dried plants exposed on top. The wind was fierce and biting, certainly a tough place for anything to survive. But because of this winter wind and the resulting lack of summit snow, here is a place where the summit plants actually bloom before those lower down (where the ground is still covered with snow). Here the 'tide' is a little out of sequence—by the time flowers are fully in bloom in August on the shoulders, they have passed their prime on the top.

Despite a few anomalies like Mt. Rose, the 'tide' of wildflower blooming is pretty steady in its movement up the slopes, from the Central Valley in late February and March to the highest peaks in August and even September. Of course, just because the 'tide' has moved on through an elevation doesn't mean there won't be some flowers in bloom there; it can be very rewarding to return to a lower elevation later in the year to see the late-bloomers in blossom and the early-bloomers in seed.

Wouldn't it be fascinating some year to take seven months off and follow the blooming on its journey skyward! In the meantime, why not take a few short trips up and down the mountains every now and then to where the 'tide' is high, and celebrate the glory and the beauty of the flowers of the Sierra.

view from Mt. Rose

40

Families and their Flowers

Probably the easiest and most effective way to identify wildflowers in the field is to know the visible characteristics of flower families. Being able to turn to the right family in a wildflower field guide goes a long way toward identifying the flower. But learning families does more than this; it also helps you understand the flowers—their structure and function, their lifestyles, their place in the 'big picture.'

Of course, it's important to remember that families are human constructs, to help us understand and make sense of the complexities of nature. Presumably, flowers that are in the same family are closely related in evolution (and thus in genetic composition), but botanists don't always agree on family membership or even on family designation. Botanists occasionally change their minds on a flower's family membership or even on a family's existence. For example, the entire amaryllis family has recently been merged into the lily family; the fumitory family has been merged into the poppy family; the buckbean has been split off from the gentian family into its own separate family. Sometimes these changes are a result of 'better' genetic information; sometimes they seem a bit more arbitrary!

In this book you will find 17 families of wildflowers, chosen as those you are most likely to encounter and those that have the most interesting flowers and/or spectacular flower displays.

Lily—three or six 'petals' all alike (if six, actually three petals and three sepals)
Amaryllis (now considered in lily family)—six 'petals' all alike; umbel form
Mustard—four petals; superior ovary
Poppy—four (six) petals; many stamens
Pink—five separate petals, which are usually lobed or notched
Saxifrage—five separate petals, often 2-beaked ovary
Waterleaf—five separate, overlapping petals; usually cymes
Stonecrop—five (four) petals flaring out of tube; succulent leaves
Snapdragon—five petals in 2-lipped tube
Mint—five petals in 2-lipped tube; square stem; mint aroma
Bellflower—five petals in 2-lipped tube; inferior ovary
Phlox—five petals in tube or bowl; narrow (often needle-like) leaves
Gentian—five (four) petals in tube; superior ovary; branched stigma
Pea—five irregular petals (banner, wings, keel)
Purslane—variable number of petals all alike
Buttercup—irregular number and/or shape of petals; many reproductive parts
Composite—many ray flowers and/or many disk flowers

Of course you may come across in the California Floristic Province many other families that have intriguing and beautiful flowers that are not included in this book. Below are some of these other families you might encounter.

Orchid—six tepals (five alike and the other quite different in shape, size, and/or color)
Buckwheat—usually clusters of small, white flowers with no true petals (the flowers appear to have no sepals)
Carrot—clusters of small flowers on pedicels all coming from the same place on the stem (like Queen Anne's lace)
Violet—usually large, bilaterally symmetrical, 5-petaled flowers with two petals up, two out, and one down, with a conspicuous nectar spur
Borage—five uniform petals forming a bowl or tube often with a raised ring in the center of the flower throat
Rose—five regular and uniform petals, many reproductive parts
Wintergreen—five petals united into (usually) a hanging, urn-shaped flower

The Flower Parts

To identify families and flowers within families, it is often extremely useful to be able to recognize and characterize the key parts of flowers. The variation of these parts often distinguishes one family or flower from another.

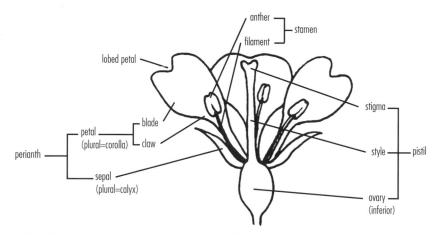

A helpful way to understand the key parts of a flower is to visualize the flower closed in bud with the parts in concentric circles, somewhat like a series of nested cradling hands.

green sepals under the petals

If you visualize a prototype '5-merous' flower (having parts in fives or multiples of five), the outside layer of the bud will be five tough, green sepals cradling the rest of the flower parts within. In the typical flower, the sole function of the sepals is to protect the fragile developing flower within the bud from cold and perhaps also from predation. The word for all the sepals collectively is the 'calyx.'

When the bud opens, the sepals unfold as do the petals, which are the next 'circle' in. The sepals—no longer serving a function—now lie under the unfolded petals. In some flowers (e.g., many poppies), the now-useless sepals actually fall off when the petals open. In most flowers, however, the sepals remain like green fingers or a green bowl hidden under the petals.

In some families (mostly the monocots, e.g., lily, orchid, iris, onion) the sepals remain on the opened flower and continue to serve a vital function, for they have adapted to look like petals and so help attract pollinators. In these flowers (usually with three petals and three petal-like sepals), the petals and sepals are both sometimes called 'tepals.'

more green sepals

But back to our typical 5-merous flower: the five sepals are green, the five petals are brightly colored and showy, attracting pollinators into the flower. Frequently, the flower produces nectar in glands at the base of the petals to help lure the pollinator; often the pollinator is guided to the 'good' parts of the flower by nectar guides—lines, dots, 'eat-at-Joe's' signs—decorating the petals. (Some of these markings may reflect only ultraviolet light and so be highly visible to insects but invisible to humans.) The word for all the petals collectively is the 'corolla.'

When the petals unfold, the next circle of parts is revealed—the male reproductive parts (stamens). In this typical 5-merous flower we're investigating, there will be five (or 10) stamens forming a more or less symmetrical ring around the periphery of the flower. Each of these male parts consists of a fleshy, cylindrical tip (anther), which produces the pollen, attached to the end of a column-like stalk (filament). The insect or other pollinator lured to the flower by the petals (and often the nectar) will pick up pollen from the anthers to take to the female part of the next flower of the same species.

6 tepals, 6 stamens

Finally, going further into the center of the flower, we reach the 'inner sanctum' consisting of, typically, one female part (pistil). The pistil consists of the fleshy tip (stigma), which is attached to the end of a column-like or thread-like structure (style), whose lower end swells into the ovary. Ideally, the pollinator deposits pollen from another plant onto the stigma, and the pollen grows a thread or tube that tunnels down through the style into the ovary where it fertilizes the egg(s). Seeds then begin to mature within the ovary.

nectar glands and nectar guides

When the ovary begin to swell and ripen, the now unneeded parts (the petals and the stamens) often shrivel up and fall off the plant. In late summer or early fall, you may find nearly naked flower stems supporting only swelling ovaries (seedpods) from which may project the now shriveled slender style and delicate (often branched) stigma—neither the petals nor the male parts are anywhere to be found!

stamens (yellow)

poppies, some in seed with petals dropped

pistil with stigma

Variability in Flower Parts and Identifying Families

green sepals

2 sepals

4 petals

All of these key flower parts (petals, sepals, stamens, pistil) can help in identifying families and flowers. The answers to the following questions about these parts may be especially helpful:

1) The sepals:

a. are they green and fleshy or are they petal-like?
b. are there the same number of sepals as petals or not?
c. do there appear to be any sepals under the petals?

2) The petals:

a. what color are they?
b. how many are there—five, four, three, lots, a variable number, hard to tell?
c. are they separate from each other to the base so you could (but, of course, you wouldn't!) pull off one petal without bringing the rest with it, or are they united in a bowl, cup, tube, or pinwheel?
d. are they all the same shape and size (regular) or not (irregular)?
e. are they arranged symmetrically on the flower (uniform) or asymmetrically (e.g., a 2-lipped tube with two petals in the upper lip and three petals in the lower lip)?
f. are they smooth on the edges or 'pinked' or lobed?

3) The stamens:

a. are there the same number of stamens as petals (or multiples of the number of petals) or not?
b. are there a few (an easily countable number) or a great many?

petal-like sepals

3 petals

variable number of petals

separate petals

irregular flowers

4) The pistil(s):
a. is there one pistil or are there two or more?
b. are there a great many pistils?
c. is the stigma branched or unbranched?
d. is the ovary attached above the petals or below?

Being able to recognize the parts and to answer these questions about them will go a long way in helping you identify a flower's family and often its genus and even species. Of course, there are sometimes other aspects to look for too, e.g., how the flowers are arranged on the stems, the shape of the leaves, the elevation and environment where the flower lives, and the time of year it blooms.

If you become familiar with the 17 families described and illustrated here, you should know the flowers in this book, and you should have a great head-start on identifying and knowing any flowers that belong to these families.

2-lipped flowers

lobed petals

many stamens

mariposa lily—branched stigma

many pistils and stamens

45

Lily Family
(Liliaceae)

When you think of a lily, you probably think of a large, showy, fragrant flower (perhaps an Easter lily). Although wildflowers are rarely as large as domestic flowers, many members of the lily family are exceptionally large and flamboyant for wildflowers. The genus *Lilium*, especially, contains numerous species with colorful (usually bright orange or red), fragrant, bell- or trumpet-shaped flowers up to 2" or even 3" long and at least as wide. The plants, too, are on a grand scale, with many species growing up to 3–4' tall and some up to 10'.

Several other lily family genera have species with stunning flowers, though somewhat smaller than those of the *Lilium* genus. Whether growing in great masses in foothill grasslands or mountain meadows, or soloing in splendid solitude on dry slopes or in forest clearings, many flowers of the *Trillium, Erythronium, Fritillaria, Camassia*, and *Calochortus* genera are dazzling in size, shape, and coloring.

However, not all large, showy flowers are members of the lily family; nor are all members of the

tiger lily

camas lily

avalanche lily (*Erythronium montanum*)

47

trillium (*Trillium ovatum*)

leaves of twisted stalk (*Streptopus amplexifolius*)

lily family large and showy (though many of its species with small flowers are still large plants with clusters of many flowers). So, what are the characteristics that reliably indicate the lily family?

Most importantly, the lily family is one of the few families of 'monocots' (most families are 'dicots'). Lilies, and other monocots, have '3-merous' flowers (i.e., they have flower parts in threes or multiples of three) with leaves that are parallel-veined and usually grass-like (though sometimes broader). In addition to a few families of conspicuously flowering plants, the monocots also include all the grasses and grass-like plants.

Members of the lily family have three petals, three sepals, usually six stamens, and one ovary usually with three stigmas (or a 3-branched stigma). In most genera, the sepals are almost identical to the petals (in color, size, and shape); in only a few genera (e.g., *Calochortus*) are the petals and sepals noticeably different.

Lily family members are usually perennials growing from bulbs, corms, rhizomes, or fleshy roots—some are important food sources, and others are extremely poisonous.

The lily family has approximately 300 genera and some 4000 species (not counting the estimated 500 species of onions and brodiaeas that botanists have recently moved into the lily family from the amaryllis family, which we will continue to consider separately in this book).

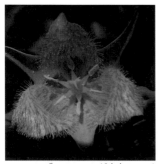

yellow pussy ears (*Calochortus* spp.)

Lily family species occur worldwide, especially in dry temperate and subtropical regions. In our area members of this family occur from the Central Valley to the high mountains, but rarely extend above timberline.

Fremont's Camas
Zigadenus fremontii
CENTRAL VALLEY

Fremont's camas is as beautiful as it is dangerous: although not as lethal as death camas (*Z. venenosus*, p. 60), it is still **highly toxic** to animals and humans. • **Several (5–15) ¹/₂" white flowers grow on a loose raceme at the end of the fleshy 1–3' stem.** The flowers have a delicate, pastel look to them. The **pointed, white tepals have yellow glands (flattened on top) near their base**, creating a subtle yellowish tinge that is enhanced by the six yellow stamens. The stamens are only about half as long as the tepals; the three stigmas are snouted. • Several long, grass-like leaves (often folded inward) arch out from the stem.

Distribution: *Zigadenus* is composed of approximately 15 species in temperate North America and Asia. *Z. fremontii* occurs in damp grassland in the Sacramento Valley. It reaches up to 3000' in western California and south to Baja. **Names:** *Zigadenus* means 'yoke-gland' in reference to the shape of the glands in some species. John C. Fremont was a 19th-century explorer of the western U.S.—one of the first white men to see Lake Tahoe. **Typical location:** Wet grasslands along Route 99 near Vina north of Chico (200').

white • 6 separate tepals • perennial

Tolmie's Pussy Ears
Calochortus tolmiei
CENTRAL VALLEY

Calochortus (the mariposa lilies) is one of the few genera in the lily family that has flowers whose sepals are noticeably different than the petals. Whereas the three petals are broadly ovate or wedge-shaped and usually hairy inside (if not all over, at least around the conspicuous nectar gland), the sepals are generally narrower, smaller, and smooth inside. The anthers are large and rectangular or spear-shaped; the pistil ends in three fleshy stigmas. The plants usually have one long, grass-like basal leaf and perhaps a few small, narrow stem leaves. • Tolmie's pussy ears is a striking pastel flower: the 1/2–1" **rounded petals are white to purplish and are covered by dense purplish hairs; the narrower, shorter, pointed sepals have a definite purple-lavender tint**. One to several erect, open flowers grow on short pedicels off the upper part of the 1/2–11/2' stem. The grass-like basal leaf is about the same length as the stem. The long, slender anthers are a beautiful silvery blue; the delicate 3–parted stigma is an intense red-purple.

Distribution: The genus *Calochortus* is composed of approximately 65 species across western North America and Central America. *C. tolmiei* is common on dry, grassy flats and slopes in the northern Sacramento Valley. It extends up to 6000' in the mountains of northwestern California, Washington, and Idaho. **Names:** *Calochortus* means 'beautiful grass' in reference to its showy flowers and its relationship to grasses (also monocots). William F. Tolmie was a 19th-century Scottish physician with the Hudson's Bay Company. **Typical location:** Grassy flats along Route 99 north of Marysville (100').

Related Plant: Globe lily/fairy lantern (*C. albus;* bottom photo) is an unusual *Calochortus* in that its delicate **white (often pink tinged) flowers remain closed in a tight globe and hang pendant on the end of long, arching pedicels**

coming out of the leaf axils of the 1–3' plant stem. The fruit is a 3-sided seed capsule nodding at the end of the pedicel, resembling a green version of the blossom it succeeds. *C. albus* is widespread on shady hillsides in the foothills. It occurs in the California coastal ranges and on the northern Channel Islands. *Albus* means 'white.' Perennial. Range: Foothills.

purple-lavender • 3 separate petals • perennial

50

Gold Nuggets
Calochortus luteus

CENTRAL VALLEY, FOOTHILLS

Of the 65 species of *Calochortus* (all of which occur in western North America and/or Central America), more than 40 grow in California. Of the 40, about 30 grow only in California. What a gift to California to have so many species of these gorgeous flowers—ranging from yellow to white to blue and from densely hairy to satin smooth. • Gold nuggets is **one of the smoothest and shiniest—its three 1–1¹/₂" rounded, wedge-shaped petals are a very bright golden yellow,** lighting up the plant's grassland habitat considerably, especially when the plants grow in clusters or masses. Each petal is usually marked by a **central reddish-brown splotch** below which are thin, vertical lines of the same color. At the base of the petal is a nectar gland near which is a cluster of fine, golden hairs. The six anthers are cylindrical, angled, and creamy white. The thick, creamy-white pistil ends in a 3-branched, sticky, yellowish stigma. • The one or several flowers grow on a¹/₂–2' stem. The 4–8" grass-like leaf is basal.

Distribution: *C. luteus* occurs in grasslands of the Sacramento Valley and in the foothills below 2000'. It occurs in the California coastal ranges and on the northern Channel Islands. **Names:** *Calochortus* (see p. 50). *Luteus* means 'yellow.' **Also known as** yellow mariposa lily. **Typical location:** Grassy slopes along Independence Trail off Route 49 near Nevada City (1200').

Related Plant: Yellow pussy ears (*C. monophyllus*; bottom photo) also has **bright yellow flowers, but they are not at all smooth—the insides of the petals are covered with dense yellow hairs.** The flowers are smaller and grow on shorter (3–8") stems, often outreached by the long, grass-like basal leaf. Yellow pussy ears occurs on wooded slopes in the foothills of the central and northern Sierra from 1200–3000'. *Monophyllus* means '1-leaved.' Perennial. Range: Foothills.

golden yellow • 3 separate petals • perennial

White Fritillary

Fritillaria liliacea

CENTRAL VALLEY

Species of the genus *Fritillaria* are typical members of the lily family: the three sepals and three petals of the large, nodding flowers are almost exactly alike in size, shape, and color. You can tell them apart when you look closely at a flower in bloom because you'll see that the sepals and petals alternate, with the sepals (which form the outside layer when the flower is in bud) being set slightly lower. When petals and sepals look alike, they are all usually called 'tepals.' • White fritillary has **one to a few large (to 2"), white flowers hanging from short pedicels that arch off the 4–15" stem**. The petals may have faint greenish vertical stripes. Most of the narrow leaves are in a cluster just above ground level; there may be a few smaller stem leaves as well. The 3-parted stigma is thick and circular in cross section; the six anthers are cylindrical and yellow. • Although sometimes known as fragrant fritillary, the flower only occasionally has a sweet scent—usually it is odorless.

Distribution: The genus *Fritillaria* is composed of approximately 100 species extending across the world's Northern Temperate Zone. *F. liliacea* is **rare**, usually occurring in open fields below 500' near the coast in central California, but it can also be found in the open, grassy fields of Jepson Prairie near Sacramento. **Names:** *Fritillaria* means 'dice box' possibly in reference to the shape of the seedpod or to the checkered pattern on the tepals. *Liliacea* means, of course, 'lily-like.' **Also known as** fragrant fritillary. **Typical location:** Only known location in our area is in the Jepson Prairie Preserve outside of Dixon, south of Sacramento (50').

white • 6 separate tepals forming bell
• perennial

52

Camas Lily
Camassia quamash
FOOTHILLS, LOW MONTANE

Many species of the lily family have spectacular showy blossoms; some dazzle us with fields solid with flowers (e.g., the avalanche lilies of the Cascades [see photo, p. 47] and sometimes the gold nuggets (p. 51) of the Central Valley and foothills). But no lily display is more glorious than the camas lily fields of the lower montane elevations of the northern Sierra.

• Each 1–3' plant is gorgeous on its own: **the deep blue or blue-purple (occasionally white) of the many 1–2" flowers packed on the stout stem** contrasts sharply with the bright yellow of the six large anthers, the bright green of the ovary, and the lush green of the long (¹/₂–2'), grass-like basal leaves. Now imagine multiplying this colorful image by thousands! **Frequently camas lilies will fill an acre or more of wet (usually very wet) meadow.** And because they bloom early for their elevation (usually in late May, a couple weeks ahead of the crowds), there may be little else in bloom with them. From a distance, it is not uncommon to mistake a field of camas lily for a small lake!

Distribution: The genus *Camassia* contains only four species, all of which are limited to North America. *C. quamash* grows in wet meadows in the northern Sierra (Tahoe and north) from 3000–6500'. It extends to the Modoc Plateau (in northeastern California) and to Canada. **Names:** Camas and *quamash* are Native American words for 'sweet' in reference to the importance of this plant as a food source. **Typical location:** Solid masses in Sagehen Meadow on west edge of Stampede Reservoir north of Truckee (5900').

blue (blue-purple) • 6 separate tepals forming star • perennial

Plain-leaf Fawn Lily

Erythronium purpurascens

LOW MONTANE

If you are at all familiar with the flowers of the Pacific Northwest, you probably have a special place in your heart for the genus *Erythronium*. The bright white avalanche lily (*E. montanum* [see photo, p. 47]) and the lemon-yellow glacier lily (*E. grandiflorum*) are two of the first flowers to bloom after the snow melts, often covering entire hillsides or mountain meadows with their cheery colors.
• In low elevations of the Sierra, we have our own beautiful *Erythronium* harbinger of spring—the white nodding flowers of plain-leaf fawn lily are **one of the first to bloom in the wake of retreating snow**. One to several 2"-wide flowers grow on each 4–10" stem. **The creamy-white petals are bright yellow at their base and are completely bent back.** The pair of nearly basal leaves (without mottling) are rather broad and are wavy on the edges. • As exciting as it is to see this fawn lily when it first blooms, it is a wonderful flower to visit late in its bloom as well, for **after fertilization the petals turn pink, then purple.** To see this, you have to time it just right because the blooming season is very short (1–2 weeks) and the petals fall off when the seeds begin to swell.

Distribution: The genus *Erythronium* is composed of approximately 25 species, most prevalent in temperate parts of North America. *E. purpurascens* occurs in forest openings in the central and northern Sierra from 5000–7000'. It extends to the Cascades of northern California. **Names:** *Erythronium* means 'red' in reference to the color of a few species. *Purpurascens* refers to the pink-purple fade of the petals. The common names refer to the broad, tongue-like leaves without the mottling characteristic of other species of fawn lily. **Also known as** adder's tongue. **Typical location:** Forest clearings along trail to Loch Leven Lakes west of Truckee (5800').

white (fading purple) • 6 separate tepals • perennial

Scarlet Fritillary

Fritillaria recurva

LOW MONTANE

The petals and petal-like sepals (collectively called 'tepals') of most fritillarys have a striking mixture of colors—usually some interspersing of brown-purple and yellow-green. However, there are a few species of this genus whose flowers dazzle more by their intensity and purity of color than by the strangeness of their design or variegation of hues. • Whereas *Fritillaria liliacea* (p. 52) is almost pure white, *F. recurva* is nearly as purely scarlet. Although the outsides of scarlet fritillary's ¹/₂–1¹/₂" tepals may be tinged with purple and their insides are usually checkered with pale yellow, these markings are subtle, so **the overall impression of the flower is still overwhelmingly scarlet.** • One to a few nodding flowers grow near the top of the 2–3' stem, each hanging on the end of its own arching pedicel. The six yellow-orange anthers protrude slightly from the trumpet-like flower tube; the scarlet stigma is 3-cleft. **Distribution:** *F. recurva* frequents dry openings in woods from Tahoe north from 3000–6300'. It extends to the Cascades and the mountains of northwestern California. **Names:** *Fritillaria* (see p. 52). *Recurva* refers to the petals being bent back at the tips. **Typical location:** Forest openings along Route 20 east of Nevada City (4500').

red • 6 separate tepals forming trumpet
• perennial

55

Leopard Lily
Lilium pardalinum
LOW MONTANE

It is difficult to decide which of the many genera of the lily family have the most spectacular flowers. If we want to see the satiny-shiny or densely furry *Calochortus*, we can go to the Central Valley grasslands or the rolling foothills; if we want to see the intense or slightly bizarre *Fritillaria*, we can explore shrubby hillsides or dry forest openings; if we want to see 'lakes' of deep-blue *Camassia*, we can search wet mountain meadows. And if we want to glory in the 'tigers' and 'leopards' of *Lilium*, we can prowl the banks of creeks and streams cutting openings in lower montane woods.
• Although there are some exceptions, most species of *Lilium* have bright orange, yellow, or red flowers growing on tall, stout stems with whorls of grass-like leaves. Leopard lily fits this description to a tee: 1–35 large (1–4") flowers nod from the 3–8' stem, which also bears 1–8 whorls of narrow 2–10" leaves (sometimes the leaves are scattered along the stem instead of in whorls). **The flowers are clearly 2-toned: yellow or pale orange (with maroon spots) turning abruptly to a darker orange at the tips. The petals are strongly bent back.** The six stamens, protruding far out of the flower, end in large (¹/₄–¹/₂") maroon or orange anthers that dry brown. The pistil protrudes even farther out of the flower than do the stamens. • Leopard lily is highly variable with numerous subspecies and much intergrading.

Distribution: *L. pardalinum* grows in large colonies along streambanks in the central and northern Sierra from 3000–6500'. It is widespread in the coastal ranges of California. **Names:** *Lilium* is the Latin form of the original Greek name. *Pardalinum* means 'leopard-like,' i.e., spotted. **Typical location:** Wet meadows along creek near Sardine Lake in Sierra Buttes area (6000').

orange • 6 separate tepals • perennial

Tiger Lily

Lilium parvum

LOW MONTANE, MID TO HIGH MONTANE

Tiger lily is similar in many ways to leopard lily (p. 56): both plants have tall, stout stems bearing several whorls of narrow leaves and a few or many large, orange, maroon-spotted flowers. The flowers of both plants provide spectacular color to their wet habitats, often seeming to light up their lush-meadow or willow-thicket environment with a strong orange 'beacon.' • Tiger lily can grow to about 6' with as many as six whorls of 2–6" tongue-like leaves (other leaves are scattered along the stem). There can be **as many as 40 large (1–2"), bright orange flowers,** though sometimes there will be only one or two. The **petals are more orange (less yellow) than those of leopard lily and they are much less recurved—** they flare out perpendicular to the flower tube and bend back only at the tips. Tiger lily's flowers usually are horizontal or ascending, whereas leopard lily's definitely nod.

Distribution: *L. parvum* occurs in wet meadows and along streams only in the central and northern Sierra from 5000–9000'. **Names:** *Lilium* (see p. 56). *Parvum* means 'small'—maybe for a lily, but not for most wildflowers! **Typical location:** Willow thickets bordering creek along Castle Peak Trail in Tahoe area (7600').

Related Plant: Washington lily (*L. washingtonianum,* bottom photo) is a stunning exception to the orange/yellow lily 'norm' in our area: its **enormous (3–4") flowers are creamy white with a hint of yellow and small reddish spots.** It grows on dry slopes in the central and northern Sierra (and Cascades) from 4000–7500'. *Washingtonianum* is after Martha Washington, wife of our first president. Perennial. Range: Same.

orange • 6 separate tepals • perennial

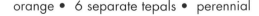

Purple Fritillary

Fritillaria atropurpurea

LOW MONTANE, MID TO HIGH MONTANE

Although a few species of fritillary have flowers with more or less solid colors (see pp. 52 and 55), most have distinctive mottled flowers in some combination of brown-purple and yellow-green. *F. atropurpurea* is one of the more typical *Fritillaria* with several rather small (¹/₂–³/₄") mottled flowers nodding from the ¹/₂–2' stem. **The six tepals are purplish-brown with yellowish or white mottling and are narrow and widely separated.** Sometimes they curve into a bell-shaped flower; sometimes they form an almost flat star. The lower stem is leafless; the upper stem has several clusters of grass-like leaves (2–3 leaves per cluster) and/or has several individual leaves alternating up the stem. • Purple fritillary is somewhat variable in coloration and flower shape.

Distribution: *F. atropurpurea* grows in forest openings and under trees throughout the Sierra from 6000–10,500'. It extends widely to the Cascades in Oregon and east into the desert mountains. **Names:** *Fritillaria* (see p. 52). *Atropurpurea* refers to the purplish (well, sort of) tepals. **Also known as** spotted mountain bells. **Typical location:** Along trail to Marlette Lake in the Tahoe area (7000').

Related Plant: Another of the strange, mottled *Fritillaria* found in our area is Davidson's fritillary (*F. pinetorum*; bottom photo). The flower is reddish-brown with yellowish-green mottling, but the major differences between this fritillary and *F. atropurpurea* are in the flower size, shape, and orientation on the plant: the flowers of *F. pinetorum* are **generally larger (1–1¹/₂" across) and more erect on the plant (less nodding); the tepals are less widely separated, sometimes almost fused into a bowl; and the anthers are a rich red.** *F. pinetorum* is uncommon on granite slopes in the central Sierra and in the mountains of southern California from 6000–10,500'. *Pinetorum* means 'of pine forests.' Perennial. Range: Same.

reddish-brown mottled yellow • 6 separate tepals • perennial

Corn Lily
Veratrum californicum
LOW MONTANE, MID TO HIGH MONTANE

'Corn lily': the name makes it
sound nutritious and beautiful. This
lily is undoubtedly beautiful, but
nutritious...don't try to find out! All
parts of the plant contain alkaloids that
are extremely **poisonous** to humans,
animals, and insects. Pollinating this
flower can be an adventure (Native
Americans reputedly made an insect-
icide from the flowers and leaves),
but apparently many insects meet
the challenge! It may be true that
'what is poison is also cure': there
are many stories of Native Americans
using this plant and other species of
Veratrum (e.g., *V. viride* of northern
California and the Pacific Northwest)
for miraculous cures for everything
from a cold to heart troubles and
from rotting teeth to tuberculosis!
• **An amazing number of 1"-wide
greenish-white flowers crowd the**

top 1–2' of the stout 3–6' stem. Many large (up to 1¹/₂' long and ¹/₂' wide)
corn-like leaves alternate on this stem. • Corn lily can put on quite a show in a
good year because the plants often grow in dense stands, filling a wet meadow
with thousands of blooms.

Distribution: The genus *Veratrum* is composed of
approximately 25 species in northern temperate
environments. *V. californicum* is widespread in wet areas
throughout the Sierra and as far away as Washington,
Colorado, and Mexico. It has a wide elevational range
from 3500–11,000'. **Names:** *Veratrum* means 'dark
roots.' *Californicum*, of course, means 'of California.'
Typical location: Solid masses along trail up east side of
Castle Peak a few miles west of Truckee (7500').

greenish-white • 6 separate tepals • perennial

Sand Corm
Zigadenus paniculatus

LOW MONTANE, MID TO HIGH MONTANE

Zigadenus is one of the most **poisonous** of all genera of flowering plants in our area (even more lethal than *Veratrum*, p. 59). Its species are all at least moderately **toxic**; *Z. venenosus* (see Related Plant), as the 'venomous' name suggests, is deadly **poisonous!** • Sand corm and death camas have similar **small** (¹/₄–¹/₂"), **greenish-white flowers** (white petals with yellowish-green nectar glands at their bases). However, sand corm is a more open-looking plant because its flowers, as the species name indicates, are often in a panicle (with branches off the main stem from which the pedicels then branch), whereas the flowers of death camas are in a simple raceme (where the pedicels branch directly off the main stem). • Both plants have slender stems that may reach 2', a few long (4–20"), grass-like leaves, and clusters of many flowers.

Distribution: *Z. paniculatus* grows in dry sagebrush scrub in the northern Sierra from 4000–7000'. It extends to Washington. **Names:** *Zigadenus* (see p. 49). *Paniculatus* refers to the flower panicle. **Typical location:** Sagebrush scrub along Sagehen Creek in Tahoe area (5900').

Related Plant: Death camas (*Z. venenosus*; bottom photo) grows in wet areas (though it sometimes occurs on dry, rocky hillsides) throughout the Sierra (and north to British Columbia and south to Baja) below 8000'. *Venenosus* means 'poisonous.' Perennial. Range: Same.

white • 6 separate tepals • perennial

Lesser Star Tulip
Calochortus minimus

LOW MONTANE, MID TO HIGH MONTANE

Although we think of *Calochortus* as one of the jewels of the Central Valley grasslands and the foothills, where so many showy species thrive (see pp. 50–51), a few of the over 40 species in our area extend up into the montane elevations. • *C. minimus* is a lovely example: usually one, but as many as five or so, open 3/4" flowers grow erect on the 1–4" stem. **The wedge-shaped petals are a delicious silvery white; the anthers are silvery with a purplish tinge.** The thick, creamy-white pistil ends in three stigmas. **The grass-like leaf is basal, reaching higher than the rest of the plant.**

Distribution: *C. minimus* occurs in open woods throughout the Sierra from 4000–9500'. **Names:** *Calochortus* (see p. 50). *Minimus* refers to the diminutive size of the plant. **Typical location:** Open woods in Crane flat in Yosemite (6000').

Related Plant: Leichtlin's mariposa lily (*C. leichtlinii*; bottom photo) lights up its sandy or gravelly Sierra habitat with its bright white flowers with yellow centers. Around the nectar gland at the base of each petal are yellow hairs; above the gland is a dramatic, dark-maroon splotch. Leichtlin's mariposa lily is common on dry flats throughout the Sierra from 4000–10,000'. Max Leichtlin was a 19th-century German horticulturalist. Perennial. Range: Low Montane, Mid to High Montane.

silvery white • 3 separate petals • perennial

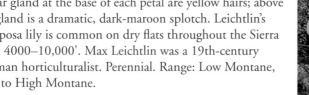

Amaryllis Family
(Amaryllidaceae)

Based on recent genetic studies, botanists have merged the entire amaryllis family into the lily family. The genera formerly considered to be in the amaryllis family certainly do share numerous observable physical characteristics with the genera of longstanding in the lily family: they all are monocots and so have flower parts in threes and they all have more or less grass-like leaves. In all but the *Calochortus* genus (one of the longstanding lily genera), the sepals and petals are identical or extremely similar in size, shape, and coloration, and so are all called tepals. (In *Calochortus*, the sepals are usually smaller and greener than the petals.)

Ithuriel's spear

However, the former-amaryllis genera do have an obvious and dominating characteristic that distinguishes them from the longstanding lily genera—their plants are in umbel form, i.e., the pedicels (the stems of each flower) all radiate from the same spot on the plant stem, like the spokes of an umbrella.

As the flowers 'awaken' in spring, these pedicels and the buds they bear burst forth dramatically from the sheath that has been holding them.

So, to ease identification and umbel-understanding, in this book we will consider the former-amaryllis genera separately from their new siblings in the lily family...perhaps we could call these *former-amaryllis* genera the '*fa*-lilies!'

And these 'fa-lilies' are a spectacular and frequent part of our wildflower display especially in the lower elevations where some of these species dazzle hillsides and grasslands with great masses of their showy, fascinating, and gorgeous flowers.

onion bursting from its sheath

The old amaryllis family is composed of approximately 90 genera and about 1200 species in temperate and warm regions worldwide, but only nine of these genera are represented in the California Floristic Province (CA-FP), and of these only four are found with any frequency in our area. But what a glorious four! They include the onions (*Allium* genus, with about 500 species worldwide and approximately 50 in the CA-FP) and the large and showy *Brodiaea* and their very close relatives.

field of three-bracted onion

63

harvest brodiaea

The *Brodiaea* genus (with 14 species, all of which are in the CA-FP) and the two genera that have been split off the *Brodiaea* genus—*Dichelostemma* (with five species, all in the CA-FP) and *Triteleia* (with 14 species, 12 of which occur in the CA-FP)—contain some of the showiest, most well-known and well-loved spring wildflowers of the Central Valley and the Sierra foothills. These wonderful 'umbrella' flowers are one of the greatest wildflower treasures of California—of the 33 species in these three brodiaea-like genera, 31 occur in the CA-FP, and most of these occur *only* in the CA-FP!

Though the onions tend to be smaller (shorter plants, smaller and tighter umbels, and smaller flowers) than the brodiaeas and the former brodiaeas, all these genera formerly considered to be in the amaryllis family have species with umbels of

beautiful and intriguing flowers, which help make the California flora so dazzling and unique.

If you look through this chapter on the 'fa-lilies' and the preceding chapter on the lilies (of longstanding), you will no doubt agree that the lily family is truly a precious and amazing gift! The native Californians certainly would have agreed, as they ate (raw or roasted) corms of many species.

glassy onion

Ithuriel's Spear
Triteleia laxa
CENTRAL VALLEY, FOOTHILLS, LOW MONTANE

Rising well above most flowers of the grasslands on stiff 1–3' stems are the loose umbels of the silver-blue Ithuriel's spear. It is a striking plant both for its size and its delicate but intense color. Each umbel consists of 5–50 spoke-like, upcurving pedicels that are 1–4" long.
• The **large (to 1¹/₂") flowers** at the tips of these pedicels **are funnel-shaped (partly closed) and are usually horizontal or upright, but sometimes droop.** The **six tepals (three petals and three sepals) are a pale blue-violet (to white) with dark-purple mid-veins.** • Taken together, the characteristics of stiff stems, loose umbels of flowers, and six fertile stamens make Ithuriel's spear a *Triteleia* instead of a *Brodiaea* or a *Dichelostemma.* In Ithuriel's spear, the six stamens are attached to the flower tube at two different levels—three high and three low. • The grass-like leaves of *T. laxa*, which often wither at flowering, are 8–16" long.

Distribution: The genus *Triteleia* (split off from *Brodiaea*) is composed of 14 species, all of which are in western North America, 12 of which occur in the CA-FP. *T. laxa* is common in open grasslands below 4500'. It extends to the California coast and to southwestern Oregon. **Names:** *Triteleia* means 'three complete' in reference to the 3-merous flower parts. *Laxa* means 'loose' in reference to the openness of the umbel. **Also known as** grass nut. **Formerly called** *Brodiaea laxa.* **Typical location:** Grassy fields in Phoenix Park in Sacramento (50').

pale blue (white) • 6 tepals flaring out of tube • perennial

Hyacinth Brodiaea

Triteleia hyacinthina

CENTRAL VALLEY, FOOTHILLS, LOW MONTANE

Hyacinth brodiaea is an exquisite plant, bearing an umbel of many (10–40) bright white flowers. Its six tepals and umbel form immediately tell you it's a fa-lily (see p. 63 for an explanation); determining its genus takes a closer look. Stem stiff rather than bent or twining, umbel loose with long pedicels, and six fertile stamens (i.e., with anthers): these characteristics are enough to tell you it is a member of the *Triteleia* genus. • Hyacinth brodiaea is smaller than many of the other *Brodiaea*-like plants you will encounter in the lower elevations: its stem rarely exceeds 2' tall, its pedicels are ¹/₂–2" long, and the flowers are usually less than ³/₄" wide. It is, nonetheless, extremely showy because **its tepals are bright white with vivid dark-green or black midveins** and the six anthers are yellow, white, or pale lilac. The tepals flare out from the stubby, urn-like flower tubes to form a cup or small bowl. • The 4–16" leaves are typical of the 'fa-lilies'—grass-like and often withering at or before flowering.

Distribution: *T. hyacinthina* grows in wet meadows throughout the Sierra below 6500' (so it reaches higher elevations than most of the Brodiaea-like plants). It extends into the Cascades and into Canada. **Names:** *Triteleia* (see p. 65). Hyacinth is the name of several species, including water hyacinth of the pickerel-weed family and grape hyacinth of the lily family. James Brodie was a Scottish botanist of the late 1700s and early 1800s. **Also known as** white brodiaea. **Formerly called** *Brodiaea hyacinthina*. **Typical location:** Wet, grassy fields in Phoenix Park in Sacramento (50').

white • 6 tepals flaring out of tube
• perennial

Blue Dick

Dichelostemma capitatum

CENTRAL VALLEY, FOOTHILLS

Blue dick is a frequent and **showy blue-purple** *Brodiaea*-**like flower of lower elevation grasslands and slopes.** Sometimes it will create **extensive wavering patches of purple** as the rather weak 1–3' stems sway in the breeze.
• If you know what to look for and you look carefully, you can recognize the characteristics that place blue dick in the *Dichelostemma* genus rather than the *Brodiaea* or *Triteleia* genera: the stem is often weak and bent rather than stiff, the umbel is closely crowded rather than loose, and there are conspicuous append-ages on some of the anthers. Although all the other members of the *Dichelostemma* genus have only three fertile stamens, *D. capitatum* has six—three with large anthers alternating with three small anthers. These stamens are hard to see, because they are partly hidden by the upright, 2-forked appendages. • The pedicels are short, so the 2–15 small ($^1/_2$"), blue-purple or pink-purple flowers are crowded tightly together. Underneath the umbel (surrounding it in bud) is a lush, metallic-purple bract. • The $^1/_2$–2' grass-like leaves often wither before the flowers appear.

Distribution: The genus *Dichelostemma* is composed of only five species, all of which are in the CA-FP. *D. capitatum* is common throughout in grassy fields below 3000'. It extends to Oregon and south to Mexico. **Names:** *Dichelostemma* means 'toothed crown' in reference to the forked stamen appendages. *Capitatum* means 'head' in reference to the tight umbels.
Formerly called *Brodiaea pulchella.* **Typical location:** Along Old Foresta Road west of Yosemite (2000').

blue-purple (pink-purple) • 6 tepals
flaring out of tube • perennial

67

Wild Hyacinth
Dichelostemma multiflorum
CENTRAL VALLEY, FOOTHILLS

Wild hyacinth is among several tall (1–3'), purplish *Brodiaea*-like flowers of lower elevation grasslands and slopes. It is identifiable as a *Dichelostemma* (rather than a *Brodiaea* or *Triteleia*) by its often bending stem, its tight umbel of flowers, and its three fertile stamens with conspicuous upright appendages. • Whereas in blue dick (p. 67), with which it might be confused, there are only 2–15 flowers on a plant, in *D. multiflorum*, as the species name suggests, there are **many more flowers per umbel: 10–35 (usually closer to 35)**. The ¹/₂" flowers are usually a pinker-purple or bluer than the blue-purple blue dick and **do not have the deep purple bract under the umbel**. The delicate pinkish or bluish color of the tepals of wild hyacinth is accentuated with dark-purple midveins. The anthers (often yellow) are bordered by erect, white, rounded appendages. The flower is strongly pinched just below where the tepals flare out of the tube. • The 3–4 grass-like leaves can be as long as 3', equaling or exceeding the length of the flower stem. • Wild hyacinth brings quite a sparkle to its grassy habitat, especially when you get close, because its pastel tepals often glisten in the sun.

Distribution: *D. multiflorum* occurs occasionally on grassy hillsides in the central and northern Sierra foothills from 50–3000'. It extends to northeastern California and into Oregon. **Names:** *Dichelostemma* (see p. 67). *Multiflorum* refers to the dense, many-flowered umbels. Hyacinth (see p. 66). **Also known as** many flowered brodiaea. **Formerly called** *Brodiaea multiflora.* **Typical location:** Grassy slopes on Table Mountain near Oroville (1000').

pink-purple • 6 tepals flaring out of tube • perennial

Harvest Brodiaea
Brodiaea elegans

CENTRAL VALLEY, FOOTHILLS, LOW MONTANE

B. elegans is elegant indeed. The 1–1¹/₂" funnel-shaped flowers are a gorgeous, intense violet to purple with dark-purple veins. They grow in a loose umbel of 3–10 flowers atop a 4–16" stem. These flowers would stand out whatever their surroundings, but they do so even more dramatically because they don't start blooming until late in the foothills' blooming season (sometimes as late as July) when most of the grasses and other plants have gone to seed and are drying out.
• What makes *B. elegans* a member of the *Brodiaea* genus whereas so many other species formerly considered to be in this genus were moved to *Triteleia* or *Dichelostemma* is its stiff stem, its loose umbel of flowers, and its three fertile stamens and three infertile staminodes. These staminodes are white and flat. • The leaves are typical of most *Brodiaeas* and *Brodiaea*-like plants: they are grass-like and long (as long or nearly as long as the plant stem) and wither early.

Distribution: The *Brodiaea* genus is composed of 14 species, all of which are in the CA-FP. *B. elegans* occurs in open fields throughout the Sierra below 7000'. It extends to Oregon. **Names:** *Brodiaea* (see p. 66). *Elegans* does indeed mean 'elegant.' **Also known as** elegant brodiaea **Typical location:** Grassy fields in Jepson Prairie outside Dixon (50').

blue-purple • 6 tepals flaring out of tube • perennial

69

Glassy Onion
Allium hyalinum
CENTRAL VALLEY, FOOTHILLS

Typical of the amaryllis family, the onions have umbels of 6-tepaled flowers. They differ from the brodiaeas (the genera *Brodiaea, Dichelostemma,* and *Triteleia*) by having smaller, tighter umbels (i.e., shorter pedicels), tepals that are separate all the way to the base instead of being fused into flower tubes, and an onion odor and flavor. • *A. hyalinum* is **an unusual onion in that it has roundish (rather than pointed) tepals with a glassy shine** that sparkles in the sun. Although the pedicels are only 1/2–11/2", the umbel of 5–25 flowers is rather loose for an onion. The 1/4–1/2" flowers are white (sometimes pale pink). The stem is only 1/2–1' tall; the grass-like leaves are not as long as the stem.

Distribution: The *Allium* genus has about 500 species worldwide, many of which are in California. *A. hyalinum* grows in grassy areas in the San Joaquin Valley and in the Sierra foothills from 100–4000'. **Names:** *Allium* is the Latin word for garlic. *Hyalinum* means 'translucent' or 'transparent.' **Typical location:** Grassy flats along road up Table Mountain near Oroville (800').

Related Plant: Paper onion (*A. amplectens;* bottom photo) is another *Allium* with unusual petals for an onion. Instead of being shiny as in glassy onion, the petals of paper onion are the **texture of dry paper**. At the tip of the 1/2–2' stem is the tight umbel of 10–50 white flowers. There are 2–4 grass-like leaves that are shorter than the stem. You may have to look closely in the grass to find them because they usually wither at or before flowering time. *A. amplectens* has a noticeable onion odor. *A. amplectens* occurs in dry, open areas throughout the Central Valley and the Sierra below 6000' and extends to British Columbia. *Amplectens* means 'embrace' perhaps in reference to the tight umbel of flowers. Perennial. Range: Central Valley, Foothills, Low Montane.

white • 6 separate tepals • perennial

Common Muilla
Muilla maritima
CENTRAL VALLEY, FOOTHILLS, LOW MONTANE

Someone sure had fun with this name: muilla is allium spelled backwards! And muilla does indeed bear a very strong resemblance to the onions but **without the distinctive onion odor.**
• The stem of common muilla may grow to 2' though ¹/₂–1' is more common. Several of the grass-like leaves may rise nearly as high as the stem, though they usually arch out away from it. • Several to many (**4–20**) **shiny, ¹/₂",** **greenish-white flowers cluster loosely in each umbel** at the tips of the ¹/₂–2" pedicels. The umbels are more open than those of most onions. Immediately beneath each umbel are three papery bracts. The six tepals are arranged in two whorls; these tepals are not completely separated, being slightly fused at the base.

Distribution: The genus *Muilla* is composed of six species in the southwestern U.S. and northern Mexico. *M. maritima* occurs uncommonly in grasslands in the Central Valley and in the central and southern Sierra foothills below 5000'. It is more common in western California.

Names: *Muilla* is indeed a backwards allium (onion). *Maritima* means 'maritime' perhaps in reference to its occurrence near the California coast.

Typical location: Grassy fields in Jepson Prairie (50').

white • 6 separate tepals joining at base • perennial

Twining Snake Lily

Dichelostemma volubile

FOOTHILLS

A crowded umbel of flowers under which are membranous bracts, flowers with six tepals flaring out of a flower tube, three fertile, appendaged stamens (alternating with three sterile stamens)—it's a 'fa-lily' for sure (see p. 63 for an explanation) and it sounds like a species of *Dichelostemma*. When you see the 2–5' stem (and it's hard to miss!), you're certain it's a member of that genus because the stem is so long and weak it can't support itself—it twines tightly around anything in its vicinity...other flowers, poison oak, rocks, even itself! • This plant is truly distinctive with **a tight umbel (with pedicels only** ¹/₂–2**") of small (**¹/₂**"), pink flowers atop a long, slender, snaking stem**. The flower tubes are short and stubby urns with six angular sacs and the tepals flare only partially, making the flowers appear partly closed. The three fertile stamens are bordered by erect, forked appendages; these fertile stamens alternate with three infertile stamens. • The vine-like stem is extraordinary—even if it breaks off the flowers will continue to bloom and seed for quite some time. As you would expect from a *Dichelostemma* (and related genera), the leaves are long and grass-like.

Distribution: *D. volubile* occurs occasionally in shaded grassy areas throughout the Sierra foothills from 1000–3000'. It extends to the Coast Range of northern California. **Names:** *Dichelostemma* (see p. 67). *Volubile* means 'twining.' **Also known as** twining brodiaea. **Formerly called** *Brodiaea volubilis.* **Typical location:** Along Hite's Cove Trail just west of Yosemite (1500').

pink • 6 tepals flaring out of tube • perennial

Pretty Face
Triteleia ixioides

FOOTHILLS, LOW MONTANE, MID TO HIGH MONTANE

Pretty face is a wonderfully apt name for this cheery flower—**its six tepals are bright yellow (or straw-colored) with dark-purple midveins**, and they flare out of the flower tube to form a wide-open, almost flat 'face.' There are several subspecies of *T. ixioides*, varying somewhat in coloration and location, but all subspecies have widely flaring and showy flowers. • *T. ixioides* has the typical features of the *Triteleia* genus: loose umbels (pedicels of ½–3") of many flowers (15–40), stiff stems, and six fertile stamens (three tall alternating with three short). Each stamen has an erect, forked appendage behind it. • The umbel of flowers grows atop a 6–18" stem; the 8–16" leaves are grass-like and usually wither early.

Distribution: *T. ixioides* has several subspecies that have somewhat different ranges. One subspecies is primarily a Sierra foothills dweller (top photo) while another reaches elevations as high as 10,000' (bottom photo). *T. ixioides* occurs in meadows and dry openings throughout the Sierra from 500–10,000'. **Names:** *Triteleia* (see p. 65). *Ixioides* means 'ixia-like'—*Ixia* is a genus in the iris family. **Formerly called** *Brodiaea lutea*. **Typical location:** Grassy fields on Table Mountain outside Oroville (1200'); gravelly flats along Castle Peak Trail in Tahoe area (7500').

yellow • 6 tepals flaring out of tube
• perennial

Swamp Onion
Allium validum

LOW MONTANE, MID TO HIGH MONTANE

Swamp onion is among our tallest and most robust onions. The **umbel of 15–40 rose flowers (sometimes dark red-purple, sometimes white) sits atop a stout stem that may exceed 3'.** • The six tepals are more or less erect (rather than flaring), making the flowers appear partly closed. The dark anthers stick up above the tepals. The 3–6 leaves are usually flat and are much shorter than the stem. • *A. validum* **often grows thick in wet, boggy areas filling the air with a distinct onion odor.**

Distribution: *A. validum* is common in wet meadows throughout the Sierra from 4000–10,500'. It extends to British Columbia. **Names:** *Allium* (see p. 70). *Validum* means 'strong' in reference to its onion odor. **Typical location:** Along creek above Tioga Lake just east of Yosemite (10,000').

Related Plant: Sierra onion (*A. campanulatum*; bottom photo) has a fairly loose umbel (at least loose for an onion) of exquisite rose-purple, star-shaped flowers growing on a 6–12" stem. Each tepal has a darker rose-colored crescent at its base. It is common on dry, sandy flats throughout the CA-FP from 2500–9000'. *Campanulatum* means 'bell-shaped.' Perennial. Range: Same.

red-purple • 6 separate tepals
• perennial

74

Three-bracted Onion
Allium tribracteatum
LOW MONTANE, MID TO HIGH MONTANE

You're standing in the middle of a vast field of pink-purple flowers (see photo, p. 33) a mild onion aroma lies thick like a fog just above the ground in the warm air of this early-summer day. Your shoes are a bit soggy from the wet ground you've had to cross to get out here in the middle of this field, but you and the flowers are now on slightly higher ground—dried clay cracked in odd polygons amid scatterings of flat volcanic rocks. These glorious onions love this volcanic terrain; their great low masses nearly conceal the rocks and the clay. The field of pink shades in places to dark rose-purple, in other spots to patches of bright white. • You have come across a rare member of our flora—though certainly not rare in this particular

place! Three-bracted onion is named for the **three (or two) transparent, white bracts under the head of 10–20 purple to pink to white** 1/4" **flowers.** The heads are fairly tight as the 1/4–1/2" pedicels are nearly erect. The six tepals are elliptic and erect; the six stamens stick out of the flower and end in large purplish-blue or yellow anthers. If you look closely inside the flowerhead, you will see the silvery glisten of the nectar glands. • The **two leaves are flattened and channeled** (i.e., folded over along their length creating a hollow groove) and are longer than the 2–9" flower stems.

Distribution: *A. tribracteatum* is **rare**, found on volcanic slopes and flats in the central Sierra (mostly around Yosemite but also in the Tahoe area) between 4000–8000'. **Names:** *Allium* (see p. 70). *Tribracteatum* means '3-bracted' in reference to the three (two) papery white bracts under the flowerheads. **Typical location:** Drying volcanic fields along Sagehen Creek in Tahoe area (5900').

pink (rose-purple or white) • 6 separate tepals • perennial

Flat-stemmed Onion

Allium platycaule

LOW MONTANE, MID TO HIGH MONTANE

Our onions are all very striking—sometimes for the intricate and elaborate beauty of their flowers, sometimes for their unusual texture (see glassy onion, and paper onion, p. 70), and sometimes for their extensive, nearly solid displays. Flat-stemmed onion has beautiful rose or pink-purple flowers, but is most spectacular when it almost completely covers large areas of otherwise bare, rocky flats. • At the tip of the short (1–6") stem is a large 'ball' thick with flowers. The pedicels are only ¹/₂–1" long, so the **30–90 small** (¹/₄–¹/₂") **flowers form a very close-packed umbel** indeed! The flower tube is constricted above the ovary; above this constriction the very narrow and pointed (almost thread-like) tepals flare out into pink-purple stars. • The stem and two leaves are broad, flattened 'ribbons.' The blue-green leaves are about twice as long as the stem.

Distribution: *A. platycaule* occurs on rocky or sandy slopes or flats in the northern Sierra (from Tahoe north) from 5000–9000'. It extends to southern Oregon. **Names:** *Allium* (see p. 70). *Platycaule* means 'broad-stemmed.' **Also known as** pink star onion. **Typical location:** Large masses on sandy slopes below Ward Peak in Tahoe area (8200').

pink-purple • 6 separate tepals • perennial

Red Sierra Onion
Allium obtusum
LOW MONTANE, MID TO HIGH MONTANE, ALPINE

Red Sierra onion is an odd little plant that is full of paradoxes: it appears to be quite fragile yet grows in difficult environments including rocky flats well above timberline; the flowers are quite showy yet are often almost invisible; the flowers, common name notwithstanding, are most often white. • The **tight umbel of 6–30 small flowers nearly rests on the ground** because the stem rarely exceeds 3" and can be much shorter. **The six tepals are white (sometimes slightly greenish) with a red-purple midrib.** These midribs, and/or the large red-maroon bract under the umbel, are probably the source of the common name. Even though these color contrasts are quite vivid, it is often difficult to see this plant because of its short stature and camouflage—it blends easily into its rocky or sandy environment. Once you see a red Sierra onion, however, you seem to see them everywhere. • The one or two leaves are flat and are usually considerably longer than the stem.

Distribution: *A. obtusum* occurs on rocky (sometimes damp) flats from 5000–12,000'. It extends into the Cascades. **Names:** *Allium* (see p. 70). *Obtusum* means 'broad' in reference to the rather blunt ends of the tepals. **Also known as** dwarf Sierra onion. **Typical location:** Rocky flats in Carson Pass area (9000').

white • 6 separate tepals • perennial

Mustard Family
(Brassicaceae)

When you think mustard, you probably think yellow and acrid. You'd be right of course, though you'd probably be thinking of the mustard genus (*Brassica*)—a single genus among the many genera in this large and varied family. In our area, field mustard (p. 83) is one of the earliest signs of spring as it spreads its bright yellow flowers thickly under the blossoming fruit trees in cultivated orchards.

field mustard in orchard

There are many food (and condiment) plants in the mustard family (including cabbage, cauliflower, broccoli, radish, Brussels sprout, turnip, horseradish, and of course, mustard), but there are also some very interesting wildflowers. What is it about these flowers that tells you they are in this intriguing family?

Latin names are sometimes very helpful in pointing out distinctive characteristics. The former name for the mustard family— Cruciferae (meaning 'cross')—is a prime example of this because all members of this family have four petals forming a symmetrical cross.

western wallflower

The other most identifying trait is the seedpods: they are very distinctive, often more conspicuous than the flowers. They form long, slender siliques or short, squat silicles that have two chambers separated by a membrane.

Although there are occasional 4-petaled species in other families, there are only a small number of families where 4-petaled flowers are the norm. Of these, the mustard family alone has flowers with four petals in a cross, showy seedpods, and superior ovaries. How do you tell if an ovary is superior? It's not as easy as you might think! It may be very difficult to determine the position of the ovary when a flower is in bloom; however, if you can wait until it starts to go to seed, things get much easier. If you are looking at a mustard (with

shieldleaf seedpods

a superior ovary) soon after pollination, you may find remnants of the shriveled petals still attached to the receptacle at the base of the now-swelling ovary. (If you were to find shriveled petals attached to the top of the ovary, the ovary would be considered inferior and you would probably be looking at a member of the evening-primrose family.)

Mustards usually have six stamens (four long and two short), though some species have two or four stamens.

superior ovary of wallflower

The mustard family is a large family with approximately 300 genera and about 3000 species distributed worldwide, especially in the cool regions of the globe. In our area the genera with the most species that you are likely to encounter include *Arabis* (rock cress), *Cardamine* (bittercress), *Draba, Lepidium* (pepper-grass), and *Streptanthus* (jewelflower).

Many species of this family grow rampant in disturbed areas and grassy fields (some becoming 'problem weeds'), but the family also includes species that inhabit difficult environments such as the rocks on the highest peaks (e.g., *Draba*) and running water (e.g., some *Cardamine* and *Rorippa*).

Though many people may think of mustards as primarily food plants or noxious weeds, many species have beautiful and fascinating flowers (and seedpods), which bring bright color and fascination to our Sierra springs and summers.

Draba in alpine environment

Lacepod

Thysanocarpus curvipes

CENTRAL VALLEY, FOOTHILLS

Lacepod is a prime example of a plant more notable for its fruits than for its flowers. The ¹/₂–2' stem bears numerous tiny (less than ¹/₈"), white (sometimes purple-tinged) flowers hanging from slender pedicels. You might not even notice this plant, except that when it goes to seed (and it does so early), its **fruits are conspicuous ¹/₄–¹/₂" 'flying saucers.'** Each silicle is flat and circular with a green center (the actual seedpod) from which radiate numerous narrow spokes. The spokes are connected by a papery white membrane that often is tinged pink-purple at the periphery. Because these translucent 'saucers' usually hang on edge from the pedicels, you can look through them at a low sun—with backlighting they fairly glow! • The 1–2" lower leaves are narrow and usually lobed and are shed soon after the flowers bloom; the higher stem leaves are more oval and clasp the stem.

Distribution: The genus *Thysanocarpus* is composed of five species, all of which are in North America. *T. curvipes* is common in open meadows and on grassy slopes throughout the CA-FP below 3500'. It occurs from British Columbia to Baja. **Names:** *Thysanocarpus* means 'fringed fruit' in reference to the spokes radiating from the seedpod. *Curvipes* means 'curved' probably in reference to its circular pods. **Typical location:** Grassy slopes along Hite's Cove Trail east of Yosemite (1500').

white • 4 petals forming symmetrical cross • annual

Shiny Peppergrass
Lepidium nitidum

CENTRAL VALLEY, FOOTHILLS, LOW MONTANE

Many mustards, including peppergrass, are more noted for their seedpods than for their flowers. • In shiny peppergrass, **many of the tiny (¹/₈") white, 4-petaled flowers branch off a slender 4–16" stem**, though they are barely noticeable until they go to seed. Then each flower becomes a ¹/₄", **shiny, oval seedpod— green at first, then reddish-purple with age.** At the tip of each spoon-like pod there is a tiny but distinctive notch. • The leaves are narrow and mostly divided into linear lobes. • Usually shiny peppergrass grows in large clumps, often in disturbed areas.

Distribution: The genus *Lepidium* is composed of approximately 175 species worldwide. *L. nitidum* is common throughout California in dry flats and on grassy slopes below 3000'. It extends to the central U.S. **Names:** *Lepidium* means 'little scale' and *nitidum* means 'shiny,' both in reference to the seedpods. The common name peppergrass refers to the peppery taste of these pods. **Typical location:** Grassy flats along Route 140 near El Portal west of Yosemite (1800').

Related Plant: Shepherd's purse (*Capsella bursa-pastoris*; bottom photo) is another member of the mustard family with distinctive seedpods. The **tiny, white flowers turn into flat, heart-shaped pods.** The mostly basal leaves are dandelion-like. Shepherd's purse occurs commonly throughout the CA-FP in disturbed areas below 5000'. *Capsella* means 'little box.' *Bursa-pastoris* is Latin for 'shepherd's purse.' Annual. Range: Same.

white • 4 petals forming symmetrical cross • annual

Field Mustard

Brassica rapa

CENTRAL VALLEY, FOOTHILLS

Although the **yellow** ¹/₂" **flowers of field mustard are quite bright and flashy, the real show is the fields full of these 1–6' robust plants**. Each stem ends in a long raceme from which branch numerous 1–2" ascending pedicels. When the flowers go to seed and the petals fall off, the flowers lose their color but remain interesting because each pedicel then bears a 2" elongated, cylindrical silique. • The large, lower leaves are deeply lobed and the upper leaves are smaller and entire; all the leaves clasp the stem. • Fields of this mustard are quite an exhilarating sight, especially in spring orchards under the soft white and pink blossoms of the fruit trees (see photo, p. 79). One of the earliest of the low-elevation spring flowers, it is a welcome harbinger of the spring to follow!

Distribution: The genus *Brassica* (from which the present name of the mustard family is derived) has some 35 species most commonly found in Eurasia. *B. rapa* was introduced from Europe and is now widespread throughout the U.S. in agricultural areas (especially orchards) and other disturbed areas below 4000'. **Names:** *Brassica* means 'cabbage.' *Rapa* means 'turnip.' **Also known as** *B. campestris. Campestris* means 'of the fields.' **Typical location:** Orchards along Route 80 near Roseville (150').

Related Plant: Another showy 'alien' mustard from Europe that sometimes grows with field mustard is wild radish (*Raphanus sativus;* bottom photo). Its flowers are considerably larger than those of field mustard, though the plants don't usually grow in such large masses. **The petals of wild radish are purple to white or yellow with reddish or purplish veins.** *Raphanus* means 'appearing rapidly' in reference to its quick seed germination. *Sativus* means 'cultivated.' Annual or biennial. Range: Same.

yellow • 4 petals forming symmetrical cross • annual

Tropidocarpum
Tropidocarpum gracile
CENTRAL VALLEY, FOOTHILLS

Although tropidocarpum is another of the mustards whose seedpods are more conspicuous than the flowers, this phenomenon is not so pronounced in this plant as in many of its mustard relatives. The flowers of *T. gracile* are small (¹/₄–¹/₂") but not tiny, and they are a **showy bright-yellow** (rather than the less conspicuous white of plants like peppergrass, shepherd's purse, and lacepod). • You may not notice tropidocarpum at first because the stems (though 4–20") are often prostrate, so the **flowers frequently lie somewhat concealed in their grass-field habitat**. However, once you notice a flower, you will probably then see many of them, for they are quite common in fields and along roadsides throughout the Central Valley and Sierra foothills. • The leaves are deeply pinnately lobed with linear, needle-like segments. The seedpods are long (1–2"), narrowly linear, and erect on short pedicels. Much of the plant is covered with short, white hairs.

Distribution: The genus *Tropidocarpum* has only two species, both occurring only in California. *T. gracile* is common in grassy fields and pastures and along roads below 2500'. It extends to the coastal ranges and into the Mojave Desert. **Names:** *Tropidocarpum* means 'keeled fruit.' *Gracile* means 'slender' in reference to the fruit. **Typical location:** Grassy fields in Jepson Prairie south of Dixon (50').

yellow • 4 petals forming symmetrical cross • annual

Milkmaids

Cardamine californica

FOOTHILLS

Milkmaids is an especially striking mustard: for its toothed, compound leaves; for its **large** ($^1/_2$–$^3/_4$"), **creamy-white flowers**; and for its early blooming. One of the first spring wildflowers to bloom, milkmaids' bright, white blossoms can be found lighting up shady canyons and slopes in the foothills as early as mid-February. • The $^1/_2$–2' stem bears several **compound leaves whose edges are toothed or wavy.** Several broader leaves grow on petioles coming directly off the rhizome (underground runner). Off the top several inches of the plant stem branch many of the showy flowers. When the plant goes to seed, the flowers are replaced by slender, erect seedpods that can be as long as 2".

Distribution: The genus *Cardamine* is composed of approximately 170 species occurring in most temperate areas of the world. *C. californica* occurs in shady canyons and woods throughout the CA-FP below 3500'. It extends to Baja. **Names:** *Cardamine* means 'heart-subdue' in reference to the medicinal qualities of some of these plants. *Californica* refers to its predominantly Californian distribution. **Also known as** toothwort, referring to the oddly shaped tuberous rootstalk that was sometimes eaten raw. **Formerly called** *Dentaria californica.* **Typical location:** Shady slopes along Independence Trail off Route 49 (1200').

white • 4 petals forming symmetrical cross • perennial

Brewer's Bittercress

Cardamine breweri

LOW MONTANE, MID TO HIGH MONTANE

If you've gotten used to seeing mustards growing in grassy fields and disturbed areas, you may be in for a surprise with the *Cardamine* genus. Nearly all of its species grow in wet areas, sometimes even in slow-moving water (although *C. californica*, p. 85, inhabits shady canyons). Brewer's bittercress **prefers very wet areas including creek shallows.** • But *C. breweri* is a typical mustard in many ways: it has a long raceme at the top of a sturdy (1–2') stem that bears many flowers, the **flowers have four petals and are brightly colored (in this case, white), and it has long siliques when it goes to seed.** The pure white flowers are about ¹/₂" across. • Several bittercress grow in our area; *C. breweri* is distinctive for its oddly lobed leaves. Most of the leaves, especially those lower down, have three holly-like lobes—the two lateral are small and opposite, the terminal is much larger and wavy-margined or toothed. • Brewer's bittercress is a very striking plant: with its bright white blossoms it stands out from the other creekside plants or stands alone in the creek itself.

Distribution: *C. breweri* is widespread in wet areas throughout the Sierra from 3000–10,000'. It extends north to British Columbia and east to Colorado. **Names:** *Cardamine* (see p. 85). William Brewer was a professor of agriculture at Yale who worked on the botany of California in the late 1800s. He was the first botanist on the U.S. Geological Survey (USGS)/Whitney survey of California from 1860–64. **Typical location:** Along and in Sagehen Creek in Tahoe area (6200').

white • 4 petals forming symmetrical cross • perennial

Tahoe Yellow Cress

Rorippa subumbellata

LOW MONTANE

Tahoe yellow cress is certainly not an imposing or showy plant—its **stems are only 2–6" long and they usually trail on the ground**; it has small (1–3") leaves (pinnately lobed or wavy on the edges); and it bears **tiny ($^1/_8$–$^1/_4$") pale yellow flowers that are scarcely noticeable against their sandy environment**. But, despite all this, it radiates a certain mystique, a poignancy that stirs reflection. • When you look at this plant growing on the sandy shores of a lake in the Tahoe Basin (most commonly on the shores of Lake Tahoe itself), you know that this is the only place in the world where it grows: *R. subumbellata* is a federal- and state-listed **endangered** plant.

Distribution: The genus *Rorippa* is composed of approximately 75 species worldwide. *R. subumbellata* occurs only on sandy lake margins in the Tahoe area from 6000–7000'. **Names:** *Rorippa* is the old Saxon name for these mustards. *Subumbellata* refers to the umbel-like inflorescence. **Typical location:** Sand along west shore of Lake Tahoe 6230'.

Related Plant: Water cress (*R. nasturtium-aquaticum*; bottom photo) is another sprawling cress, but in this case on mud or in quietly flowing streams rather than on sandy lakeshores. Its $^1/_4$" white flowers grow in clusters above pinnately compound leaves. When this plant **floats in shallow streams, you will find thin roots hanging down**. In dramatic contrast to the endangered yellow cress, water cress is very common worldwide below 8000' and was introduced to America from Europe. *Aquaticum* means 'aquatic.' Perennial. Range: All zones except alpine.

yellow • 4 petals forming symmetrical cross
• perennial

87

American Wintercress

Barbarea orthoceras

LOW MONTANE, MID TO HIGH MONTANE

Though small-flowered, as most mustards are, American wintercress brings quite a splash of color to its thick grass habitat. Each ¹/₂–2' **stout stem bears a raceme densely packed with the** ¹/₂" **bright yellow flowers.** After pollination, the petals fall off and the ovaries grow into long, narrow, ascending seedpods (siliques). • The leaves are interesting and helpful in identification: they **have 2–3 pairs of small lateral lobes and one much larger, oval terminal lobe.** The upper stem leaves have the same general form, though usually with fewer lateral lobes, and often clasp the stem.

Distribution: The genus *Barbarea* has about 20 species in North America, Europe, and Asia. *B. orthoceras* is common in damp areas throughout the Sierra from 3000–11,000'. It ranges widely from Baja to Alaska (and into temperate areas of Asia). **Names:** *Barbarea* is after Saint Barbara. *Orthoceras* means 'straight-beaked' in reference to the long, straight siliques. **Typical location:** Grassy meadows along Sagehen Creek in Tahoe area (6200').

Related Plant: Mountain tansy mustard (*Descurainia incana*, formerly *D. richardsonii*; bottom photo) is another **stout-stemmed, tall (1–4') mustard with a dense raceme of small yellow flowers.** It differs from American wintercress by having **delicate fern-like leaves** and short seedpods and by growing in more open, drier areas. *D. incana* is widespread throughout the Sierra and north to Alaska from 5000–10,000'. F. Descourain was a French botanist of the late 1600s and early 1700s. *Incana* means 'hoary' in reference to the grayish stems. Biennial. Range: Same.

yellow • 4 petals forming symmetrical cross
• biennial

Shieldleaf
Streptanthus tortuosus

FOOTHILLS, LOW MONTANE, MID TO HIGH MONTANE

Shieldleaf continues the mustard 'tradition' of directing our attention away from its flowers to other aspects of the plant. Although its seedpods are intriguing—very long (2–6"), arching siliques—it is the leaves, especially the upper leaves, that draw the most attention. The lower leaves are petioled, oblong, and toothed; the **upper leaves are shield-like—round and smooth and completely surrounding the stem. In fall, these upper 'shields' turn shiny bronze**, ready to do battle (against the oncoming winter perhaps). • The upper part of the ¹/₂–3' stem is a raceme bearing many of the rather odd urn-shaped flowers. The four purplish (sometimes yellow) petals arch out of the somewhat twisted 'vase' of four green (or purple or yellow) sepals. Visit this fascinating plant at intervals throughout the seasons, for you can see some dramatic new developments in flowers, seedpods, or leaves almost every week!

Distribution: The genus *Streptanthus* is composed of approximately 40 species in the southwestern U.S. and northern Mexico. *S. tortuosus* (in several variations) occurs in rocky or sandy areas throughout the Sierra from 1000–11,000'. It extends to the California coastal ranges and southwestern Oregon. **Names:** *Streptanthus* means 'twisted flower.' *Tortuosus* also refers, a little more dramatically, to this same quality of the sepals. **Also known as** jewelflower. **Typical location:** Rocky areas along trail to Long Lake in Sierra Buttes area (6400').

purplish (white) • 4 petals forming symmetrical cross
• annual (or subshrub)

Western Wallflower
Erysimum capitatum

ALL ZONES EXCEPT CENTRAL VALLEY

Though a typical mustard in many ways (with a dense raceme of 4-petaled flowers and seedpods that are long, slender siliques), the flowers of western wallflower are unusual for a mustard in several regards. • The **flowers are larger (to 1¹/₂") and showier than usual, they are sometimes the usual yellow but are sometimes orange**, and the cluster of flowers is more rounded than elongated. • The leaves are narrow and, in some subspecies, somewhat toothed, growing in a basal cluster and at intervals along the 1–3' stem. • The many subspecies and varieties of *E. capitatum*, with slightly different characteristics and range, often intergrade, making precise description difficult. Douglas wallflower (formerly *E. perenne*) is now considered to be a subspecies of *E. capitatum*. Whatever the variety, *E. capitatum* is a striking plant with very showy and fragrant flowers.

Distribution: The genus *Erysimum* is composed of approximately 160 species across the temperate areas of the Northern Hemisphere. *E. capitatum*, in its various subspecies, is very widespread and common in open areas throughout California from the foothills to the highest peaks. **Names:** *Erysimum* means 'help' in reference to medicinal uses. *Capitatum* refers to the rounded head of flowers. **Typical location:** Dry flats along Glacier Point Road in Yosemite (7000').

yellow or orange • 4 petals forming symmetrical cross • biennial

90

Lemmon's Draba

Draba lemmonii

MID TO HIGH MONTANE, ALPINE

Although a tiny plant (1–5" stem) with small flowers (¹/₄"), Lemmon's draba puts on quite a show on the rock ledges and talus slopes of its high Sierra habitat. **Its tiny, oval, hairy basal leaves form extensive mats that contour the ground. Just above these leaves are dense clusters of the bright yellow flowers**, which from a distance could easily be mistaken for patches of lichen plastering the rocks.

• Many of the numerous Draba species in our area have yellow flowers and grow among the rocks above timberline. *D. lemmonii* is distinguished by its bizarre, twisted seedpods (bottom photo).

Distribution: The genus *Draba* has about 350 species in the Northern Hemisphere and the mountains of South America. *D. lemmonii* is a Sierra endemic of rocky areas above 8000'. It is one of the few species that you will find growing at or near the summit of the Sierra's highest peaks. **Names:** *Draba* means 'acrid.' John and Sara Lemmon were a 19th-century husband-and-wife botanical team who collected and discovered plants throughout the American West. **Typical location:** Rocks near the summit of Mt. Rose in the Tahoe area (about 10,750').

yellow • 4 petals forming symmetrical cross • perennial

Poppy Family
(Papaveraceae)

Poppies and the California dream...they just seem to have always gone together. Hills of gold as far as the eye could see; streets of gold as rich as the mind could imagine. Even today there's something about standing in the middle of a field of brilliant orange California poppies on a burning sunny day that seems to melt away time and flesh. Those thousands of orange satin suns warm your heart and quiet your mind and stir forgotten memories of simpler times, of childhood and innocence and simple sensuality.

California poppies

Apparently others felt similar sentiments for the poppy, because the California poppy is the California state flower. But 'poppy' is also a family, and the California poppy has relatives with their own stories to tell.

This family is full of surprises: many stamens but only one pistil; four petals (or six) and two sepals (or three); 'disappearing' sepals falling off early in the blooming cycle; often crinkly, 'crepe-papery' petals; often milky sap; a species with the largest flower of any plant native to California (Matilija poppy, p. 98).

The poppy family contains approximately 40 genera and approximately 400 species worldwide, and is especially prevalent in northern temperate and northern tropical areas and in southern Africa. (Botanists recently merged the fumitory family—the bleeding hearts and their close relatives—into the poppy family, but I have chosen not to include them here.)

Not counting the bleeding hearts and other former fumitories, the genera of the

Matilija poppy

93

steershead (*Dicentra uniflora*) of the former fumitory family

California poppy closed

poppy family you are most likely to encounter in our area are *Eschscholzia* (containing, among others, the California poppy), *Platystemon* (cream cups), *Romneya* (Matilija poppy), *Stylomecon* (wind poppy), *Argemone* (prickly poppy), and perhaps *Papaver* (containing some aliens including the opium poppy). Of all these genera, only *Argemone* has plants you will find above the foothills and very low montane elevations.

Surprisingly, only the genus *Eschscholzia* has more than one native species found in our area, but what the poppy family may lack (in our area) in number of species and elevational range, it more than makes up for in floral displays and spectacular blossoms. And some of the poppies (e.g., California poppy) give us joy by blooming over and over again: they close at night and open each morning (if it's sunny).

When you hear the word 'poppy,' you can almost hear those dry seedpods popping open!

94

California Poppy
Eschscholzia californica

CENTRAL VALLEY, FOOTHILLS, LOW MONTANE

When you think of the poppy family in California, you most likely think of California poppy—the bright and showy **state flower that often turns entire fields and slopes in the lower elevations into flaming orange or burnished gold.** The claim has been made that for early settlers in California this flower was so bright and grew in such large masses that it could be used as a landmark by ships at sea! • *E. californica* is a typical member of the poppy family in that it has four petals, two fused sepals that are shed as a unit at flowering, and a cluster of many stamens. The four petals form a large (up to 2" wide), bowl-shaped flower that sits alone atop its slender 2–24" stem. The flowers are usually bright orange but may sometimes be more yellow (especially in the smaller flowers that bloom later in the season). The leaves are blue-green and lacy. • *E. californica* is highly variable, but all varieties are distinguished from other species of this genus by the **conspicuous, flat, pink rim (platform) beneath the petals** (see photo, p. 94). This platform is especially noticeable when the petals fall off (after pollination) or when the flower closes (at night and during overcast weather).

Distribution: The genus *Eschscholzia* is composed of 12 species, all of which are in western North America. *E. californica* is widespread in grassy areas from sea level to 5000' (sometimes higher as an escaped garden plant). It extends (in its many variations) from southern Washington to Baja. **Names:** J.F. Eschscholtz was the ship's doctor on the Russian ship *Rurik*. *Californica* (see p. 85). **Typical location:** Grassy hillsides along Route 49 through the foothills (1500').

Related Plant: Caespitose poppy (*E. caespitosa*; bottom photo) often grows with California poppy and greatly resembles it, but the caespitose poppy is **smaller and lacks the platform beneath the petals.** It occurs throughout California and southern Oregon from sea level to 2500'. *Caespitosa* means 'caespitose' (i.e., tufted growth form). Annual. Range: Central Valley, Foothills.

orange (yellow) • 4 separate petals • annual or perennial

Frying Pans
Eschscholzia lobbii

CENTRAL VALLEY, FOOTHILLS

With its four petals and cluster of many reproductive parts, *E. lobbii* is easily recognizable as a member of the poppy family. Although it resembles California poppy and caespitose poppy (both p. 95) in having one flower per stem and deeply divided leaves, it does have some obvious distinguishing features as well. • Most noticeably, it is **yellow rather than orange** (though both *E. californica* and *E. caespitosa* can have yellow flowers). More reliable differences are the flower size and shape. The petals of California poppy are quite large (³/₄–2") and those of caespitose poppy are smaller (¹/₂–1"), but frying pans' petals are smaller yet (¹/₄–¹/₂"). Also **the petals of frying pans are distinctively pointed—in some cases almost diamond-shaped**—whereas those of the other two poppies are usually rounded. The shape of the flowers of California poppy and caespitose poppy are cupped or funnel-shaped, while those of frying pans are usually flat. • The flowers of frying pans are usually close to the ground: the plant stem rarely exceeds 1' and is often closer to 6". The leaves are basal and are deeply divided into very narrow segments.

Distribution: *E. lobbii* occurs in open grassy fields only in the Central Valley and Sierra foothills below 2000'. **Names:** *Eschscholzia* (see p. 95). William Lobb was a 19th-century English plant collector. **Typical location:** Grassy fields in Phoenix Park in Sacramento (50').

yellow • 4 separate petals • annual

Cream Cups

Platystemon californicus

CENTRAL VALLEY, FOOTHILLS

Often covering large areas with its **creamy yellow** color, cream cups also occurs interspersed with its close relative—California poppy (p. 95). Although a typical poppy, cream cups differs from California poppy in several ways in addition to color. Cream cups has six petals that persist after pollination; three hairy sepals that fall off when the flower opens; **a densely hairy (4–12") stem that bears several flowers and droops (especially when the flowers are in bud)**; and narrow, undivided leaves (2–3") mostly on the lower plant. The buds are deliciously pink and hairy. • Like most poppies, however, *P. californicus* has rather large flowers (1–1¹/₂" wide) with many stamens.

Distribution: Cream cups is the only species of the *Platystemon* genus, though it is highly variable. It occurs throughout the Sierra in open grasslands and burn areas from sea level to 3000'. It extends from Oregon to Baja and east to Utah. **Names:** *Platystemon* means 'wide stamen.' *Californicus* means 'of California.' **Typical location:** Along Old Foresta Road into Yosemite (2500').

creamy yellow • 6 separate petals • annual

97

Matilija Poppy
Romneya coulteri
CENTRAL VALLEY, FOOTHILLS

Although *R. coulteri* does have the most obvious characteristics of a typical poppy (six separate petals that fall off after pollination and a central cluster of many stamens), the immense flowers growing on their tall shrub (to 10') might lead you to doubt this identification. But keep the faith, it is indeed an extraordinary poppy. • **The white, crinkly petals form a flower that can be up to 7" across**—the largest flower of any plant native to California. Many of the fragrant flowers grow on the shrub, which also bears numerous broadly lobed, gray-green 2–8" leaves. The many stamens are golden yellow, dramatically contrasting with the snow-white petals.

Distribution: The genus *Romneya* has only two species, both of which grow only in California. *R. coulteri* is quite uncommon, occurring only in the southern parts of the central Sierra and in southern California from sea level to 4000'. **Names:** T. Romney Robinson was an Irish astronomer of the 19th century. Thomas Coulter was an Irish naturalist who collected in Mexico and the southwest U.S. in the 1800s. **Typical location:** Along Route 140 west of Yosemite (2500').

white • 6 separate petals • shrub

Prickly Poppy
Argemone munita

LOW MONTANE, MID TO HIGH MONTANE

Prickly poppy is clearly both prickly and a poppy. It resembles a much smaller version of Matilija poppy (p. 98) with **six crinkly, white petals forming a shallow bowl around the dense central cluster of many yellow stamens.** One or a few 2–5" flowers grow on each **1–4' prickly stem.** The 2–6" toothed leaves are spiny on top and bottom. The small stamens number an amazing 150–250!
• Like most members of the poppy family, *A. munita* contains alkaloids that are **toxic** to humans.

Distribution: The *Argemone* genus is composed of approximately 30 species across North America, South America, and Hawaii. *A. munita* occurs in open, often sandy, areas on the eastern edge of the high Sierra to 9000'. It grows down the eastern slope of the Sierra into the Great Basin and in the coastal ranges of California. **Names:** *Argemone* is Greek for 'cataract of the eye,' an affliction supposedly remedied by the sap of some species of this genus. *Munita* means 'armed' in reference to the spines on the plant's stems and leaves. **Typical location:** Dry flats along road up Ward Canyon in Tahoe area (6600').

white • 6 separate petals • annual or perennial

Pink Family
(Caryophyllaceae)

Beautiful, delicate, intense pink. Most of the showiest and well-known species in the pink family you are likely to encounter in our area do have pink (or red) flowers (e.g., wild carnation, p. 102; California Indian pink, p. 106; meadow pink [*Dianthus deltoides*]).

But the pink family was not named after the color pink. It is so named because many (though not all) of its genera have flowers whose petals are 'pinked,' i.e., lobed or ragged on the tips. Sometimes the petals are 2-lobed, sometimes 3-lobed, sometimes just notched. In some cases (e.g., mountain chickweed, p. 107), the cuts are so deep that the five lobed petals appear to be 10 petals.

wild carnation

With certainly some notable exceptions, many species of the pink family have rather small, inconspicuous flowers. Whether notched, lobed, or entire, the flowers have five (rarely four) separate petals and five or 10 stamens.

Most species of the pink family have simple, unlobed leaves that are in opposite pairs on the stems. The stems often have very conspicuous swollen nodes.

This family is composed of approximately 85 genera and about 2400 species, most of which occur in temperate and arctic/alpine areas of the Northern Hemisphere. Some of the alpine species form magnificent, tight cushion plants.

California Indian pink

The most noticeable and frequent genera in our area are *Arenaria* (sandwort), *Cerastium* (mouse-ear chickweed), *Minuartia* (sandwort), *Silene* (catchfly), and *Spergularia* (sand-spurrey). Worldwide, the most widespread genera with the most species are *Silene* and *Dianthus* (meadow pink).

moss campion (*Silene acaulis*) at Mt. Ranier

Wild Carnation

Petrorhagia dubia

CENTRAL VALLEY, FOOTHILLS, LOW MONTANE

One of the most delicately beautiful of all grassland flowers is the intense, almost florescent-pink wild carnation. Perched atop the **single wiry 4–24" stem** is a small cluster of $^1/_4$–$^1/_2$" flowers. However, it often appears that each stem has only one flower because the stemless flowers emerge from a 'cocoon' of papery bracts and often only one flower in a cluster blooms at a time. • The **five petals are bright pink, blending at their base into the white of the inside of the flower tube.** The base of each petal has deep red-purple markings, creating the appearance of two small, pale pink 'rabbit ears' outlined in red-purple. The overall effect is a 5-petaled bright pink flower with a smaller 10-petaled pale-pink flower lying on top of it! The anthers are a striking lavender.

• Typical of the pink family, each separate petal is lobed or deeply notched at the tip, creating a somewhat heart-shaped petal. Several pairs of short, opposite leaves occur at intervals along the stem; the leaves are sheathed at their base.

Distribution: The genus *Petrorhagia* has approximately 20 species, which range from the Mediterranean to southern Asia. *P. dubia* is an alien introduced to the CA-FP from southern Europe. It occurs in disturbed areas and fields in the Sacramento Valley and bordering foothills below 5000'. It extends to the California coastal ranges and the foothills of the Cascades. **Names:** *Petrorhagia* means 'rock fissure' in reference to the habitat of some species (not ours). *Dubia*...sounds 'doubtful!' **Formerly called** *Kohlrauschia velutina.* **Typical location:** Grassy fields along Route 16 near Sloughhouse outside Sacramento (100').

pink • 5 separate notched petals • annual

Mouse-ear Chickweed
Cerastium glomeratum
CENTRAL VALLEY, FOOTHILLS, LOW MONTANE

Mouse-ear chickweed is a **small, bristly plant with tiny ($^1/_8$"), white flowers.** • The 3–15" stem bears several pairs of narrow, opposite leaves; both stem and leaves are covered with more or less sticky, silvery hairs. Several flowers branch off the top of the stem on short pedicels. • Typical of the pink family, the five tiny petals are each notched, though in *C. glomeratum* these **notches are quite shallow.** The green sepals, covered with those same fine, silvery hairs, are just slightly shorter than the petals and usually show through between the petals when the flower is fully open.

Distribution: The genus *Cerastium* is composed of approximately 60 species worldwide. *C. glomeratum* is an alien introduced from Europe. It occurs in disturbed areas and grassy fields in the central and northern Central Valley and Sierra below 5000'. **Names:** *Cerastium* means 'horn' in reference to the shape of the fruit. *Glomeratum* means 'clustered' in reference to the many-flowered inflorescence. **Typical location:** Grassy edges of Route 140 around Catheys Valley (500').

Related Plant: Meadow chickweed (*C. arvense*; bottom photo) is a much showier plant than mouse-ear chickweed, with tufts of **large ($^3/_4$"), silvery-white flowers. Each petal, with its deep notch at the tip, resembles a satiny silver heart.** Meadow chickweed occurs in seep areas, grassy meadows, and rocky or sandy slopes throughout the central and northern Sierra (and in the eastern U.S. and Eurasia) from 1000–9000'. *Arvense* means 'of cultivated fields.' Perennial. Range: Foothills, Low Montane, Mid to High Montane.

white • 5 separate notched petals
• perennial

103

California Sandwort

Minuartia californica

CENTRAL VALLEY, FOOTHILLS, LOW MONTANE

Although many of the pink family members are rather rough-looking aliens (e.g., see common catchfly, p. 105), California sandwort is a very **delicate-looking plant, both for its small flowers and its slender, hairless, branching stems**. The 2–6" thread-like stems bear several very small ($^1/_8$–$^1/_4$"), **needle-like leaves** and a few small ($^1/_2$"), white flowers. The five separate petals (often purple-veined) gracefully curve up to form a small bowl. The 10 thread-like stamens bear small orange to yellow anthers. The ovary is round and shiny green. The sepals are small and pointed or rounded. • Because the stems are so slender, the slightest breeze will be enough to set these flowers dancing—a delight for the eyes though a problem for the camera!

Distribution: The *Minuartia* genus has about 120 species from the Arctic to Mexico and to Africa and Asia. *M. californica* occurs on gravelly or sandy slopes in the Sacramento Valley and in the Sierra foothills below 3000'. It extends to southern Oregon. **Names:** J. Minuart was an 18th-century Spanish botanist and pharmacist. *Californica* (see p. 85). **Formerly called** *Arenaria californica*. **Typical location:** Sandy slopes along Hite's Cove Trail west of Yosemite (1500').

white • 5 separate petals • annual

Common Catchfly
Silene gallica
CENTRAL VALLEY, FOOTHILLS

Common catchfly is a rather unfriendly looking plant. Its 4–16" stem, pairs of opposite leaves, and flower sepals are all rough-hairy or bristly. **The sepals are united into a yellowish-green, swollen tube with 10 red-purple, bristly ribs.** The five white (sometimes pink or lavender) petals flare out of this tube to form a 'star.'
• Several flowers branch off one side of the top 1–6" of the stem, and very small bristly leaves branch off the other side. The lower stem bears several pairs of larger, opposite leaves. • Unlike most catchflies (and unlike many members of the pink family), the petals of common catchfly are not lobed and usually are not even notched.

Distribution: The genus *Silene* has about 500 species in the Northern Hemisphere. *S. gallica* is an alien introduced from Europe. It occurs in fields and disturbed areas throughout the CA-FP below 3000'. It extends to British Columbia and occurs in the eastern U.S. (and in Europe). **Names:** *Silene* is derived from the mythological Silenus, intoxicated foster-father of Bacchus (god of wine). Catchfly seems to be a bit of a misnomer. It apparently refers to the sticky secretion on the calyx of many species, which sometimes entraps tiny gnats; it is unlikely a fly would be stuck, though it might be distracted! *Gallica* is of uncertain meaning. • **Typical location:** Edges of grassy fields along Route 49 near Angels Camp (1500').

white • 5 separate petals • annual

105

California Indian Pink
Silene californica
FOOTHILLS, LOW MONTANE

Indian pink is a **large (1")**, **stunning, bright scarlet flower** that is all the more dramatic for its startling contrast to its wooded environment. Coming across a cluster of these amazing flowers in the shade is always a delight and a surprise—the brilliant splashes of color seem like joyful shouts in a library! • The stems are 1/2–11/2' tall, but frequently the terminal flowers are closer to the ground than that because the stems usually partly recline. Each stem bears several pairs of downy, tongue-shaped leaves, the lower pairs often withering early in the blooming. The stem usually branches, bearing several of the flowers, and because several plants often grow together, you may come across a patch of scarlet rather than a few 'dabs.' • As you would expect with a member of the pink family, each of the five flaring petals is lobed—in this case with four lobes, the inner two longer and broader than the outer two. There are 10 protruding stamens with creamy-white anthers.

Distribution: *S. californica* occurs in the partial shade of wooded slopes throughout the Sierra below 4000'. It extends to the California coastal ranges and to the Cascades. • **Names:** *Silene* (see p. 105). *Californica* (see p. 85). • **Typical location:** Oak-shaded slopes along Old Foresta Road just west of Yosemite (2000').

red • 5 separate lobed petals • perennial

Mountain Chickweed

Stellaria longipes

LOW MONTANE, MID TO HIGH MONTANE

Mountain chickweed is a delightful flower of grassy meadows and fields throughout the Sierra. Part of its charm may be its rather mysterious nature—you need to spend some quality, close-up time with it to penetrate its secrets.
• Even locating this chickweed is a bit tricky: the plant is only **4–12"** **tall, so the small (**$^1/_4$–$^1/_2$"**), white,** **terminal flowers are often hidden** **in the grass**. When you do find this flower, you may initially think it's some kind of daisy-like composite (see composite family, pp. 261–81) because it **appears to** **have many narrow, ray-like** **petals**—10, you realize, when you get close enough to count them. But an even closer look soon shows you that there are only five petals, each of which is deeply lobed

almost but not completely to the base. Aha! These are the characteristic lobed petals of the pink family. • Another mystery now unfolds: some flowers seem to have red spots on the petals and others don't. But again, up-close exploration reveals the secret: the red 'spots' are actually the ripe anthers pressed against the petals. Later in the blooming cycle, the anthers start shriveling and the filaments rise up and lift the anthers up away from the petals, removing the 'spots.'

Distribution: The genus *Stellaria* is composed of approximately 120 species worldwide. *S. longipes* occurs in moist, grassy meadows throughout the Sierra from 4000–11,000'. It is circumboreal, occurring in much of the Northern Hemisphere. **Names:** *Stellaria* means 'star' in reference to the flaring petals. *Longipes* means 'long-stalked' in reference to the long pedicels. **Also known as** long-stalked starwort. **Typical location:** Damp, grassy meadows along Sagehen Creek in Tahoe area (5900').

white • 5 separate lobed petals • perennial

Douglas Catchfly
Silene douglasii
LOW MONTANE, MID TO HIGH MONTANE

Douglas catchfly is a typical *Silene* and a typical member of the pink family: its flowers have a swollen, ribbed calyx out of which the five petals flare into a star, and the petals are lobed, though just barely. • The slender 4–16" stem is covered with tiny, barely visible hairs and bears 2–8 pairs of narrow, opposite leaves. Each stem may bear one terminal flower or several more flowers branching on slender pedicels. • **The ¹/₂" swollen calyx tube is usually a greenish-white with 10 distinct, dark ribs running its length.** The five flaring petals are white (sometimes pinkish or purplish). Each petal is barely 2-lobed with a shallow notch at its tip. • *S. douglasii* tends to grow in clumps, so usually you'll find many of these intriguing flowers dancing above a thick cluster of lush green leaves.

Distribution: *S. douglasii* occurs in dry flats and openings in woods throughout the central and northern Sierra from 5000–9000'. It extends to the coastal ranges of northern California and to the Cascades. **Names:** *Silene* (see p. 105). David Douglas was a British horticulturalist and explorer who made three collecting trips to America in the 1820s and 1830s. Many flowers and the Douglas-fir are named after him. **Typical location:** Dry, gravelly flats along the trail to Silver Lake in Sierra Buttes/Lakes Basin area (6800').

Related Plant: Lemmon's catchfly (*S. lemmonii*; bottom photo) has many ¹/₂", **greenish-yellow (to pink) flowers nodding gracefully on short, arching pedicels off a ¹/₂–1¹/₂' stem**. With their **deeply cut, fringe-like petals** and slender, silky, long-protruding reproductive parts, these flowers have a soft, delicate grace. *S. lemmonii* occurs in forest openings throughout the Sierra and into southern Oregon from 3000–9000'. *Lemmonii* (see p. 91). Perennial. Range: Low Montane, Mid to High Montane.

white • 5 separate notched petals • perennial

108

King's Sandwort
Arenaria kingii
MID TO HIGH MONTANE, ALPINE

King's sandwort is a **short (4–8")**, **delicate plant whose small (¹/₂"),** **white blossoms look a bit like** **floral stars hovering just off the** **ground**. The plant stem and several branching pedicels bearing the flowers are slender and nearly leafless and blend in so well against their gravelly or sandy background that you might not notice them at first glance. The delicate flowers apparently float unattached in the air. • When you do notice the stems and examine them closely, you will see that they are sticky-hairy and rise above a tuft of needle-like basal leaves. • There are five widely separated petals with blunt or rounded tips, sometimes smooth-tipped, sometimes with slight notches. The green sepals are pointed and shorter than the petals and show through between them. The 10 stamens arch up, holding the red (or reddish-brown) anthers well above the petals.

Distribution: The genus *Arenaria* is composed of 150 species in northern temperate areas, especially in the mountains. *A. kingii* occurs in rocky or sandy areas throughout the Sierra from 7000–13,000'. It extends to Oregon and east to Utah. **Names:** *Arenaria* means 'sand' in reference to the sandy or gravelly habitat of many species. Clarence King was a California geologist connected with the California Geological Survey in the 1860s and author of *Mountaineering in the Sierra Nevada*. **Typical location:** Rocky flats around Cathedral Peak in Yosemite (10,000').

white • 5 separate petals • perennial

Saxifrage Family
(Saxifragaceae)

Although the name 'saxifrage' sounds like some sort of strange cross between sassafrass and saxophone, it is actually a bit less exotic: saxifrage means 'stone-breaker,' apparently in reference to the rock-cliff habitat of some species. This family contains some of our daintiest and most interesting flowers; you'll need a magnifying glass to fully appreciate and understand their beauty and intricate forms. The prototype saxifrage family member has many small ($1/4$"), white flowers in a branched inflorescence (panicle) and has lush-green, basal leaves with scalloped edges.

scalloped basal leaves

The flowers typically have five separate petals, five sepals, five or 10 stamens, and an ovary split into two beaked pistils. There are usually many small seeds.

The genus whose flowers are dramatically atypical in some regards is *Parnassia* (grass-of-Parnassus): its flowers are solitary and quite large (to 1") and have five glandular staminodes in addition to the five 'regular' stamens.

2-beaked ovary

The saxifrage family is composed of approximately 40 genera and approximately 600 species that are especially prevalent in northern temperate areas and in arctic and alpine environments. The genera you are most likely to encounter in our area are *Heuchera* (alumroot), *Lithophragma* (woodland star), *Mitella* (mitrewort), and *Saxifraga* (saxifrage). *Saxifraga* is by far the largest genus worldwide (approximately 400 species) and in our area (10 species).

grass-of-Parnassus

Foothill Saxifrage

Saxifraga californica

CENTRAL VALLEY, FOOTHILLS, LOW MONTANE

Noting its broad, basal leaves, its slender, leafless stem, and the open, branched inflorescence of many small ($^1/_4$–$^1/_2$"), white flowers, you probably suspect that you are looking at some kind of saxifrage (family and genus). Careful inspection of the pistil strengthens your suspicion because it is split into two curving beaks all the way down to the ovary—a characteristic common to many members of the saxifrage family and especially prominent in species of the *Saxifraga* genus. • Foothill saxifrage has a **rosette of 2–4" ovate, basal leaves whose edges are shallowly toothed or smooth**. If you look very closely, you will notice that their edges are fringed with tiny white hairs. The $^1/_2$–1$^1/_2$' leafless stem is also hairy (and glandular) and branches freely. Many bright white flowers are perched on the ends of short pedicels. • The five elliptic or round petals provide a bright background for the 10 yellow anthers. Unlike many members of the *Saxifraga* genus, **the petals are pure white without colored spots**. • *S. californica* is especially showy in early spring (even February): then you are likely to find large clusters of these flowers in full bloom before much else around them has blossomed.

Distribution: The genus *Saxifraga* is composed of approximately 400 species in northern temperate areas worldwide. *S. californica* occurs in moist, shady places throughout the CA-FP below 4000'. It extends from southwest Oregon to Baja. **Names:** *Saxifraga* means 'stone-breaker' in reference to the rocky habitats of some species and probably to the use of some species in dissolving gallstones. *Californica* (see p. 85). **Also known as** California saxifrage. **Typical location:** Shady areas along Hite's Cove Trail just west of Yosemite (1500').

white • 5 separate petals • perennial

Fringed Woodland Star

Lithophragma parviflorum

FOOTHILLS, LOW MONTANE

One of the great delights of spring in the foothills is welcoming the dancing stars of *Lithophragma*. Woodland stars are aptly named: they look like delicate stars stuck to a magic wand because the pedicels are usually so short that the flowers appear to be attached almost directly to the slender plant stem.
• The 1–3' short-hairy stem is mostly bare of leaves; other than the 3-lobed basal leaves whose long petioles branch off the very base of the stem, there are only a few small stem leaves. The broad (1–2" wide), basal leaves almost appear to be toothed because each of the three lobes is again lobed. • Several (4–14) of the showy ¹/₂" flowers are arranged alternately along the upper ¹/₂–1¹/₂' of the stem. **The five separate petals are white to pink/ lavender and are more than fringed—they are distinctly 3-lobed.**

Distribution: The genus *Lithophragma* has 12 species in western North America. *L. parvi-florum* occurs on open (often partially shady) slopes in the foothills of the central Sierra. It occurs in the California coastal ranges and from Oregon to Baja up to 6000'. Especially in northern California it intergrades with *L. affine*, another wood-land star with lobed petals. **Names:** *Lithophragma* means 'rock hedge.' *Parviflorum* means 'small-flowered.' **Typical location:** Grassy, shady slopes along Hite's Cove Trail just west of Yosemite (1500').

Related Plant: Smooth woodland star *(L. bolanderi,* formerly *L. scabrella;* bottom photo) is a very similar plant, but its **petals are white and unlobed and without fringes.** It occurs on open slopes throughout the Sierra foothills from 500–5000'. H.N. Bolander was an American naturalist of the early 19th century. Perennial. Range: Same.

white or pink to lavender • 5 separate 3-lobed petals • perennial

113

Rock Star

Lithophragma glabrum

LOW MONTANE, MID TO HIGH MONTANE

Star-gazers are fortunate in the Sierra, for stars penetrate the dark of crisp, clear nights, and also shine brightly in broad daylight! As early as February you can find various woodland stars in the foothills (see p. 113) and by summer you can find rock star nearly all the way to timberline. • In rock star, only a few (1–7) dainty $^1/_2$" flowers branch off a slender $^1/_2$–$1^1/_2$' stem. **The five separate petals of the pink or white flowers appear fringed because each petal has numerous (usually four or five, sometimes three) deep lobes.** • You will sometimes notice fuzzy, red, BB-size 'bulbils' attached to the leaf axils in place of a flower. These bulbils will later fall off the plant and sprout—a tricky, non-sexual way of spreading the plant! • The leaves are mostly basal, lobed, and hairless.

Distribution: *L. glabrum* occurs in dry, gravelly flats and forest clearings throughout the Sierra from 500–10,000'. It extends north to British Columbia and east to Colorado. **Names:** *Lithophragma* (see p. 113). *Glabrum* means 'smooth' in reference to the hairless leaves. **Typical location:** Dry borders of Paige Meadows in Tahoe area (7000').

pink or white • 5 separate petals • perennial

Brewer's Mitrewort
Mitella breweri

LOW MONTANE, MID TO HIGH MONTANE, ALPINE

From a distance, Brewer's mitrewort looks like a swarm of greenish
spiders climbing up a stem. Each
4–12" stem may have **as many as
60 small (¹/₄"), yellowish-green
flowers** clinging to it. The spidery
look comes from the petals, which
consist of 2–5 pairs of thread-like
segments that extend out beyond
the tiny (¹/₈") flower cup. From
closer range, the flowers look more
like some strange, antennaed space
satellite! • These tiny, feathery
flowers are quite a contrast to the
leaves: like those of many members
of the saxifrage family, they are
basal, broad (1–3" wide), round in
outline, shallowly lobed, and
toothed. • Often you will find these
plants growing in thick clusters
along creeks or in damp places in
woods, their flowers bringing a lacy,
subtle, yellowish-green beauty to
their usually densely vegetated
habitat. • This plant is intriguing in
fall when the petals fall off, for then
the flower cup brims over with
dozens of the tiny, black seeds.

Distribution: The genus *Mitella* is composed of 12 species in temperate and
arctic North America and Asia. *M. breweri* grows in moist to wet areas throughout the Sierra from 6000–11,000'. It extends to British Columbia. **Names:**
Mitella means 'small cap' in reference to the fruit. *Breweri* (see p. 86). **Typical
location:** Along Round Lake Trail in Sierra Buttes/Lake Basin area (6600').

greenish-yellow • 5 separate petals • perennial

Pink Alumroot
Heuchera rubescens

LOW MONTANE, MID TO HIGH MONTANE, ALPINE

You have been out all day exploring and scrambling in the rocks around a beautiful, granite-encircled lake of the high Sierra. It's getting late in the afternoon, and the sun is dropping fast; the granite cliff ahead of you turns a cold, steely gray as it is cast in shadow. You shiver slightly in the chill. But then, in a crack in the granite wall, you see a sight that warms and delights you—a pinkish-white glow of sun not yet departed. The long, slender, many-flowered stems of alumroot stick out from the rock just far enough to catch the sun's last rays, which have already left the rock. • Alumroot's 6–12" stems rise above clusters of broad (1–2"), **roundish, lobed and toothed, basal leaves.** The stems bear **many-branched racemes of tiny** (¹/₄–¹/₂"), **white to pink flowers** that dangle in the breeze. • Pink alumroot clearly illustrates the meaning of its family name (saxifrage, meaning 'rock-breaker') because its tough roots penetrate into cracks and fissures in the rock wall.

Distribution: The genus *Heuchera* is composed of approximately 50 species in North America. *H. rubescens* occurs in rocky areas throughout the Sierra from 6000–12,000'. *H. rubescens* has several varieties, most of which occur only in the Sierra. One variety extends south to Mexico and east to Colorado. **Names:** J. von Heucher was an 18th-century German professor of medicine. *Rubescens* means 'becoming red' in reference to the pinkish tinge of the sepals and sometimes the petals. **Typical location:** Rock cliffs around Fontanillis Lake in Tahoe area (8400').

white to pink • 5 separate petals • perennial

Fringed Grass-of-Parnassus

Parnassia fimbriata

LOW MONTANE, MID TO HIGH MONTANE

Grass-of-Parnassus is very unusual for a saxifrage: rather than having spikes or racemes of many small flowers, its stems bear only **one large** (¹/₂–1"), **showy flower**. Like many saxifrages, however, the flowers of *Parnassia* are white, sometimes with a slight greenish tinge. • Fringed grass-of-Parnassus is a peculiar-looking flower. Its **five white, obovate petals are fringed along their lower edges with white, yellow-tipped threads**, and attached to the base of each petal is a stubby, lobed, orange staminode. The five fertile stamens radiate out flat between the petals (see photo, p. 111) • Each ¹/₂–2' stem, bearing only one flower at its tip, rises above the mostly basal ¹/₂–1" heart-shaped leaves. Often there will be one additional clasping leaf at or above the mid-point of the stem.

Distribution: The genus *Parnassia* is composed of 25 species in northern temperate and arctic areas. *P. fimbriata* occurs rarely in wet areas in the northern Sierra from 6000–10,000'. It extends north to Alaska and east to the Rockies. **Names:** *Parnassia* refers to Mt. Parnassus in Greece, mistakenly thought to be home of a *Parnassia* species by an early Greek naturalist. *Fimbriata* means 'fringed' in reference to the petals. **Typical location:** Base of cliff along the source of Pole Creek in Tahoe area (7400').

Related Plant: Smooth grass-of-Parnassus (*P. californica*, formerly *P. palustris*, bottom photo) has similar flowers but **does not have fringed petals**. It occurs along creeks and in wet meadows throughout the Sierra (and to southern Oregon) from 5000–10,000'. *Californica* (see p. 85). Perennial. Range: Same.

white • 5 separate petals • perennial

Brook Saxifrage
Saxifraga odontoloma
MID TO HIGH MONTANE

If you picture a saxifrage (*Saxifraga* genus) in your mind, you probably are visualizing a plant and flowers very much like brook saxifrage. • Its ¹/₂–1¹/₂' leafless stem rises above basal leaves and is slender and delicately branched into an open inflorescence. The **leaves are large and round (to somewhat kidney-shaped) and are scalloped with sharp teeth**; their petioles may be as long as 8" although they can be much shorter. Many small (¹/₄"), white flowers hang gracefully from short pedicels. Each of the five separate, white petals looks like a spade with a short, narrow handle and has a pair of beautiful yellow dots, contrasting with the petals and also with the red of the 10 anthers and the fleshy, 2-beaked ovary (especially red after fertilization).

Distribution: *S. punctata* occurs in wet meadows and along streams throughout the Sierra from 6500–11,000'. It extends widely to the Coastal Range of northern California and into the Cascades north to British Columbia. **Names:** *Saxifraga* (see p. 112). *Odontoloma* means 'toothed' in reference to the jagged-edges leaves. **Formerly called** *S. punctata.* **Typical location:** Along creeks on south face of Castle Peak in Tahoe area (8200').

Related Plant: Bog saxifrage (*S. oregana;* bottom photo) has the small (¹/₄"), white flowers with 2-beaked ovary and basal leaves (oval) typical of the *Saxifraga* genus, but the flowers are not in the usual loose panicle. They are **crowded into a cylindrical cluster at the end of the thick, succulent, glandular stem.** *S. oregana* occurs in **very wet areas** throughout the Sierra (and Cascades) from 3500–11,000'. *Oregana* refers to part of its location. Perennial. Range: Low Montane, Mid to High Montane.

white • 5 separate petals • perennial

Tolmie's Saxifrage

Saxifraga tolmiei

MID TO HIGH MONTANE, ALPINE

Think of a typical member of the *Saxifraga* genus: small, white flowers with five narrow, widely separated petals and a 2-beaked ovary; slender, mostly leafless stems; basal leaves. Now think of a typical alpine plant: short stems rising only slightly above a tight mat or cushion of tiny hairy and/or waxy leaves. Now combine these images and you have *S. tolmiei*—an alpine saxifrage of the Sierra and the Cascades. • **The 1–6" reddish stem rises above a very dense mat of tiny ($^1/_8$–$^1/_2$"), succulent, spoon-shaped leaves.** There are a few stem leaves, which remain clinging to the stem even after they die—dry, stiff, and red. • You often find great masses of the flowers and leaves huddled behind rocks on open, windswept ridges high above timberline. A few small ($^1/_4$") flowers, each on its own short pedicel, cluster at the top of the short stem above the shiny, fleshy leaves. The flowers may appear to have many white petals. Close inspection will show, however, that there are only five petals; the narrower club-shaped white structures are actually stamens.

Distribution: *S. tolmiei* occurs in moist areas where snow lies late on rocky ridges in the high mountains throughout the Sierra from 8500–12,000'. It is much more common outside our area, extending through the Cascades all the way to Alaska. **Names:** *Saxifraga* (see p. 112). *Tolmiei* (see p. 50). **Also known as** alpine saxifrage. **Typical location:** Rocky flats near summit of Freel Peak in Tahoe area (10,700').

Related Plant: Sierra saxifrage (*S. aprica;* bottom photo) is another short-stemmed saxifrage of wet areas in high elevations. Many of its tiny ($^1/_8$–$^1/_4$"), **white flowers form a rounded cluster atop the 1–5" leafless, reddish-purple stem**. The basal leaves are relatively large (to 1$^1/_2$"), oval, and purple-tinged. *S. aprica* occurs in moist, stony places throughout the Sierra (and Cascades) from 6000–12,000'. *Aprica* means 'exposed to the sun.' Perennial. Range: Same.

white • 5 separate petals • perennial

Waterleaf Family
(Hydrophyllaceae)

Visualize a plant with large, slightly cupped leaves in a gentle rain. Slowly, small drops of water begin to accumulate in the bottom of the leaf. Clinging to the edge of the leaf, trying to stay out of the pool, is what looks like a very fuzzy caterpillar. The significance of the water in the leaf is probably obvious—the waterleaf family name came from some of its species that do have leaves that can hold a bit of water—but what is the fuzzy caterpillar? Be patient: it won't take long to get to know this interesting family.

Waterleaf is one of the many families that have flowers with five petals united into a bowl, funnel, or bell, five sepals, five stamens, and one pistil (sometimes with two styles, sometimes with a 2-parted stigma). However, it does have some very distinguishing characteristics. Most of the species of the waterleaf family look fuzzy. The plants are usually hairy, the reproductive parts protrude way out of the flower bowl, and most distinctively the flowers are often arranged in coiled cymes that resemble curled up caterpillars!

typical waterleaf leaves on ballhead phacelia

Some species in this family have none of these fuzzy characteristics, but most species have at least one, if not all, of them. One interesting characteristic that is universal to waterleaf family species is that the five petals overlap to some degree.

The waterleaf family is relatively small with only 20 genera and about 300 species, but its species are widespread, occurring on all the world's continents except Australia. The western United States (and the California Floristic Province [CA-FP] in particular) is the world's waterleaf center: almost half of the world's estimated 300 species occur in the CA-FP!

baby blue eyes

The genera you are most likely to encounter in our area are *Phacelia, Nemophila, Pholistoma, Nama,* and *Hydrophyllum. Phacelia* is by far the largest genus both worldwide (approximately 175 species) and in our area.

An exception to the many fascinating 'caterpillar' plants (without the cyme, the dense hairiness, or the long, protruding reproductive parts), is a most enchanting and delightful flower of spring in the foothills: *Nemophila menziesii* (baby blue-eyes, p. 123).

typical cymes

Baby Blue-eyes
Nemophila menziesii
CENTRAL VALLEY, FOOTHILLS

Baby blue-eyes is one of the great joys of spring in the foothills—looking into the faces of these glorious flowers is almost like looking up into a bottomless blue sky flecked with fleecy white clouds. • Each 4–12" stem bears several **large (to 1¹/₂")**, **bowl-shaped flowers**. The bowl is **bright blue with a white center** and the five petals are blue-veined. The five anthers are short with dark (purple or black) pollen. • As is the case with many species of *Nemophila*, the stem is rather weak, sometimes sprawling slightly on neighboring plants. The 1–2" deeply lobed leaves are in opposite pairs on the stem and are sparsely hairy. Also typical of many *Nemophila* species are the tiny bent-back spurs (auricles) between the five green sepals. • Baby blue-eyes often look like large pieces of blue sky on the earth because they frequently grow in large clusters in the grass.

Distribution: The genus *Nemophila* is composed of 11 species in western North America and the southeastern United States. *N. menziesii* grows in meadows and woodland openings throughout California from 50–5000'. It extends to the Mojave Desert. **Names:** *Nemophila* means 'woodland-loving,' because many of its species (though not baby blue-eyes, which seems to prefer the sun) grow in the shade. Archibald Menzies was a naturalist on the Vancouver Expedition at the end of the 18th century. **Typical location:** Grassy flats along Old Foresta Road just west of Yosemite (1500').

blue • 5 petals overlapping in bowl • annual

Blue Fiesta Flower

Pholistoma auritum

CENTRAL VALLEY, FOOTHILLS

Blue fiesta flower is somewhat like a taller baby blue-eyes (p. 123) of the shade. Its weak stem bears several large (to 1¹/₂") **blue bowl-shaped flowers, which have white centers and five protruding stamens with dark anthers.** If you look underneath the overlapping petals, you'll even see the five bent-back spurs (auricles) between the sepals also characteristic of baby blue-eyes. • Though they are close relatives, there are some very distinct differences between these two waterleafs. Fiesta flower grows much taller (to 3') and has a much weaker stem than baby blue-eyes. This weak stem makes fiesta flower unable to stand by itself, so it usually hangs on for dear life to whatever is near it! If you want to find out how it hangs on, brush up against the stem or leaves. You will find that it is **covered with reverse-barbed prickles that cling in a raspy sort of way.** • The flowers are a much darker blue (to lavender or purple), all the more intense for its shade environment. The leaves have deep pinnate lobes that are swept back, looking like some kind of supersonic jet. • Fiesta flower is quite dazzling, despite (or perhaps because of) its shady environment, for many plants typically sprawl together and on other flowering plants (e.g., on twining snake lily, p. 72) creating quite a jungle of rich blossoms.

Distribution: The genus *Pholistoma* has only three species, all of which occur in the southwestern United States and Baja. *P. auritum* occurs primarily in shaded woodlands of the central Sierra from sea level to 4000'. It extends to southern California. **Names:** *Pholistoma* means 'scale mouth' in reference to the five 'nipples' on the flower tube. *Auritum* means 'eared' in reference to the auricles. **Typical location:** Shady slopes along Hite's Cove Trail just west of Yosemite (1500').

blue to purple • 5 petals overlapping in bowl • annual

Foothill Phacelia

Phacelia egena

FOOTHILLS, LOW MONTANE

Foothill phacelia is a perfect example of waterleaf fuzziness. The flowers are packed closely together in a **caterpillar-like cyme**, the inflorescence (pedicels, sepals, even the lower parts of the stamens) are **densely white-hairy**, and the stamens and pistil protrude way out of the bell-shaped flower tube. • The ¹/₂–2' stem bears several deeply dissected, basal leaves, a few undissected stem leaves, and a tightly packed cyme of many flowers. The ¹/₂" flowers are a **creamy white with brown specks at the base of the petals**. The five green sepals are very narrow and pointed and are covered with white hairs.

Distribution: *P. egena* grows on slopes and in woodland openings throughout the Sierra foothills from 300–5000'. It extends to the Cascades. **Names:** *Phacelia* means 'cluster' in reference to the densely packed cyme. *Egena* is of unknown origin. **Typical location:** Grassy slopes along Hite's Cove Trail just west of Yosemite (1500').

Related Plant: Mariposa phacelia (*P. vallicola*; bottom photo) is a very uncommon phacelia with beautiful ¹/₄–¹/₂" **blue-purple flowers**. It grows in open rocky or gravelly areas in the Sierra from 1500–7000'. Formerly reported to be limited to a few canyons in the Merced and Tuolumne river drainages, it is now reported to reach as far north as the southern Cascades. I have found this exquisite phacelia along the Merced River just west of Yosemite at 2000'. *Vallicola* means 'wall-dwelling' in reference to its rocky habitat. Annual. Range: Same.

dirty white • 5 petals overlapping in bell
• perennial

125

Caterpillar Phacelia

Phacelia cicutaria

FOOTHILLS

The *Phacelia* genus is by far the largest genus in the waterleaf family, and it has the most prototypical fuzzy flowers. Caterpillar phacelia is well named indeed because it is **one of the fuzziest of the phacelias**. At the end of the 1–2', bristly-hairy stem are numerous **coiled cymes, each packed tightly with many ¹/₂" yellowish-white flowers**. The reproductive parts stick ¹/₂" or so out of the flowers and the narrow sepals are long-hairy. Everywhere you look on this plant you see fuzz! • Many large (to 8"), deeply lobed and toothed leaves alternate along the stem, which more often than not is leaning against other plants or against the dry, rocky banks where this plant grows.

Distribution: The genus *Phacelia* is composed of approximately 175 species, most in western North America. *P. cicutaria* occurs on rocky or grassy slopes throughout the Sierra foothills from 500–4000'. It extends to southern California (including the deserts) and Baja. **Names:** *Phacelia* (see p. 125). *Cicutaria* means 'resembling *Cicuta*,' *Cicuta* is the water-hemlock genus in the carrot family. **Typical location:** Rocky slopes along Hite's Cove Trail just west of Yosemite (1500').

white • 5 overlapping petals in bell • annual

Varied-leaf Phacelia

Phacelia heterophylla

FOOTHILLS, LOW MONTANE, MID TO HIGH MONTANE

In case you have any doubt that this plant is a *Phacelia, P. heterophylla* gives you numerous opportunities to confirm its identity. The single, stout stem can grow as high as 4', and 1¹/₂' of it can be the inflorescence, which bears **hordes of caterpillar-like cymes.** Each of these tight, curled 'caterpillars' is composed of many ¹/₄" **greenish-white (sometimes greenish-yellow) flowers crammed tightly together.**

• As the species name suggests, the leaves of *P. heterophylla* are quite varied. The basal (and lower stem) leaves are deeply lobed with one or two pair of lateral lobes and one much larger terminal lobe. The much smaller upper stem leaves are usually ovate and unlobed.

Distribution: *P. heterophylla* grows in dry areas on slopes and flats (sometimes along roadsides) throughout the central and northern Sierra over a remarkable elevational range from 500–9500'. It extends north to the Cascades of Oregon and east to the Great Basin. **Names:** *Phacelia* (see p. 125). *Heterophylla* means 'varied-leaf.' **Typical location:** Dry flats along trail to Smith Lake in Sierra Buttes area (6000').

Related Plant: Low phacelia (*P. humilis*; bottom photo) also has dense 'caterpillars' of flowers but they grow on a much smaller and more delicate plant. Often **large mats** of these graceful **blue-purple bowl-shaped flowers** cover patches of the dry flats where they grow. *P. humilis* occurs throughout the Sierra (especially its eastern edge) and into Washington from 5000–8500'. *Humilis* means 'low.' Annual. Range: Low Montane, Mid to High Montane.

white • 5 overlapping petals in bell • biennial

127

Varied-leaf Nemophila

Nemophila heterophylla

CENTRAL VALLEY, FOOTHILLS, LOW MONTANE

Although not the prototypical fuzzy waterleaf with caterpillar-like cymes and long-protruding reproductive parts (see *Phacelia,* pp. 125–27 and 132–33), *N. heterophylla* does have the typical bell-shaped flowers with five overlapping petals and the usual hairy stems and sepals. You might recognize it as a member of the *Nemophila* genus by its **weak stem** (often sprawling on other plants), its opposite pairs of deeply lobed leaves, its **shade habitat**, and its reflexed auricles between the sepals. • In *N. heterophylla* the **small** ($^1/_4$–$^1/_2$"), **white (sometimes bluish) flowers** grow on $^1/_2$" pedicels coming out of the axils of the upper stem leaves. When the plant is in fruit, these pedicels elongate to as long as 2". • This *Nemophila* occurs on grassy foothill slopes in the shade under oaks or other trees or tall shrubs. Because many of the weak 4–16" stems often tangle together, you will frequently find these shady environments liberally sprinkled with these graceful and delicate blossoms.

Distribution: *N. heterophylla* occurs in shady areas in grasslands and foothill slopes throughout the Central Valley and Sierra from 100–4000'. It extends to the mountains of the central and northern coast of California and into Oregon. **Names:** *Nemophila* (see p. 123). *Heterophylla* means 'varied-leaf.' **Typical location:** Shady areas under oaks on grassy hillsides along the Merced River west of Yosemite (1500').

white • 5 overlapping petals in bell • annual

Mitten-leaf Nemophila

Nemophila spatulata

LOW MONTANE, MID TO HIGH MONTANE

Five overlapping petals, prostrate (very weak) stems, and hairy bent-back auricles between the sepals allow you to recognize the waterleaf family and also the *Nemophila* genus...perhaps even before consciously noting these specific characteristics. It is reassuring when your 'feel' for flowers is confirmed by detailed observation! • *N. spatulata* is a particularly charming *Nemophila*, as the small (¹/₄"), bright white flowers seem to be offered up for us to appreciate by many adorable mitten-clad hands. **These ¹/₄–1" leaves just below the flowers are 3-lobed and prickly white-hairy,** looking for all the world like some dwarf's homemade handwarmers! • Close inspection of the flowers will show delicate patterns and coloration—the white petals are vertically veined with purple and

often are sprinkled toward the base with dark dots. Sometimes larger purple spots adorn the petal tips as well. • The stems are only 4–8", but the flowers are often even closer to the ground because the stems are frequently prostrate.

Distribution: *N. spatulata* grows in damp meadows and open areas (sometimes even on the drying mud bottoms of short-lived shallow pools) throughout the Sierra from 3500–10,000'. It extends north to the Cascades and south to southern California. **Names:** *Nemophila* (see p. 123). *Spatulata* refers to the 'spoon-shaped' (in outline) leaves. **Typical location:** Caked, dried mud where water had been pooling along trail to Paige Meadows in Tahoe area (6700').

white • 5 overlapping petals in bell • annual

California Waterleaf

Hydrophyllum occidentale

LOW MONTANE, MID TO HIGH MONTANE

With the genus *Hydrophyllum* (meaning 'water-leaf') we have the name-source for the waterleaf family, so we might expect *Hydrophyllum* plants to typify that family. In most ways, they do. • The leaves are large and deeply lobed, somewhat hairy, and often slightly cupped, capable of holding a bit of dew or rainwater. The flowers have five rounded petals that overlap to form small, bell-shaped flowers. The overall appearance of the plant is quite fuzzy because the stamens and pistil stick $^1/_2$" out of the flower and many of the flowers are crammed together into a dense inflorescence. This inflorescence is a **dense head with flowers packed** about as tightly as possible. The hairy sepals and 'cottonball' buds further enhance this cuddly 'fuzzball' appearance. • In *H. occidentale* the head of **lavender (sometimes white with lavender markings)** flowers sits atop a $^1/_2$–2' stem. Most of the large, deeply pinnately lobed leaves rise vertically on their own stems (petioles). These leaves may reach as high as $1^1/_2$', but the flowers usually are clearly displayed above them.

Distribution: The genus *Hydrophyllum* is composed of eight species, all of which are in North America. *H. occidentale* occurs in forest openings throughout the Sierra from 2500–9500'. It extends to the Cascades of Oregon and south to Arizona. **Names:** *Hydrophyllum* means 'water-leaf.' *Occidentale* means 'western' in reference to the plant's distribution. **Typical location:** Openings in woods along Castle Peak Trail in Tahoe area (7500').

Related Plant: Star lavender/cat's breeches (*H. capitatum*; bottom photo) has almost identical flowers in very similar dense heads, but the **flowers are nearly on the ground, often hidden by the tall, deeply lobed leaves**. *H. capitatum* is common in sagebrush flats throughout the northern Sierra and Cascades from 3000–7000'. *Capitatum* means 'head' in reference to the inflorescence. Perennial. Range: Low Montane, Mid to High Montane.

lavender • 5 overlapping petals in bell • perennial

130

California Hesperochiron
Hesperochiron californicus
LOW MONTANE, MID TO HIGH MONTANE

There are only two species in this genus, both of which grow in our area. The flowers (and plants) of both species are very odd for waterleafs: the flowers are not in caterpillar-like cymes or even dense heads, the reproductive parts do not stick out, there are no auricles, the leaves are neither opposite nor lobed, and to top it off the flowers sometimes have six petals! • California hesperochiron has a **basal rosette of shiny, tongue-like 2–3" leaves among which several large (1"), white, funnel-shaped flowers nestle** (on short pedicels). The flowers have yellowish throats; the petals are veined with lavender or purple.

Distribution: The genus *Hesperochiron* has only two species, both in the western United States. *H. californicus* occurs in wet meadows throughout the Sierra from 4000–9000'. It ranges widely from Baja to Washington. **Names:** The meaning of *Hesperochiron* is somewhat uncertain: it derives from words for 'evening' or 'western' and Chiron—a mythic centaur skilled in medicine. *Californicus* (see p. 97). **Typical location:** Grassy meadows in Kyburz flat in Tahoe area (5800').

Related Plant: Dwarf hesperochiron (*H. pumilis*; bottom photo) is similar but the **flower is more flat than funnel-shaped. Its white petals are streaked purple, and the flower throat is bright yellow.** Though there are usually five petals, sometimes there are six. *H. pumilis* occurs in wet meadows throughout the Sierra and the Cascades and south to Arizona from 1500–9000'. *Pumilis* means 'dwarf.' Perennial. Range: Foothills, Low Montane, Mid to High Montane.

white • 5 overlapping petals in bell • perennial

131

Ballhead Phacelia
Phacelia hydrophylloides
LOW MONTANE, MID TO HIGH MONTANE

Although recognizable as a *Phacelia* with its long, protruding reproductive parts and dense cluster of 5-petaled bell-like flowers, *P. hydrophylloides* is a bit unusual for this genus. The flower is really more tubular than bell-shaped, with a broader and deeper tube and less conspicuous flaring petals than most *Phacelia*. Also the petals are less noticeably overlapping, appearing instead to be fused into that conspicuous tube. But the most apparent difference from the *Phacelia* norm is the arrangement of the flowers in the inflorescence—it is more a **dense, spherical head** than a caterpillar-like cyme. • The hairy stems are 4–12" tall and bear several of the **large, broad, felt-like leaves that are often deeply lobed.** These leaves, as the species name suggests, just might be able to hold some water! • The petals are shiny blue-violet (sometimes white) and the inside of the flower tube is often a bright yellow-green. The delicate stamens and style protrude up to $1/2$" out of this tube.

Distribution: *P. hydrophylloides* occurs in openings in woods throughout the Sierra from 5000–10,000'. It extends to the Oregon Cascades. **Names:** *Phacelia* (see p. 125). *Hydrophylloides* means 'like water-leaf.' **Typical location:** Partial shade of forest openings along trail to Barker Peak in Tahoe area (7600').

blue-violet • 5 petals in bell • perennial

Timberline Phacelia

Phacelia hastata ssp. *compacta*

MID TO HIGH MONTANE, ALPINE

Caterpillars above timberline? These 'caterpillars' are stiff-hairy and stay close to the ground. You will easily recognize the flower of timberline phacelia as a waterleaf and as a *Phacelia* because it has very long, protruding reproductive parts and it clusters with its neighbors into dense caterpillar-like cymes. • The **stems grow only 2–8" tall and frequently are decumbent, so the many ¹/₄" creamy-white (sometimes lavender) flowers stay down out of the threatening alpine wind.** As further protection, the stems and the clustered, elliptic 1–4" leaves are covered with stiff, white hairs. • The stamens and pistil stick out as much as ¹/₂" from the flower tube, completing the overall fuzzy look.

Distribution: Timberline phacelia occurs in gravelly and rocky places throughout the Sierra from 7000–13,000'. It extends to the Cascades into Washington. **Names:** *Phacelia* (see p. 125). *Hastata* means 'spear-shaped' in reference to the pointed leaves. *Compacta* refers to the compact growth form (typical of high elevation plants). **Also known as** silverleaf phacelia. **Formerly called** *P. frigida*. **Typical location:** Rocky ridges on the Dana Plateau just east of Yosemite (10,800').

white • 5 overlapping petals in bell • perennial

Stonecrop Family
(Crassulaceae)

The name 'stonecrop' refers to the typical habitat of members of this intriguing family. The stonecrops usually grow in dry, rocky areas—frequently on rock ledges or even out of cracks in sheer rock cliffs, where they often rival the lichen for showiness.

One look at a typical stonecrop plant will tell you how it survives in its dry environment. The leaves are soft and fleshy (succulent), containing a considerable amount of watery sap in their cells. As a further strategy for reducing evaporation, the leaves of many stonecrops are waxy and grow in a basal 'rosette'—an intricate pattern of ground-hugging leaves where each leaf gets maximum exposure to the sun with minimum exposure to the dessicating wind.

live forever

The flowers of this family are tubular, with petals flaring out into stars. Although there are usually five petals, sometimes there are four (e.g., rosy sedum, p. 141), or three, or more.

Most species of this family have bright yellow petals, sometimes tending toward yellow-orange or even red. There are 3–5 triangular sepals, 3–5 pistils, and stamens that are either the same number as the sepals or twice the number of sepals.

typical leaf rosette

The stonecrop family is composed of approximately 30 genera and some 1500 species with worldwide distribution, especially in dry temperate areas. The most widespread genera (both in the wild and in cultivation for ornamentals) are *Sedum* and *Dudleya*, but other genera you might encounter in our area are *Parvisedum* and *Crassula*.

dwarf cliff sedum

Dwarf Cliff Sedum
Parvisedum pumilum

CENTRAL VALLEY, FOOTHILLS

Although it has the 5-petaled star flowers and succulent leaves typical of the stonecrops, *P. pumilum* is unusual for both its leaves and its favored habitat. **The tiny (¹/₄") leaves are tightly woven together on the delicate, reddish 2–10" stems**, creating something resembling those lanyards some of us laboriously constructed in summer camp!

• Seemingly resting here and there on these 'lanyard' stems are several bright yellow flowers, whose five widely separated petals form graceful stars. Ten small, yellow (to brown) anthers tip the thread-like filaments, which splay out symmetrically from the center and form their own star.

• Although *P. pumilum* does occur in rocky areas, it is usually found blooming around drying vernal pools.

Distribution: The genus *Parvisedum* is composed of four species, all endemic to California. *P. pumilum* occurs in the Central Valley and in the foothills from 100–3000'. It grows in the coastal ranges of northern California. **Names:** *Parvisedum* means 'little sedum.' *Pumilum* means 'dwarf.' **Also known as** sedella. **Typical location:** Rocky flats around wet depressions on top of Table Mountain near Oroville (1200').

yellow • 5 petals united in tube flaring into star • annual

136

Pacific Sedum

Sedum spathulifolium

FOOTHILLS, LOW MONTANE, MID TO HIGH MONTANE

In a family noted for its distinctive and striking, succulent leaves, the leaves of Pacific sedum are extraordinarily interesting and beautiful. As with most of the stonecrop family members and almost all of the *Sedum* species, most of the leaves of Pacific sedum form a basal rosette (there are a few smaller stem leaves as well). However, whereas the basal leaves of *Dudleya* (p. 138) and most *Sedum* are up-turned and often pointed and rather cactus-like (see pp. 139–40), those of *S. spathulifolium* are **layered flat and tight** and are rounded. They are so **soft-looking** (not at all cactus-like) and so tightly layered that they look almost like flower petals rather than leaves. • Many (5–50) yellow, star-shaped flowers cluster in the branched inflorescence atop the 2–12" stem. Unlike the other sedums in our area whose petals unite at their base to form tubes, the petals of this sedum are completely free from each other.

Distribution: The genus *Sedum* has about 350 species in northern temperate areas and in mountains in the tropics. *S. spathulifolium* occurs on rock outcrops usually in the shade throughout the Sierra from 200–7500'. It extends to British Columbia. **Names:** There is some disagreement about the origins of the word *Sedum*—it may mean 'to assuage' in reference to its healing properties or it may mean 'to sit' in reference to its growth form. *Spathulifolium* means 'spatulate-leaved.' **Typical location:** Shady rock outcrops along Independence Trail off Route 49 near Nevada City (1200').

yellow • 5 separate petals • perennial

Live-forever
Dudleya cymosa
FOOTHILLS

Live-forever dazzles with its acrobatics and tenacity, often seeming to grow right out of solid rock cliffs. The plant's most conspicuous feature is its gorgeous **rosette of broad, fleshy, pointed 2–6" leaves**, which store water from fall rains to sustain the plant through the rest of the year in its hot, dry environment. By the end of summer, the leaves are usually quite withered, but will engorge again with the next fall's showers—hence 'live-forever.' • Out of the side of this basal rosette of leaves ascends **one or a few 4–12" stout, red stems, each bearing numerous striking ¹/₂" flowers**. The five triangular sepals form a tube out of which the five pointed petals flare. The colors of the flowers vary somewhat, but often the sepals are orange-red and the petals are bright yellow. Both sepals and petals are shiny-waxy. There are 10 yellow anthers and five fused pistils.

Distribution: The genus *Dudleya* is composed of approximately 45 species, all of which are in southwestern North America. *D. cymosa* grows in rocky areas throughout the Sierra from 200–9000', but is much more frequent in foothill elevations. It occurs in the coastal ranges of California and into southwest Oregon. **Names:** W.R. Dudley was a botanist of the American West around the turn of the 20th century. *Cymosa* means 'bearing cymes' in reference to the growth form of this plant. **Also known as** canyon dudleya. **Typical location:** Rock cliffs along Hite's Cove Trail just west of Yosemite (1500').

yellow (orange-red) • 5 petals united in tube flaring at tips • perennial

Sierra Stonecrop
Sedum obtusatum
LOW MONTANE, MID TO HIGH MONTANE, ALPINE

S. obtusatum is a typical stonecrop: it grows in the rocks and has clusters of many (8–60) yellow, star-shaped flowers on stems that rise above a basal rosette of succulent leaves. In *S. obtusatum* the **leaves** in the basal rosette and the numerous leaves growing off the 1–8" stem **are spoon-shaped.** The stems are often reddish. • **The five bright yellow petals flare out of the flower tube, forming delicate stars with widely separated 'arms.'** Late in the blooming season, the petals fade to pink or buff and the leaves (especially the stem leaves) often turn reddish (bottom photo).

Distribution: *S. obtusatum* occurs in rock outcrops throughout the Sierra from 5000–13,000'. It occurs in the Cascades to Oregon and in the Coastal Range of northern California. **Names:** *Sedum* (see p. 137). *Obtusatum* means 'blunt,' a characteristic of the unpointed leaves. **Typical location:** Rock ledges at the source of Pole Creek in the Tahoe area (6800').

yellow • 5 petals united in tube flaring into star • perennial

Narrow-leaf Stonecrop

Sedum lanceolatum

MID TO HIGH MONTANE

Narrow-leaf stonecrop is very similar to Sierra stonecrop (*S. obtusatum*, p. 139) in appearance and in habitat. Both plants grow on rock outcrops, both plants have succulent leaves, most of which form a basal rosette, and both plants have clusters of bright yellow, star-shaped flowers. • The main differences between these two close relatives are in the leaves. *S. obtusatum* leaves are blunt and spoon-shaped, whereas *S. lanceolatum* **leaves are more narrow and pointed or 'lance-like.'** Another strong clue is in the stem leaves: if they have mostly **shriveled or fallen off by the time the flowers bloom**, it is probably narrow-leaf stonecrop. • The stem rarely exceeds 8"; the inflorescence rarely exceeds 25 flowers. The flowers are a blazing yellow!

Distribution: *S. lanceolatum* occurs on granite outcrops throughout the Sierra from 6000–9000'. It extends to the Cascades and north to Alaska. **Names:** *Sedum* (see p. 137). *Lanceolatum* means 'lanceolate.' **Typical location:** Rocky flats on Red Lake Peak near Carson Pass (9000').

yellow • 5 petals united in tube flaring into star • perennial

Rosy Sedum
Sedum roseum
MID TO HIGH MONTANE, ALPINE

For rosy sedum it is the leaves more than the flowers or growth form that tell you it is a stonecrop. The 2–12" stems grow in such dense clusters (several sprouting from one rootstock) and are covered with so many succulent leaves that the plant often appears to be a shrub. The flowers (with four petals and four sepals) are deep maroon and cluster at the tips of the stems. The leaves are oval and rather flat and are attached directly to the stems. • It is always a joy to find rosy sedum because it radiates lushness and intensity. The rich wine-red flowers (in bloom or in bud) contrast vividly with the fresh-green leaves.

Distribution: *S. roseum* grows in damp, rocky areas throughout the Sierra from 6000–12,000'. It is a circumboreal plant ranging throughout much of the northern latitudes. **Names:** *Sedum* (see p. 137). *Roseum* probably refers to the rose-like fragrance of the roots, though it could also refer to the color of the flowers or the often reddish leaves and stems. **Also known as** western roseroot. **Typical location:** Near seeps on granite on the Dana Plateau just east of Yosemite (11,000').

maroon • 4 petals united in tube flaring at tip • perennial

Snapdragon Family
(Scrophulariaceae)

'Two up, three down'—the sign of the snapdragon. The snapdragon (or figwort) family is large and varied with some 200 genera and about 3000 species worldwide, but almost without exception the flowers have five petals united into a 2-lipped tube, with two petals in the upper lip and three in the lower.

monkeyflower

Although the flowers are not radially symmetrical, they are bilaterally symmetrical—a vertical bisection will produce two halves that are mirror images. In most genera this flower structure is readily apparent; in a few (e.g., *Castilleja* and *Orthocarpus*, where the flowers are mostly atrophied and are hidden by the colorful petal-like bracts) it takes close inspection and botanical faith to ascertain this feature.

The snapdragon family is among our most fascinating, with some of our showiest, strangest, and/or most endearing flowers. In addition to dragons, this family harbors monkeys (large and small), elephants (pink even!), toads, foxes, and owls, sweet little Veronica, blue-eyed Mary, and even Indian art implements!

Some genera, *Mimulus* and *Penstemon* in particular, have flowers with delicate faces

purple owl's-clover

blue-eyed mary   foxglove

that you could swear have almost human expressions!

There are flowers of almost every color (and even some half and half!), size (from 2" to barely $^1/_8$"), shape (tubes, trumpets, bowls, beaks, trunks), and lifestyle (including parasites).

California and our area in particular is one of the world's great centers for the snapdragon family, especially for the genera *Castilleja* (paintbrushes), *Collinsia*, *Mimulus* (monkeyflowers), and *Penstemon*. The gathering of monkeyflowers here is especially impressive: of the estimated 100 species of *Mimulus* spread across western North America, Chile, eastern Asia, southern Africa, and the South Pacific, over 60 grow in California with about 40 occurring in our area.

yellow-and-white monkeyflower

On a lesser scale, of the 18 species of *Collinsia*, 17 occur in California, about half of which occur within our area.

Though so many species of the snap-dragon family are widespread and common, they are usually dramatic and striking. Whether they occur in magnificent masses or in stately solitude, they command great respect and gratitude wherever they are encountered.

field of purple owl's-clover

Kellogg's monkeyflower

Chinese Houses
Collinsia heterophylla

CENTRAL VALLEY, FOOTHILLS

When you think of great wildflower displays in the Sierra foothills, you probably visualize open, sunny slopes nearly solid with the bright oranges of poppy (see photo, p. 93), or sunny yellows of goldfield, or perhaps the mixed blues and purples of lupine and owl's-clover. But somewhat hidden in the shady areas (e.g., under oaks) you will find a great floral treasure of the foothills: Chinese houses.
• Each 4–24" stem of Chinese houses bears several to many **whorls of 2–7 gorgeous ³/₄–1" flowers.** The **two petals of the upper lip are white with carefully etched red-purple spots and lines and with deep, dark violet tips.** The two lower petals are solid with that same violet, shading to rose-purple. The middle petal of the lower lip in all *Collinsia* species is somewhat hidden—folded into a keel-like structure that houses the reproductive parts. • The several pairs of large (3"), triangular, opposite leaves along the stem add to the plant's allure. • The intense colors and exquisite markings of this flower invite you for a closer look, but watch out for that shiny-leaved plant lurking nearby...yep, it's poison oak!

Distribution: The genus *Collinsia* is composed of 18 species, all of which are in North America, especially of California. *C. heterophylla* occurs throughout California below 3000'. **Names:** Zaccheus Collins was a Philadelphia botanist of the late 1700s and early 1800s. *Heterophylla* means 'varied-leaf' probably in reference to the leaves being deeply lobed in the seedlings and only shallowly toothed in the mature plants. **Typical location:** Along Hite's Cove Trail just west of Yosemite (1500').

rose-purple • 5 petals (appears to be 4) united in 2-lipped tube
• annual

Pansy Monkeyflower
Mimulus angustatus
CENTRAL VALLEY, FOOTHILLS

Our area is one of the world's great monkeyflower playgrounds. The genus name *Mimulus* suggests the characteristic that distinguishes the monkeyflowers from other members of the snapdragon family: the five petals of the flower tube flare out into an open, showy 'face,' which is usually broader than the flower tube is long. • Most monkeyflowers are yellow, while most of the rest are some shade of red or pink; pansy monkeyflower is all of these! Each of its **five rounded petals is pink blending to white toward the flower's throat. A large red-purple spot decorates each petal where the pink goes to white.** Looking down the throat into the flower tube, you will see two bright yellow ribs covered with short, stiff, yellow hairs and several more maroon spots. Deeper down the tube, the ribs change from yellow to solid maroon. This rainbow of colors is somewhat evident on the outside of the 1–2" tube as well— a soft rose-maroon with occasional yellow markings. • Although *M. angustatus* is a typical monkeyflower in having its five petals flaring from a 2-lipped tube into a large (³/₄") face, it is unusual in that **the five petals are all nearly the same size and are arranged nearly symmetrically,** so the 2-lipped form (with two petals up and three petals down) is not as prominent as in most monkeyflowers. • Pansy monkeyflower usually grows only 2–4" tall and is often partially buried in its grassy environment. The ¹/₂–1' leaves are narrow and basal.

Distribution: The genus *Mimulus* is composed of approximately 100 species in temperate areas worldwide. *M. angustatus* grows in grassy fields and damp depressions in the San Joaquin Valley and neighboring foothills from 100–4000'. It grows in the Coast Range of northern California. **Names:** *Mimulus* means 'mime' in reference to the flower 'faces.' *Angustatus* means 'narrow' in reference to the leaves. **Typical location:** Grassy fields along Route 140 east of Merced (50').

pink • 5 petals united in 2-lipped tube • annual

Butter-and-Eggs

Triphysaria eriantha

CENTRAL VALLEY, FOOTHILLS

Whereas the 2-lipped flower tube with the 'two petals up, three petals down' so characteristic of the snapdragon family is clearly apparent in the monkeyflowers (*Mimulus*, pp. 146, 151–53, and 156–59) and penstemons (*Penstemon*, pp. 150, 160–63, and 169), in some of the other genera this flower structure is not so obvious. In the paintbrushes and the owl's-clovers in particular (*Castilleja, Orthocarpus, Triphysaria*), even finding the flower is sometimes a challenge, as it can easily be confused with the colorful leaf bracts. • In *T. eriantha* the flowers are easy enough to find, as the long, white flower tubes extend beyond the narrow, lobed leaves and purplish bracts. The **three lower petals are conspicuous, swollen, yellow sacs with white at their bases** (hence the name butter-and-eggs). The two upper petals are more difficult to recognize, however, as they are united into a purple, pointed beak that sticks out only slightly farther than the sacs.
• Sometimes you will find an acre or more solid with the creamy yellow blossom of *T. eriantha*. All *Triphysaria* (and *Castilleja* and *Orthocarpus*) species are green root-parasites (i.e., they have some green leaves for photosynthesis but also parasitize the roots of other plants).

Distribution: The genus *Triphysaria* has five species, all of which grow in western North America. Butter-and-eggs grows all through the Sierra in grassy fields below 4000'. It extends all through lowland California and southwest Oregon. **Names:** *Triphysaria* means '3 bladders'—very descriptive of this plant! *Eriantha* means 'woolly-flowered' in reference to the plant's soft hairs. **Formerly called** *Orthocarpus erianthus*. **Typical location:** Grassy fields along Route 140 east of Merced (100').

yellow • 5 petals united in 2-lipped tube • annual

147

Purple Owl's-clover
Castilleja exserta
CENTRAL VALLEY, FOOTHILLS

Several *Castilleja* species can form glorious masses of color in fields and on slopes on lower elevations, but purple owl's-clover may be the most spectacular. Sometimes **entire hillsides will be covered solid with its exuberant pink to purple 'flowers'** (see photo, p. 144); sometimes its masses will be delightfully intermingled with the bright blue to purple of various lupines. • As in most *Castilleja* (and *Orthocarpus*) the most conspicuous parts of the 'bloom' are actually the bracts (modified leaves), which in *C. exserta* are pink-purple and grow dense on the upper part of the 4–16" stem. Though the actual flowers are less obvious than these bracts, they have their own showy beauty. The lower three petals are a rich red-purple with white tips; the upper two petals form a narrow red-purple beak with a hairy 'cap.' If you look closely at the plant, it appears to be a purple tree with strange Dr. Seuss-like characters with purple spike hairdos peering out of its branches! • The 4–16" stems are stiff-hairy with numerous thread-like lower leaves.

Distribution: The genus *Castilleja* is composed of approximately 200 species, especially in western North America. *C. exserta* grows all through the CA-FP in grasslands and on open slopes below 4000'. **Names:** Domingo Castillejo was a Spanish botanist. *Exserta* is in reference to the flower's protruding beak. Early Californians called owl's-clover 'escobita' ('little broom'). **Formerly called** *Orthocarpus purpurascens*. **Typical location:** Grassy slopes along Hite's Cove Trail west of Yosemite (1500').

red-purple • 5 petals united in 2-lipped tube • annual

Valley Tassels
Castilleja attenuata
CENTRAL VALLEY, FOOTHILLS

Valley tassels and cream sacs (see Related Plant) have several characteristics in common: the bracts are colored the same as the petals (typical of paintbrush and owl's-clover); **the bracts and flowers are both white;** the flowers are almost as conspicuous as the bracts and resemble some bizarre cartoon character; and both species have been moved by botanists from the owl's-clover genus (*Orthocarpus*) to the paintbrush genus (*Castilleja*). • Valley tassels is generally a smaller plant than cream sacs—both shorter (4–12") and with a less robust, less dense inflorescence. The green leaves and the white-tipped bracts are divided into very narrow 'fingers.' • **The upper two petals of valley tassels form a short, white beak; the lower three petals form white pouches.**

Distribution: *C. attenuata* frequents grasslands throughout the CA-FP below 3000'. It extends from British Columbia to Baja. **Names:** *Castilleja* (see p.148). *Attenuata* means 'narrowed to a point' in reference to the leaf lobes. **Formerly called** *Orthocarpus attenuatus.* **Also known as** narrow-leaved owl's clover. **Typical location:** Grassy slopes along Hite's Cove Trail east of Yosemite (1500').

Related Plant: Cream sacs (*C. rubicundula,* formerly *Orthocarpus rubicundulus;* bottom photo) is a more robust plant with a wide-spreading inflorescence thick with bright white flowers and bracts. The **lower three petals form large, swollen, white sacs; the upper two petals form a strange, curved, white beak covered with long, white hairs.** *C. rubicundula* grows in open, grassy places below 3000'. *Rubicundula* means 'reddish.' Annual. Range: Same.

white • 5 petals united in 2-lipped tube • annual

Foothill Penstemon

Penstemon heterophyllus

CENTRAL VALLEY, FOOTHILLS

Along with about 40 species of monkeyflowers (*Mimulus*) and some 30 species of paintbrush and owl's-clovers (*Castilleja* and *Orthocarpus*) gracing our area, there are almost 20 species of their close relatives, the penstemons (*Penstemon*). Like the monkeyflowers, the penstemons have large, showy, 2-lipped flower tubes where the '2 petals up, 3 petals down' insignia of the snapdragon family is quite apparent and dramatic. The most visible difference between these two genera is the flower shape: whereas *Mimulus* flowers have a large face compared to the length of the tube, *Penstemon* flowers have a long, narrow tube with a relatively small face. • Although some penstemons are red or pink (p. 160) and some are white (p. 163), the typical penstemon is deep-blue, blue-purple, or violet. Foothill penstemon fits this prototype well: its **long (1–1¹/₂"), tubular flowers are a rich blue or violet with touches of magenta**. • Unlike its higher elevation blue relatives, which rarely exceed 2' in height, foothill penstemon plants **often reach 3' or 4' (sometimes even 5') tall**, with flowers branching off the upper 2' or so! Very narrow, pointed, 1–4" leaves with tapered bases alternate up the stem. The upper stem leaves are much shorter and are usually in opposite pairs. Being a perennial, the stem is woody below.

Distribution: The *Penstemon* genus is composed of approximately 250 species, all of which are in North America (most in the American West). *P. heterophyllus* occurs in grasslands and forest openings from 200–3000' in the Sacramento Valley and bordering foothills. **Names:** *Penstemon* means '5 stamens' (see p.160 for an explanation). *Heterophyllus* means 'varied-leaf' probably in reference to the dramatic difference between the lower and upper stem leaves. **Typical location:** Grassy road banks along Route 32 east of Chico (1500').

blue • 5 petals united in 2-lipped tube • perennial

Douglas Monkeyflower
Mimulus douglasii
FOOTHILLS

In a genus of so many diverse and showy species, Douglas monkeyflower stands out for its unusual shape and vivid coloring. The long flower tube (to 1¹/₂") opens into a deep-magenta face: the upper two petals are broad and rounded, the **lower three petals are very unusual in that they are almost non-existent, forming little more than the rim of the flower's throat.** Looking down inside the tube, you will be dazzled by the gold and purple spots and stripes. The four anthers pressed against the roof of the tube look very much like a golden butterfly; the yellow stigma protrudes above the anthers. • One to several of the showy flowers rise out of the basal cluster of shiny-green, ovate leaves. The entire plant rarely exceeds 2–3" tall.

Distribution: *M. douglasii* occurs on bare soils throughout the Sierra foothills from 200–4000'. It extends to the foothills of the Cascades and to the coastal ranges of central and northern California. **Names:** *Mimulus* (see p. 146). *Douglasii* (see p. 108). **Typical location:** Bare ground in Sutter Buttes area (1800').

Related Plant: Small-flowered monkeyflower (*M. inconspicuus*; bottom photo) has, as its name suggests, very small flowers (¹/₄"), but it is nonetheless quite attention-grabbing: its **five pink and white petals are deeply notched and lead to a white throat colored with yellow ribs and pink spots.** *M. inconspicuous* is uncommon along seeps in the Sierra foothills and low mountains south of Tahoe from 500–7500'. Annual. Range: Foothills, Low Montane.

magenta • 5 petals united in 2-lipped tube
• annual

151

Kellogg's Monkeyflower

Mimulus kelloggii

FOOTHILLS

The 2-lipped tube with 'two petals up, three petals down' is quite apparent on Kellogg's monkeyflower because the **upper two petals are very noticeably broader and longer than the lower three.** All five petals of this flower are the same stunning pink to magenta, deepening to a rich red-purple toward the throat. The flower face is large ($^1/_2$–$^3/_4$") but the flower tube is considerably longer (up to almost 2"). • This beautiful flower grows on a 2–12" stem, which also bears many lush-green, ovate leaves, often purple-tinged on the veins and on the undersides. You will usually find *M. kelloggii* growing in dense mats.

Distribution: *M. kelloggii* grows in bare or disturbed areas in fields or on slopes in the foothills below 3000'. It extends to the foothills of the Cascades. **Names:** *Mimulus* (see p. 146). Albert Kellogg was a 19th-century California doctor and botanist who helped create the California Academy of Sciences. **Typical location:** Along Route 140 west of Yosemite (1200').

Related Plant: Bolander's monkeyflower (*M. bolanderi*; bottom photo) is another pinkish monkeyflower, but very different in appearance from Kellogg's with lighter pink and less dramatic markings (pale white throat with red-purple spots), and **a longer lower middle petal resembling a pink tongue sticking out of the flower face.** The large, dark green leaves sometimes almost hide the flowers. *M. bolanderi* occurs in the foothills (and in the Coastal Range of northern California) from 1000–6000'. *Bolanderii* (see p. 113). Annual. Range: Foothills, Low Montane.

red-purple • 5 petals united in 2-lipped tube
• annual

Yellow-and-White Monkeyflower
Mimulus bicolor
FOOTHILLS, LOW MONTANE

If you are at all uncertain about the 'two up, three down' identifying trait of the snapdragon family, check out *M. bicolor*. On some monkeyflowers the five petals are close to symmetrical so the 'two up, three down' arrangement can be difficult to detect, but on *M. bicolor* two petals are clearly above the horizontal mid-line and three are clearly below it. And just to ensure absolute certainty, **the upper two petals are white, and the lower three are yellow with red spots.**
• The 4–12" stem bears several ¹/₂" flowers and the oval ¹/₂–1" serrated leaves.

Distribution: *M. bicolor* grows in damp places throughout the Sierra from 1000–4000'. It extends into the Cascades and Klamath ranges. **Names:** *Mimulus* (see p. 146). *Bicolor* means '2-colored.' **Typical location:** Along Route 20 east of Nevada City (3500').

Related Plant: Bush monkeyflower (*M. aurantiacus,* formerly *M. longiflorus;* bottom photo) is an unusual salmon-orange monkeyflower growing on a 2–4' shrub with sticky stems and leaves. It is highly variable and occurs on dry slopes throughout the southern part of our area below 5000'. *Aurantiacus* means 'orange-colored.' Shrub. Range: Same.

yellow and white • 5 petals united in
2-lipped tube • annual

Indian Warrior
Pedicularis densiflora
FOOTHILLS, LOW MONTANE

From a distance you might mistake Indian warrior for a paintbrush (*Castilleja*) or an owl's-clover (*Orthocarpus*), as it has their characteristic **dense spike** of colorful beaked flowers. You would be close to right because *Pedicularis*, like *Castilleja* and *Orthocarpus*, is one of the genera of the snapdragon family whose upper two petals form long, narrow beaks housing the reproductive parts. And Indian warrior, unlike most of its fellow *Pedicularis* species with well-developed lower petals, has little more than small sacs for its three lower petals. • *P. densiflora* has many 1–1^1/$_2$" **deep red to purple tubular flowers.** The lower lip consists of three very small white or yellow lobes flaring off the tube about halfway along its length. Many of the flowers grow off the purplish ^{1}/$_2$–2' stems. The leaves are typical of *Pedicularis* species—they are deeply divided like fern leaves. • Like all species of *Pedicularis* (and *Castilleja*), *P. densiflora* is a green root-parasite, supplementing its photosynthesis with thievery.

Distribution: The *Pedicularis* genus is composed of approximately 500 species widespread in wet, northern temperate environments. *P. densiflora* grows in mulch under trees (mostly oak) below 6000'. It extends to the mountains of northern California and southern Oregon. **Names:** *Pedicularis* means 'lousewort' from the belief that cattle eating these plants became susceptible to lice infestation. *Densiflora* refers, of course, to the dense spike of flowers. **Typical location:** Clearings in woods along road to Cohasset northeast of Chico (3000').

red • 5 petals united in 2-lipped tube
• perennial

Applegate's Paintbrush
Castilleja applegatei

FOOTHILLS, LOW MONTANE, MID TO HIGH MONTANE

Applegate's paintbrush is the most **common, wide-ranging,** and variable (with several identified subspecies) of the paintbrushes in our area. You can find it all the way from the foothills to 11,000' and from dry sagebrush scrub to forest openings to rock ledges. It is **usually bright red but sometimes tends toward orangish-red or even yellow.** • From a distance, it really looks like the ¹/₂–2' stems are bearing clusters of bright red flowers, but, of course, you know better. The actual 5-petaled flowers are 2-lipped—the two upper petals form the yellowish-green beak, and the lower three petals are reduced to barely discernible green bumps.
• Although the color and habitat of Applegate's paintbrush vary somewhat, it has certain characteristics that are consistent and distinctive: the entire plant is sticky, and the leaves are wavy-edged (somewhat crinkly).

Distribution: *C. applegatei* (in its many subspecies) occurs in dry or rocky areas throughout the Sierra from 1000–11,000'. It extends from Oregon to Baja. **Names:** *Castilleja* (see p. 148). Elmer Applegate (1867–1949) was a student of Oregon flora. **Typical location:** Rock ledges along Hite's Cove Trail just west of Yosemite (1500').

Related Plant: Giant red paintbrush (*C. miniata*; bottom photo) is a taller (1–3'), more robust plant with darker red bracts. It grows in wet areas throughout the Sierra (and north to Alaska) below 11,000'. Its **leaves are neither wavy-edged nor lobed.** *Miniata* means 'cinnabar-red.' Perennial. Range: Same.

red (to orange) • 5 petals in 2-lipped tube
• perennial

Primrose Monkeyflower
Mimulus primuloides
LOW MONTANE, MID TO HIGH MONTANE, ALPINE

Tip-toe into a Sierra wet meadow in the early morning and you will find many surprises; primrose monkeyflower might be the most delightful of these. Finding these perky little flowers may be the first surprise, for they often **hide beneath taller grass**; but once you find a primrose monkeyflower, they seem to pop up all over the place! Each plant has only **one small ($1/4$"), yellow flower** at the tip of a solitary 1–5" pedicel, which lifts the flower above the basal rosette of oval leaves. Each petal is shallowly 2-lobed and has a small red spot at its base. • The basal leaves may be the second surprise because they are covered with long, silky hairs that often hold drops of moisture. In early morning, you can sometimes see the rays of the rising sun sparkle in each of these tiny dew-prisms!

Distribution: *M. primuloides* occurs in very wet areas throughout the Sierra from 4000–11,000'. It extends to the Cascades of Washington. **Names:** *Mimulus* (see p. 146). *Primuloides* means 'primrose-like.' **Typical location:** Boggy meadows near Dana Lake just east of Yosemite (10,800').

Related Plant: Floriferous monkeyflower (*M. floribundus*; bottom photo) is another of the many beautiful yellow monkeyflowers of our area. Like primrose monkeyflower, its leaves hold a little surprise—you'll be amazed at how **slimy** they are to the touch. These leaves, and most of the plant, are **covered by soft, white hairs**. *M. floribundus* grows in granite outcrops near seeps, especially from foothills elevations up to 8000'. *Floribundus* means 'free flowering.' Annual. Range: Foothills, Low Montane, Mid to High Montane.

yellow • 5 petals united in 2-lipped tube
• perennial

Scarlet Monkeyflower
Mimulus cardinalis
LOW MONTANE, MID TO HIGH MONTANE

Yellow, white, salmon, pink, purple, magenta, fuschia, red...and now scarlet; monkeyflowers show an astonishing range of colors! *M. cardinalis* is a spectacular member of a spectacular genus. The **five velvety scarlet petals** form a large (to 2") flower, which stands out dramatically from the often dense foliage of willows and other shrubs growing with it along streambanks and seeps. The flower looks a bit odd— almost swollen—for the upper two petals are swept back and the lower three bend back at the tips. All the petals are fringed with short, white hairs. The long-protruding anthers and stigma are creamy yellow and hairy. • Each plant has many flowers, all growing on long

pedicels from the leaf axils. The 2–4' stem also bears numerous pairs of 1–3" broad, fleshy, opposite leaves. The leaves are oval, toothed, and sticky.

Distribution: *M. cardinalis* grows along streams and seeps throughout the Sierra below 8000'. It is widespread through the mountains of California and from Oregon to Baja and east to Utah. **Names:** *Mimulus* (see p. 146). *Cardinalis* means 'red.' **Typical location:** Along Tenaya Creek in Yosemite Valley (5000').

red • 5 petals united in 2-lipped tube • perennial

Lewis Monkeyflower
Mimulus lewisii

LOW MONTANE, MID TO HIGH MONTANE

One of the **largest and most spectacular** monkeyflowers in our area, Lewis monkeyflower must have been as much of a treat for Meriwether Lewis and the Lewis and Clark Expedition as it is for us today. Growing on a tall (1–3') hairy stem are many 1–2" **pink to rose flowers.** The flowers, on their long pedicels, usually come off the stem in pairs from the axils of the upper pairs of opposite leaves. The leaves are oval, toothed, and sticky hairy.
• Each squarish petal is a delicate pink with a darker rose splotch on the vertical mid-line. The lower three petals have yellow ridges covered with thick white to yellow hairs. • Because this is such a large flower, it provides an ideal opportunity for you to discover the secret of the monkeyflower's hinged stigma. Touch it and watch it rapidly close (as it analyzes the pollen it received). If there was no pollen or if it was pollen from a species other than *M. lewisii* or if it was pollen from the same *M. lewisii* plant, it will reject it and re-open after a few minutes. Only if the pollen was from a different plant of *M. lewisii* will the stigma remain closed, the flower having been successfully pollinated!

Distribution: *M. lewisii* is widespread in wet areas throughout the Sierra from 4000–10,000'. It extends north to western Canada and east to Utah. **Names:** *Mimulus* (see p. 146). Meriwether Lewis, 1774–1809, was co-leader of the famous Lewis and Clark Expedition. **Typical location:** Seep areas along Mt. Rose Trail in Tahoe area (9000').

pink • 5 petals united in 2-lipped tube • perennial

Mountain Monkeyflower

Mimulus tilingii

LOW MONTANE, MID TO HIGH MONTANE, ALPINE

Many species of yellow monkeyflowers grow in our study area. Mountain monkeyflower and common monkeyflower (see Related Plant) are two of the large-flowered species you are likely to see. Both have large (1–1¹/₂"), **bright yellow flowers** that are often speckled with red in the flower throat. Both can be tall plants, though *M. tilingii* peaks at about 1¹/₂' whereas *M. guttatus* can sometimes reach 4'. • There are some noticeable differences between the two species: the leaves of *M. tilingii* are **often slimy** to the touch and usually have very short petioles, whereas those of *M. guttatus* **are not slimy and often fuse around the stem**; the pedicels of *M. tilingii* are longer than the flower tubes whereas those of *M. guttatus* are usually shorter than the flower tubes; there are usually only 1–5 flowers per plant on *M. tilingii* while there are many per plant on *M. guttatus.* Not all these distinctions hold up, because the two species often intergrade! Whatever species (or combination of species) it is, this large, showy, shiny yellow flower is dazzling!

Distribution: *M. tilingii* is widespread in seeps and other wet areas throughout the Sierra from 5000–11,000'. It extends north to Alaska and east to Colorado. **Names:** *Mimulus* (see p. 146). Heinrich Tiling was a Baltic physician and botanist for a Russian-American company in Sitka (1866–68) who also collected in California and Nevada for various European botanical gardens. **Typical location:** Near Round Lake in Sierra Buttes area (7000').

Related Plant: Common monkeyflower (*M. guttatus*; bottom photo) is very common in wet areas. *Guttatus* means 'speckled' in reference to the red spots on the yellow petals. Perennial. Range: Same.

yellow • 5 petals united in 2-lipped tube • perennial

Scarlet Penstemon

Penstemon rostriflorus

LOW MONTANE, MID TO HIGH MONTANE

With its long, 2-lipped, tubular flowers with 'two petals up, three petals down,' *P. rostriflorus* should be easy to identify as a penstemon, though you might be a little surprised to see a penstemon with bright red flowers (rather than the usual blue). • *P. rostriflorus* grows 1–3' tall and bears many **1–1¹/₂" bright scarlet, bugle-like flowers.** The flowers look like scarlet seals swimming through the mountain air, for the three petals of the lower lip bend down and back like flippers in action. The inflorescence is sticky; the lower stem bears pairs of opposite, narrow 1–3" leaves.

Distribution: *P. rostriflorus* grows in forest openings and on scrubby slopes south of the Tahoe area from 5000–9000'. It extends into the southern Sierra and desert mountains and east to Colorado. **Names:** *Penstemon* means 'five stamens' in reference to the fifth infertile stamen characteristic of the genus. If you look inside a penstemon's flower tube, you will find the expected one long pistil and the four stamens pressing their showy anthers against the roof of the tube, but you will also find another thread-like structure that you may, at first, mistake for a second pistil. In fact, it is a fifth stamen without an anther. This infertile staminode is often hairy or densely bearded. *Rostriflorus* means 'beaked flower' in reference to the upper two petals projecting way beyond the bent-back lower three. **Also known as** bridge's penstemon. **Formerly called** *P. bridgesii.* **Typical location:** Brushy slopes above Hetch Hetchy Reservoir in Yosemite (6000').

red • 5 petals united in 2-lipped tube • perennial

Showy Penstemon

Penstemon speciosus

LOW MONTANE, MID TO HIGH MONTANE

'Showy' is certainly an appropriate name for this beauty. The flowers are **large (1–1³/₄" long and rather pot-bellied) and are various blends of red, purple, and blue.** On the outside the flower tube is a red-purple flaring into a sky-blue face; the inside of the tube tends toward white (or pink). The staminode usually has a fuzzy tip. • The plant is 2"–2' tall with many thick, narrow, blue-green 1–3" leaves that are often partly folded lengthwise. Each branch usually bears many of these spectacular flowers going every which way; the resulting purple clusters add glorious color to their often bare-ground habitat. For a final splash of color, the sepals are a shiny yellow-green.

Distribution: The *Penstemon* genus is the largest genus of flowering plants endemic to North America. Most of its estimated 250 species occur in the western United States. *P. speciosus* is widespread throughout the Sierra on dry slopes from 5000–9000'. It extends to Washington, the mountains of southern California, and east to Utah. **Names:** *Penstemon* (see p. 160). *Speciosus* means 'showy.' **Typical location:** Along Mt. Rose Trail in Tahoe area (9000').

Related Plant: Another large (1–1¹/₂"), showy penstemon common in the montane elevations of the Sierra (from 6000–10,000') is the **bright red** mountain pride (*P. newberryi*; bottom photo). **Tumbling down rocky slopes in large, low mats,** this striking penstemon lives up to its common name. John Newberry was a 19th-century physician and botanist. Subshrub. Range: Same.

blue to purple • 5 petals united in 2-lipped tube • perennial

161

Meadow Penstemon
Penstemon rydbergii
LOW MONTANE, MID TO HIGH MONTANE

Though the flowers of meadow penstemon are small ($1/2$"), they grow in dense whorls on the $1/2$–2' stem, and the plants often grow in huge masses. The resulting **carpet of solid blue-purple** is a dazzling sight in the grassy montane meadows where it grows. • A close look at the flower shows that the small face is bluer than the purplish flower tube. The floor of the tube is covered with white to yellow hair, and the staminode is covered with dense golden-yellow hair.

Distribution: *P. rydbergii* grows in wet meadows (often in dense masses) throughout the Sierra from 5000–9000'. It extends to the Cascades and east to the Great Basin. **Names:** *Penstemon* (see p. 160). Per Axel Rydberg was a member of the N.Y. Botanical Gardens in the late 19th and early 20th centuries. He wrote the first book on the flora of the Rockies from Mexico to Canada. **Also known as** whorled penstemon. **Typical location:** Great masses in grassy Mt. Rose meadows along Route 431 in Tahoe area (8900').

Related Plant: Gay penstemon (*P. laetus*; bottom photo) has many 1" tubular blue flowers along its $1/2$–2' glandular stem. The beautiful **blue petals, glandular on the outside**, merge to an intense red-purple at the base. *P. laetus* grows in dry, open scrub or forest openings throughout the Sierra (and Cascades) from 2500–8000'. *Laetus* means 'bright or vivid.' Perennial. Range: Same.

blue-purple • 5 petals united in 2-lipped tube
• perennial

Hot-rock Penstemon

Penstemon deustus

LOW MONTANE, MID TO HIGH MONTANE

Although clearly recognizable as a *Penstemon, P. deustus* is unusual for that genus in several regards. The $^1/_2$" flower is **creamy white (to yellowish) with red to maroon stripes** lining the lower three petals and the inside of the flower tube. The upper two petals are quite small and inconspicuous and frequently appear somewhat shriveled and dirty brown. • Many flowers grow on the low (less than $1^1/_2$') stems as do many of the pairs of opposite, toothed leaves. • The inflorescence is glandular and aromatic and the staminode is smooth or sparsely hairy.

Distribution: *P. deustus* is widespread throughout the Sierra in hot and dry rocky areas from 4000–8500'. It ranges widely into the Cascades to Washington and east to Utah. **Names:** *Penstemon* (see p. 160). *Deustus* means 'burned'—what it could easily be in its hot, exposed environment, and what the upper two petals often appear to be. **Typical location:** Along Route 89 north of Truckee in Tahoe area (6000').

creamy white • 5 petals united in 2-lipped tube • perennial

American Brooklime
Veronica americana
ALL ZONES EXCEPT ALPINE

Although it has a vague snapdragon look to it, your 'two up, three down' guideline to that family would fail you with *Veronica*. These beautiful **blue to violet** (sometimes white) flowers are in a 2-lipped tube (though the small face is much bigger than the inconspicuous tube), but they have only **four petals**. The lower lip has three petals, but the upper lip has only one petal. However, that one petal is much larger than the other three and is actually the upper two petals fused together! • In American brooklime, many of the tiny ($1/4$") flowers grow on long pedicels out of the leaf axils. The stems can be long, but the flowers are usually close to the ground (or water) because the stem is usually decumbent. You will usually find masses of flowers because the stems root at the nodes and send up many flowering splays. The oval, shiny leaves are very large (to 2") compared to the flowers and often nearly conceal them. • The petals are a gorgeous blue (to violet) with red-purple markings. There are only two stamens, which protrude from the flower like a butterfly's antennae. One pistil sticks out between the stamens.

Distribution: The genus *Veronica* is composed of approximately 250 species in northern temperate areas, especially in Europe. *V. americana* is common in wet meadows or bordering slow-moving streams throughout California from sea level to 10,500'. **Names:** *Veronica* is possibly after Saint Veronica. Brooklime presumably refers to the wet mud habitat of some plants where birds can become trapped (limed). *Americana* means 'of America.' **Typical location:** Along and in the edges of Sagehen Creek in Tahoe area (6200').

Related Plant: Alpine veronica (*V. wormskjoldii*, formerly *V. alpina*; bottom photo) is a **smaller plant** (4–12") with small, oval leaves. The flowers are nearly identical to those of *V. americana*, though perhaps a deeper blue. *V. wormskjoldii* grows in **wet areas** throughout the Sierra from 7500–11,000' (and also in the Alps). Morton Wormskjold was a 19th-century Danish plant collector. Perennial. Range: Mid to High Montane, Alpine.

blue to violet • 4 petals united in 2-lipped tube • perennial

Hairy Owl's-clover
Castilleja tenuis
LOW MONTANE, MID TO HIGH MONTANE

One of those shy flowers hiding in the grass of mountain meadows, hairy owl's-clover is somewhat reminiscent of butter-and-eggs (p. 147), that is so common in the Central Valley and Sierra foothills. The flowers of both plants are yellow and have **small sacs for their lower three petals and a thin beak formed out of their upper two petals**. In addition, on both plants the bracts are small and narrowly lobed. On butter-and-eggs these bracts are purplish and spiny; on hairy owl's-clover they are green with purple-tipped, finger-like lobes. Whereas butter-and-eggs usually grows in dense masses, hairy owl's-clover often **grows alone or in small clusters**. • The 4–16" stems (and the entire plant) are covered with short hairs and frequently are sticky.

Distribution: *C. tenuis* grows in grassy meadows throughout the Sierra from 3000–8000'. It extends to Alaska. **Names:** *Castilleja* (see p. 148). Another similarity between butter-and-eggs and hairy owl's-clover is that botanists have recently moved both of them out of the *Orthocarpus* genus, though their common names remain 'owl's-clover.' *Tenuis* means 'slender.' **Formerly called** *Orthocarpus hispidus*. **Typical location:** Damp, grassy meadows along Sagehen Creek in Tahoe area (5900').

Related Plant: Copeland's owl's-clover (*O. cuspidatus*, formerly *O. copelandii*; bottom photo) is more conspicuous than *C. tenuis* in several ways: the plants grow on barer soil, the inflorescences have more flowers, and most significantly the bracts are 'painted' with **flashy pink**. *O. cuspidatus* occurs in dry areas in the northern Sierra from 6800–9000'. *Cuspidatus* means 'with a sharp, stiff point.' Annual. Range: Mid to High Montane.

yellow • 5 petals united in 2-lipped tube
• annual

Lemmon's Paintbrush
Castilleja lemmonii
MID TO HIGH MONTANE

Filling high mountain meadows with great masses of **rich magenta** flowers, *C. lemmonii* is a typical paintbrush in most ways. Its brightly colored bracts hide the beak-like true flowers, its leaves (on the upper stem) have three narrow lobes, it is partially parasitic, and it often grows in clusters (several stems sprout from the same root stalk). • The leaves of Lemmon's paintbrush are often ascending, not sticking out very far from the 4–12" stem.

Distribution: *C. lemmonii* grows in damp meadows throughout the Sierra from 7000–11,000'. It extends into the Cascades. **Names:** *Castilleja* (see p. 148). John and Sara Lemmon (see p. 91). **Typical location:** Tuolumne Meadows in Yosemite (8600').

Related Plant: Alpine paintbrush (*C. nana*; bottom photo) is another *Castilleja* of high elevations in the Sierra, but it is much less showy than Lemmon's paintbrush. Whereas the bracts of most paintbrushes are bright and showy (usually some shade of red, orange, or yellow), those of alpine paintbrush are an **unflashy tint of gray**, blending easily into its high elevation rocky environment. • When you examine the flower carefully, however, you will begin to see color emerge: a hint of purplish-red or yellowish-green on the bracts, a touch of pale yellow and purple on the petals. *C. nana* grows in dry, rather barren and rocky flats of upper elevations, often reaching high into the alpine zone. It occurs throughout the Sierra from 7000–12,000'. *Nana* means 'dwarf.' Perennial. Range: Mid to High Montane, Alpine.

magenta • 5 petals united in 2-lipped tube
• perennial

166

Little Elephant's Head
Pedicularis attolens

LOW MONTANE, MID TO HIGH MONTANE, ALPINE

Pedicularis is a very widespread genus with approximately 500 species found throughout the northern latitudes. All of them are green root-parasites and have their upper two petals united into some kind of odd structure—usually beak-like or trunk-like. Most *Pedicularis* have deeply divided, fern-like leaves. • Elephant's head, as you have no doubt gathered by now, has its **upper two petals united into a trunk-like structure**. In little elephant's head the **'trunk' spirals down from the top** of the flower. Many small ¹/₄–¹/₂" pink to purple flowers crowd in the 1–12" flower spike at the top of the stem. • The lower three petals (forming the floppy ears and face) are pink blending to white at the bases with dark red-purple vertical lines extending their entire length.

Distribution: *P. attolens* is fairly common in wet areas throughout the Sierra from 5000–12,000'. It extends north to Oregon and east to the White and Inyo mountains. **Names:** *Pedicularis* (see p. 154). *Attolens* is of uncertain origin. **Typical location:** Wet areas growing with *P. groenlandica* along trail to Winnemucca Lake in Carson Pass area (8900').

Related Plant: Bull elephant's head (*P. groenlandica*, bottom photo) is a larger plant (to 3') with larger (¹/₂–³/₄") pink to purple flowers that bear an uncanny resemblance to elephants' heads, because the **trunk sweeps up** in just the right curl. *P. groenlandica* grows in similar environments and elevations as *P. attolens*. *Groenlandica* means 'of Greenland,' though it doesn't grow there! Perennial. Range: Same.

pink to purple • 5 petals united in 2-lipped tube • perennial

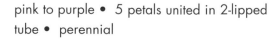

Torrey's Blue-eyed Mary

Collinsia torreyi

LOW MONTANE, MID TO HIGH MONTANE

Collinsia is another tricky snapdragon: its petals are clearly united in a 2-lipped tube, but like *Veronica* (p.164) it **appears to have only four petals**. Unlike *Veronica*, which has 'one up, three down', the blue-eyed Mary appear to have 'two up, two down.' All is not lost for our snapdragon logo, though, because if you gently open up the two lower petals, you will find a **third petal folded up between them**. This middle petal houses the reproductive parts. For a large, spectacular *Collinsia* of lower elevations, see Chinese houses (p. 145).

• Blue-eyed Mary is a much smaller flower than Chinese houses, but has the same *Collinsia* characteristics. The distinguishing characteristic of blue-eyed mary is the unusual coloration—the upper two petals are white or pale lavender and the lower two (and the third folded petal) are deep blue. • There are many species of blue-eyed Mary in the Sierra, most of which have tiny flowers. Torrey's blue-eyed Mary has somewhat bigger flowers (1/2") than many of the other species. Its white upper petals usually have tiny purple spots toward the base. The 2–10" plant is conspicuously glandular with several whorls of flowers at the tips of 1/4–1/2" pedicels.

Distribution: *C. torreyi* occurs in sandy soil throughout the Sierra from 3000–10,000'. It extends to the Cascades. **Names:** *Collinsia* (see p. 145). John Torrey was a 19th-century New York botanist. **Typical location:** Sandy soil along trail to Paige Meadows in Tahoe (6500').

blue (and white) • 5 petals (appears to be 4) united in 2-lipped tube
• annual

Alpine Penstemon
Penstemon davidsonii
MID TO HIGH MONTANE, ALPINE

Imagine what a squirrel might look like trying to play a trumpet—that's something like the **incongruity of the large (1–1¹/₂") tubular flowers of alpine penstemon growing on their dwarfed 4–6" stems**. It really looks like someone brought these large purple flowers from a lowland garden and stuck them ·on these tiny alpine plants. • The violet to blue lavender flowers bring a dazzling color to the spartan rock outcroppings where they grow, especially when the shrub-like plants form large clusters of blossoms. Frequently the beautiful violet flowers will be displayed against a background of the bright yellows, oranges, and reds of the various lichens growing on the rocks that are this penstemon's home. • The floor of the flower tube is covered with dense white hairs; the four stamens and the staminode are also densely white (or yellow) bearded. The inflorescence is glandular. The small oval stem leaves and the somewhat larger basal leaves are smooth and fleshy.

Distribution: *P. davidsonii* grows in rocky areas near and above timberline (9000–12,000') throughout the Sierra. It extends from the Cascades to the Sweetwater Mountains of eastern California. **Names:** *Penstemon* (see p. 160). Dr. George Davidson was the first to collect this plant in California. **Typical location:** Rocky outcrops atop the Tioga Crest in Yosemite (11,000').

violet • 5 petals united in 2-lipped tube • subshrub

169

Mint Family
(Lamiaceae)

You are out wandering up a dry slope in the Sierra on a hot day in late summer. All of a sudden you are enveloped in a sweet cloud of fragrance that warms you and soothes you with its gentle, oily caress. You have stepped on some pennyroyal (p.179)...a mint!

Up ahead, in a slightly damper area, you see a large 'forest' of rose-purple spikes bristling with flowers. As you get closer, but still before you can make out the details of the flowers, you start hearing a faint vibration. It gets louder and louder and more confused as you near until it becomes a furious buzzing of hundreds of bees swarming those flower spikes. You are approaching horse-mint (p. 178)...another mint!

field of pennyroyal, horsemint, and arnica

Mint is a family that appeals to all the senses. Most species of mints have a strong mint aroma, square stems, and bluish or pinkish flowers that attract mostly bees. Many members of this family (e.g., lavender, basil, rosemary, thyme) are cultivated for herbs, oils, and fragrances. The flowers of most mints are in head-like or spike-like clusters. The flowers usually have five petals in a 2-lipped tube with two petals up and three petals down (much like the snapdragons, pp. 143–69). There are only two or four stamens, usually sticking well out of the flower, and a 4-lobed, superior ovary with one style and usually two stigmas. The leaves are in opposite pairs.

The mint family is composed of approximately 200 genera and some 5500 species worldwide. The genera with several species (or common flowers) that you are most likely to encounter in our area include *Agastache* (horsemint), *Mentha* (mint), *Monardella*, *Pogogyne*, *Prunella* (self-heal), *Salvia*, *Scutellaria* (scullcap), *Stachys* (hedge-nettle), and *Trichostemma* (blue-curls). Worldwide, *Salvia* is by far the biggest genus with approximately 900 species, but in the California Floristic Province (CA-FP) *Monardella* is the largest genus with over 20 species. *M. odoratissima* (pennyroyal) is one of the most common flowers of dry mountain slopes.

horsemint

typical mint flower

Clasping Henbit
Lamium amplexicaule
CENTRAL VALLEY, FOOTHILLS

Clasping henbit is quite a bizarre and intricately beautiful mint, both for its flower and its leaves, to say nothing of its name! • The 4–16" branching stem bears **several pairs of roundish, scalloped, opposite leaves.** The pairs of leaves on the upper stem have no pedicels and almost fuse into one large leaf surrounding the stem (hence the clasping). Out of the leaf axils rise a few of the strange, **reddish-purple tubular flowers.** The flower tube is ¹/₂–³/₄" long and culminates in two lips— the upper two petals unite to form a small, pink hood covered on its outside surface with short, deep red-purple hairs, the lower petals form a pair of vertical cupped hands that pinch together and then flare into two flat lobes that resemble whale flukes! The entire lower lip is pink to white with large red splotches. • As peculiar as clasping henbit is, it does have the 2-lipped flower, the four stamens (hidden inside the hood), the square stem, and the pairs of opposite leaves typical of the mint family.

Distribution: The genus *Lamium* is composed of approximately 40 species of temperate areas in Eurasia and northern Africa. *L. amplexicaule* is an alien introduced from Eurasia that is now widespread throughout the CA-FP in disturbed places below 2500' and in much of North America. **Names:** *Lamium* means 'throat' in reference to the corolla shape. This genus name is the source of the current scientific name for the mint family—Lamiaceae. *Amplexicaule* means 'stem-clasping' in reference to the upper leaves. **Also known as** dead nettle. **Typical location:** Along road paralleling the Merced River and Route 140 west of Yosemite (1700').

red-purple (pink) • 5 petals united in 2-lipped tube • annual

Douglas Pogogyne
Pogogyne douglasii
CENTRAL VALLEY, FOOTHILLS

Several aspects of pogogyne are intriguing: its name (it doesn't seem to have a common name other than its strange Latin genus name), its structure, and its habitat.
• Whereas most mints inhabit dry flats and slopes, the pogogynes grow mostly in areas that are extremely wet at least part of the year (several species including *P. douglasii* grow in **drying vernal pools**). • Pogogyne does have several characteristics typical of mints—head-like clusters of 2-lipped tubular flowers, pairs of opposite leaves, squarish stems, and minty fragrance. In *P. douglasii* the flowerheads are 1–2" wide, and the stems can be as tall as 2', though 1' is more usual.
• The flowers are **usually pale lavender but can be white**. The two petals of the upper lip flare up to an almost erect position; the three petals of the lower lip usually flare down in the same plane as the upper petals. The lower lip is often spotted yellow, but there are many variations of this plant with somewhat different coloration.

Distribution: The genus *Pogogyne* has seven species, all located primarily in California. *P. douglasii* grows in vernal pools and swales in the Central Valley and Sierra foothills below 3000'. It extends to the California coastal ranges. **Names:** *Pogogyne* means 'bearded style' in reference to the hairs on the style slightly below the two stigma lobes. *Douglasii* (see p. 108). **Typical location:** Wet, grassy ledges on top of Table Mountain near Oroville (1200').

white • 5 petals united in 2-lipped tube • annual

Chia

Salvia columbariae

CENTRAL VALLEY, FOOTHILLS, LOW MONTANE

When you think of sage, you probably think of herbs and cooking, and the seeds of chia were used extensively by Native Americans as a food (roasted) and as a refreshing drink, and its leaves have a **strong, pungent mint aroma**. However, the flower may be even more interesting than the plant's use—it is an especially intricate and bizarre flower even for a mint. • Chia is an intriguing little plant with one or two **dense head-like clusters of strange, little blue flowers** on its 4–20" stem. One cluster is at the tip of the stem; if there is a second cluster, it is spaced slightly below the first. The clusters appear rather spiky as the red-purple sepals are tipped with spines. • Each flower has the 2-lipped tube characteristic of mints and a few other families; the odd shape of the flower leads you to strongly suspect it's a mint. The pungent aroma of the leaves confirms your suspicion. The $^1/_2$" flower tube is narrow, flaring out into a small ($^1/_4$"), 2-lipped flower face. The upper lip consists of two erect 'rabbit ears'; the lower lip forms two lateral 'arms,' a constricted 'body,' and two 'legs' parallel to the 'arms.' • The petals are a beautiful pale or deep blue with splotches of purple on the lower lip. Two delicate protruding stamens bear tiny, but showy, bright yellow anthers. • Chia's stem is squarish (as is characteristic of many mints), and bears the typical pairs of opposite leaves. All the leaves are delicately fern-like, i.e., deeply pinnately (or twice pinnately) dissected.

Distribution: The genus *Salvia* is huge, composed of approximately 900 species worldwide (especially in subtropical and tropical areas of the Americas). *S. columbariae* is common in dry, disturbed areas in the central Sierra below 4000'. It extends into the southern Sierra and into Utah and Arizona. **Names:** *Salvia* means 'to save' in reference to the medicinal uses of many species. *Columbariae* means 'Columbian,' i.e., of western North America. **Typical location:** Dry, sandy hillsides along Route 20 west of Nevada City (1500').

blue • 5 petals united in 2-lipped tube • annual

Whitestem Hedgenettle

Stachys albens

ALL ZONES EXCEPT ALPINE

Whitestem hedgenettle is another of the mints that rewards close inspection by revealing intricate forms and delicate, complex coloring. • At intervals along the upper part of the 1–5' stem are **several whorls of the ¹/₄" white to rose flowers**. Each whorl contains 6–12 tightly clustered flowers. It doesn't matter which direction you approach this plant from: at least one flower in each whorl is going to face you! • The flower tube is hidden in the dark red calyx and the five petals flare out in two lips. The upper two petals unite to form a sort of awning, the lateral two petals form small 'wings,' and the lower petal forms a large scoop-like 'tongue.' The hood is pinkish, the other petals are rose with white splotches and dark red-purple markings. • The stems are square and are covered (as is most of the plant) with white, cobwebby hairs. The pairs of opposite, ovate leaves are toothed on the edges.

Distribution: The genus *Stachys* has approximately 300 species in temperate areas worldwide. *S. albens* occurs in wet areas in the central Sierra below 9000'. It extends to the coastal ranges of central and northern California and into Washington and Idaho. **Names:** *Stachys* means 'ear of corn' in reference to the spike-like inflorescence. *Albens* means 'white' in reference to the cobwebby white hairs all over the plant. **Typical location:** Wet meadows along Pohono Trail in Yosemite (7200').

rose (pink) • 5 petals united in 2-lipped tube • perennial

Self-heal

Prunella vulgaris

ALL ZONES EXCEPT ALPINE

Self-heal is as much a balm for the spirit as for the flesh—its colors are intense and its shapes intricate. At the tip of the square 4–20" stem is a 1–2" dense, 'pinecone' spike tightly **packed with scale-like sepals that are dark red-purple or purple-tipped green.** These sepals are covered sparsely with bright white, thread-like hairs.
• In delicious contrast to the red-purple sepals are the delicate violet (sometimes pink) $^1/_2$" flowers. Their upper two petals are united into a cowl over the protruding reproductive parts, the lower three petals form a broad, fringed, central 'bib' and two smaller, smooth 'wings.' • As in many mints, there are several opposite pairs of oval, serrated leaves along the stem culminating in a pair of opposite bracts just below the flower spike. You can find these dazzling plants hidden in the grass.

Distribution: The genus *Prunella* is composed of four species in temperate areas. *P. vulgaris* is an alien introduced from Europe. It occurs in moist, grassy meadows throughout the CA-FP below 7500'. It is a circumboreal plant found in northern latitudes around the world. **Names:** *Prunella* is from a German word for 'quinsy'—a malady that this plant was used to treat. The common name self-heal also refers to its many medicinal uses, from treating heart ailments to helping heal inflammations and bruises. *Vulgaris* means 'common'—not 'vulgar'! **Typical location:** Hidden in grass near small creeks in Sagehen Meadow in Tahoe area (5900').

violet • 5 petals united in 2-lipped tube • perennial

176

Skullcap

Scutellaria californica

FOOTHILLS, LOW MONTANE

Its square stem and pairs of opposite leaves tip you off that skullcap is a mint. You're probably thankful for these clues because the flower, though quite distinctive, is rather difficult to figure out! • The $1/2$–$11/2$' stem bears numerous pairs of oval or triangular, curled leaves. Out of the axils of the upper leaves rise pairs of short pedicels, each bearing a $1/2$–$3/4$", **white (yellow-tinged) tubular flower** that looks like a smirking walrus or perhaps some kind of bemused Dr. Seuss character! The two petals of the upper lip form a rounded 'hood' that houses the four stamens; the three petals of the lower lip form a pinched 'throat' with a flaring 'mustache.' A final peculiar touch is the crest (or bumps) on the upper surface of the calyx.

Distribution: The genus *Scutellaria* has approximately 300 species worldwide. *S. californica* occurs in dry forest openings and thickets in the northern Sierra from 1000–7000'. It occurs in the Coast Range of northern California. **Names:** *Scutellaria* means 'dish-shaped' in reference to the ridge on the calyx. *Californica* (see p. 85). Skullcap probably refers to the hood-like upper lip of the flower tube. **Typical location:** Dry, rocky flats along Shirley Canyon trail in Tahoe area (6400').

white • 5 petals united in 2-lipped tube • perennial

Horse-mint

Agastache urticifolia

FOOTHILLS, LOW MONTANE, MID TO HIGH MONTANE

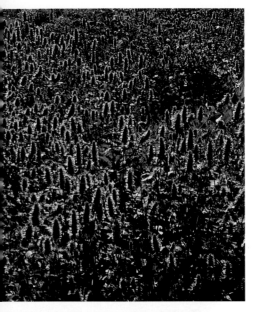

Like its close relative pennyroyal (p. 179), horse-mint announces its 'mint-ness' in no uncertain terms: its tall (3–5'), square stem bears a large (2–7"), **brush-like spike of rose or rose-purple (sometimes white) flowers** and numerous pairs of opposite, triangular, serrated leaves that are strongly fragrant. Although this fragrance is clearly mint, it (like the horse-mint plant) is much coarser than pennyroyal. • Each flower of horse-mint, however, gives a soft impression—largely because of the two pairs of long, delicate stamens that protrude out of the flower tube. The $^1/_2$" flowers are usually rose or rose-purple but pale in contrast to the darker red-purple sepals. • Like pennyroyal, horse-mint usually grows in dense clusters (actually more like miniature forests!).

Distribution: The genus *Agastache* has 22 species in North America, Mexico, and Asia. It is common in many habitats throughout the central and northern Sierra from 1000–10,000'. It occurs in the Coast Range of northern California and north to British Columbia. **Names:** *Agastache* means 'many spikes'— exactly what a 'forest' of this plant presents. *Urticifolia* means 'netde-leaf' in reference to the similarity of its opposite, triangular, serrated leaves to those of the stinging nettle. **Also known as** giant hyssop. **Typical location:** Edges of grassy meadows in Yosemite Valley (4000').

rose • 5 petals united in 2-lipped tube
• perennial

178

Pennyroyal
Monardella odoratissima
LOW MONTANE, MID TO HIGH MONTANE

Certainly one of the most noticeable and widespread of the mints in our area, pennyroyal often lets you know of its family long before you ever see the plant. Its leaves have such a strong mint aroma that just the brush of a breeze can thicken the air with their sweet and heavy scent. And if you happen to step on a leaf, you'll almost be overwhelmed by the **cloud of mint fragrance** that envelopes you. A wonderfully rich, oily tea can be made by swirling a few leaves (or even flowers) in hot water. As with any wild plant, even those you know are safe, ingesting should be done in moderation. The Native Americans used mild doses of pennyroyal for tranquillity; heavier doses acted as a purgative or even an abortive. • *M. odoratissima* is a highly variable plant whose **flowers range from white to lavender, rose, or purple.** On each square, ¹/₂–2' stem are several pairs of opposite, oval leaves. At the tip of each stem is a round, flat-topped ¹/₂–1" flowerhead under which are several overlapping bracts. This head is crammed thick with flowers. The five petals are very narrow and widely separated; the four stamens and one style are all as long as or longer than the petals. • More often than not you will find pennyroyal growing in great masses, bringing pale or rich color to its dry, sometimes rather bare habitat.

Distribution: The genus *Monardella* is composed of approximately 20 species, all of which are in western North America. *M. odoratissima* is common on dry slopes and in sagebrush scrub throughout the Sierra from 3000–11,000'. It extends to the Coast Range of northern California and to Washington. **Names:** Nicholas Monardas was a Spanish physician and botanist in the 16th century. *Odoratissima* means 'very fragrant.' **Also known as** coyote mint. **Typical location:** Dry slopes along Pacific Crest trail in Sonora Pass area (10,000').

white (purple, rose, or lavender) • 5 petals united in 2-lipped tube • perennial

Bellflower (Bluebell) Family
(Campanulaceae)

Usually blue or predominantly blue (sometimes white), the flowers of this family are of two main shapes: 1) five petals united into a broad bell, and 2) five petals united into a 2-lipped tube like the monkeyflower (see snapdragon family, pp. 143–69) with two petals up and three petals down.

type #1 flower (bluebells, *C. rotundifolia*)

Both types of bellflower family flowers are 5-merous: five petals, five sepals, and five stamens. Often the stamens are fused into the flower tube. A major distinguishing characteristic of this family is the inferior ovary. On many species, what appears to be a pedicel (i.e., the stem of an individual flower) is actually the ovary, which will swell thick after the flower has been pollinated.

You will occasionally find the bell-shaped type of flower in our area, e.g., a few species of *Campanula* (bellflower), *Githopsis* (bluecup), *Heterocodon*, and *Triodanus* (Venus looking-glass), but you are much more likely to find the tube-shaped flower. Of the genera with flowers of this second type, *Downingia* has the most species you are likely to encounter in our area, though even these are not that common, being mostly limited in occurrence to a highly specialized environment of drying vernal pools.

type #2 flower (2-horned downingia)

Despite their narrow habitat, however, when you do find *Downingia* or *Porterella* you are likely to find the flowers in great masses.

Despite their relative rarity in our area, the bellflower family is fairly large, composed of approximately 70 genera and some 2000 species worldwide. Some are cultivated for ornamentals (e.g., *Campanula* and *Lobelia*).

field of toothed downingia

181

Toothed Downingia

Downingia cuspidata

CENTRAL VALLEY, FOOTHILLS

As spring progresses toward summer in the Central Valley and low foothills, water begins to diminish. Run-off from melting snow in the high mountains decreases, and shallow pools from winter rains evaporate. In grassy fields and on rocky 'tabletops' where there were standing pools over winter and into early spring, there are now drying hollows, often bottomed with dried, cracked mud. On the bottoms and around the edges of these drying and dried vernal pools are the favorite habitats of a few intriguing and highly specialized flowers, including several species of *Downingia*.

• Toothed downingia is a species that grows in masses on the dried bottoms of these vernal pools. Its 2–6" stem has several branches, each ending in a ¹/₂–1" ovary and a charming ¹/₂"-wide blossom. • The flowers are usually bright blue with a large white patch on the lower three petals, but often the petals are very pale lavender or almost white. The lower three petals are all about the same size and shape—broadly obovate narrowing at the base. **The upper two petals are much narrower and stick up** like rabbit-ears or horns. There is a large yellow spot (partly divided into two spots) at the base of the lower corolla lip.

Distribution: The genus *Downingia* is composed of 13 species in western North America and Chile. *D. cuspidata* occurs in vernal pool and wet meadow habitats below 1600' in the San Joaquin Valley and in the foothills of the central Sierra. It extends to the California coastal ranges and to Mexico. **Names:** A.J. Downing was a 19th-century American horticulturalist. *Cuspidata* means 'with a stiff point' in reference to the pointed tips of the petals. **Typical location:** Drying vernal pools in Phoenix Park in Sacramento (50').

Related Plant: Fringed downingia/purple-spotted downingia (*D. concolor*, bottom photo) has a very distinctive, **velvety purple, square spot** at the base of the lower corolla lip and has delicate fringes on the upper 2 petals. It occurs in drying vernal pools and mudflats in the Sacramento Valley and adjoining foothills below 1000'. *Concolor* means 'colored similarly.' Annual. Range: Central Valley, Foothills.

blue or pale lavender (or white) • 5 petals united in 2-lipped tube • annual

Folded Downingia
Downingia ornatissima
CENTRAL VALLEY

Because downingias grow in dried (or drying) bottoms of vernal pools, they bloom later than most flowers of the Central Valley and foothills. The water from the rains of winter and early spring have to dry up before the plants will grow fully and flower. So, while the peak blooming in the Central Valley is mostly in March, you will look in vain for the masses of downingia in this habitat before mid to late April or early May. In the foothills, the timing will probably be a few weeks later.

You have to be patient for downingias, but the wait is well worth it—they are gorgeous, especially when they form large carpets. • Folded downingia closely resembles many others of its species with the three lower petals that are broad and blue with a large, yellow-spotted, white splotch at their base. However, this downingia is easily distinguished by the **unique folded back rather than straight growth form of its upper two petals**.

Distribution: *D. ornatissima* occurs in vernal pools only in the Central Valley.
Names: *Downingia* (see p. 182). *Ornatissima* means 'very showy.' **Typical location:** Vernal pools in Phoenix Park in Sacramento (50').

Related Plant: The species name and common name of two-horned downingia (*D. bicornuta*; bottom photo) say it all: the distinguishing characteristic of this blue-purple beauty are the **two nipple-like projections attached to the base of the lower lip**. *D. bicornuta* grows in vernal pools and lake margins throughout the Sierra below 2000'. It often grows with *D. ornatissima* (e.g., in Phoenix Park). *Bicornuta* means 'two-horned.' Annual.
Range: Central Valley, Foothills.

blue • 5 petals in 2-lipped tube • annual

Bacigalupi's Downingia
Downingia bacigalupii
LOW MONTANE

Though its common and scientific names are bigger than its flower, Bacigalupi's downingia is one of the most striking and appealing flowers of our area—its colors are lush and intense, its markings are intricate and delicate, and its shape is fascinating and endearing. • Each plant reaches only about ¹/₂–1' tall, with at least an inch or two of this being the **prominent ovary atop which perches the ¹/₂" flower.** The five petals are a **rich blue-purple with darker purple veins.** At the flower throat (at the base of the three lower petals) is a large 2-lobed white patch with an almost as large, 2-lobed, orange and yellow spot superimposed on it. The effect is a bit like a yellow and white butterfly or heart perched on the petals. The lower petals are broadly ovate while the upper two petals are narrower and point up like horns. As a finishing touch, a long, hooked, deep purple anthertube rises out of the flower like satin bait on a line!

Distribution: *D. bacigalupii* occurs in vernal pool and wet meadow habitats in the northern Sierra from 4000–7000'. It extends to the Cascades of Oregon. **Names:** *Downingia* (see p. 182). Rimo Bacigalupi was a 20th-century California botanist and curator of the Jepson Herbarium at the University of California (Berkeley). **Typical location:** Wet, grassy field in Russel Valley in Tahoe area (5800').

blue-purple • 5 petals united in 2-lipped tube • annual

Porterella

Porterella carnosula

LOW MONTANE, MID TO HIGH MONTANE

Porterella is an exquisite little flower, delightful for its mixture of bright colors, and dazzling for its **great masses of ground-hugging blooms.** • Consider yourself fortunate if you find it, for it is limited in habitat to the bottoms and edges of mostly dried vernal pools. When you do find it though, you will usually find it in large carpets with hundreds or even thousands of its cheery faces smiling back at you. The flowers are very similar to *Downingia*: the petals are blue-purple with a large, white 'field' near the flower throat on which are superimposed **large yellow spots.** The lower three petals are broad and rounded while the upper two petals are narrower and horn-like. • One to many of the ¹/₄–¹/₂" flowers grow on each plant. The blossoms are perched atop an inferior ovary and a short pedicel.

Distribution: The genus *Porterella* has only this species. It occurs in vernal pool and wet meadow habitats in the northern Sierra from 5000–10,000'. It extends to the Cascades and east to the Great Basin. **Names:** Thomas Porter was a 19th-century American botanist. *Carnosula* means 'somewhat fleshy.' **Typical location:** Mud-caked bottoms of dried vernal pools along the road to Pole Creek in Tahoe area (6100').

blue-purple • 5 petals united in 2-lipped tube • annual

185

Phlox Family
(Polemoniaceae)

Most members of the phlox family are brightly colored, especially if you consider white to be a color, and grow in dense clusters. For the most part, they're relatively small and 'normal'—botanically, they're 'regular.' Almost all phlox have five petals all alike in shape, size, and color united into a symmetrical tube. This flower tube can take the shape of a trumpet or vase, but more commonly flares into a shallow bowl or flat pinwheel.

Coville's phlox

Out of the flower tube protrude the five long stamens and the one pistil. Usually the stamens are tipped with richly colored anthers, and the stigma is 3-lobed. Most phlox, with a few notable exceptions, inhabit dry, often sandy or rocky flats or slopes and so have very narrow (often needle-like) leaves to minimize evaporation. Above timberline some phlox form dense 'shrubs' or even cushion plants—dense mounds of tightly knit stems and leaves forming their own protective micro-environments.

The phlox family contains 19 genera with approximately 320 species spread across America, northern Europe, and northern Asia. The species you are most likely to encounter in our area include *Phlox, Collomia, Allophylum, Gilia* (the largest genus), *Ipomopsis, Leptodactylon, Linanthus, Navarettia,* and *Polemonium.* As you can tell, our area is very phlox-rich!

great polemonium

granite gilia

mustang clover

187

Bird's-eye Gilia
Gilia tricolor
CENTRAL VALLEY, FOOTHILLS

From a distance, that grassy foothill slope up ahead appears to have several large patches of white mist covering parts of its colorful spring wildflower display. As you get closer, you notice that the mist seems to have a pale pink or lavender tint to it. And now, as you're standing right next to it, you see that the mist is actually dense clusters of a delicately beautiful multicolored flower—bird's-eye gilia. • Now you get out your magnifying glass and examine a flower in detail: the more you look, the more you are amazed at its wild **combination of colors** and intricate beauty. The **narrow flower tube is yellow with five deep purple lines or splotches at its mouth**. The five petals flare out of the tube into a shallow, dime-sized bowl. The petals are white (or pale blue) at the base blending into blue-violet or pink at the tips. The five stamens (which are attached to the inside of the tube and alternate with the petals) add the final delicious touch of color, for the anthers are covered with a deep-blue pollen. • Several clusters of 2–5 flowers each branch off the slender 4–12" stem. The very narrow, almost thread-like leaves are typical of the phlox family. • The bird's-eye gilia 'mist' loses much of its density on cloudy days, for the flowers close up and wait for the sun to return.

Distribution: The *Gilia* genus has approximately 70 species that spread through western North America and South America. *G. tricolor* is widespread through the San Joaquin Valley and Sierra foothills below 3000'. It grows in the California coastal ranges. **Names:** Felipe Gil was an 18th-century Spanish botanist. *Tricolor*...well, maybe it should be 'polycolor!' **Typical location:** Grassy slopes along Hite's Cove Trail west of Yosemite (1500').

lavender • 5 petals united in tube • annual

Needle Navarettia

Navarettia leucocephala

CENTRAL VALLEY, FOOTHILLS

A rather bristly, unfriendly looking plant, needle navarettia is well named, for its leaves and bracts are **clusters of sharp, shaggy-hairy needles**. The plant grows only a few inches off the ground and spreads into broad mats. • Many small (¹/₄"), pale white flowers grow out of the spiny bracts on short, narrow flower tubes. • Probably the most interesting and distinctive aspect of this plant, other than its bristly nature, is its habitat. As with many of the members of this genus, it grows most frequently on the floor of drying or dried vernal pools, its spiny green leaves and white flowers giving some life to the caked and cracked mud bottom. You will often find it intermingling with various species of *Downingia* (pp. 182–83).

Distribution: The genus *Navarettia* is composed of 30 species in western North America, Argentina, and Chile. *N. leucocephala* occurs in vernal pools in the Central Valley and Sierra foothills below 1800'. It extends to Oregon. **Names:** F. Navarrete was a Spanish physician of the 1700s. *Leucocephala* means 'dusky white head.' **Typical location:** Vernal pools in Phoenix Park in Sacramento (50').

white • 5 petals united in tube • annual

Slender Phlox
Phlox gracilis
ALL ZONES EXCEPT ALPINE

P. gracilis, as the name suggests, has small, delicate, slender flowers. The 5-petaled pinwheel flower face is no more than ¹/₂" across and is usually more like ¹/₄". The petals range from a **bright pink to a pastel lavender to white and are usually notched at the tip.** If you look carefully at a flower, you will see that the long (¹/₂–³/₄") flower tube (characteristic of the phlox family) is a soft yellow, though this might not be noticed at first because the glandular green sepals form a 'vase' that conceals much of the tube. • The plant is highly variable: sometimes a single cluster of a few flowers sits atop a single 2–8", erect stem; sometimes the stem is much-branched and partially decumbent and bears numerous clusters of flowers. Because slender phlox usually grows in thick grass and is a short plant, the flowers may be hard to see. However, once you find a slender phlox, you usually will find many. • The ¹/₂–1" leaves are narrow and in opposite pairs along the stem, becoming alternate high up on the stem.

Distribution: The *Phlox* genus has about 60 species in North America and northern Asia. *P. gracilis* is widespread in dry and moist grassy areas throughout the CA-FP all the way from Central Valley grasslands to 10,000'. It extends from British Columbia to Mexico and also occurs in South America. **Names:** *Phlox* means 'flame' in reference to the brightly colored flowers of many species. *Gracilis* means 'slender' or 'graceful.' **Formerly called** *Microsteris gracilis.* **Typical location:** Grassy meadows along Sagehen Creek in Tahoe area (5900').

pink • 5 petals united in tube • annual

Showy Phlox
Phlox speciosa
FOOTHILLS, LOW MONTANE

Showy phlox is certainly showy, and it is clearly a phlox. The narrow flower tube flaring into a 5-petaled pinwheel, the bright-yellow anthers and the opposite, narrow leaves are all typical of the phlox family. The characteristic unusual for a phlox is the 'included' stamens, hidden down in the flower tube instead of sticking out of it. • In a family of beautiful flowers, *P. speciosa* is particularly lovely. Its **flowers are unusually large (as much as 1¹/₂" across) for its family, the petals are an intense pink (turning to white at the base around the flower tube) and are heart-shaped**, and the several pairs of 1–2" lance-shaped, opposite leaves along the ¹/₂–2' stem are a rich green. Coming across this plant in its wooded habitat can be quite a surprise, for its bright pink flowers seem to leap out of the shade with an exuberant cry!

Distribution: *P. speciosa* occurs on wooded slopes throughout the Sierra from 1000–6500'. It extends to British Columbia. **Names:** *Phlox* (see p. 190). *Speciosa* means 'showy' or 'beautiful.' **Typical location:** Wooded slopes along Independence Trail off Route 49 near Nevada City (1200').

pink • 5 petals united in tube • perennial

Mustang Clover
Linanthus montanus

FOOTHILLS, LOW MONTANE

Mustang clover, despite its name (clover is in the pea family), is a textbook phlox family member. Its five petals form a long, 1–1¹/₂", slender tube flaring into a ³/₄" shallow bowl. The five stamens, attached to the inside of the tube and alternating between the petals, stick out of the bowl and are covered with bright yellow pollen. Several flowers arise from the **cluster of needle-like, white-hairy bracts at the top of the 4–24" stem**; there are several clusters of hairy, needle-like leaves at intervals along the stem. • The petals are bright white (sometime pink to lilac), each with a rich purple triangular spot at its base. The flowers actually have no pedicels, though the very long flower tubes are so slender they may appear to be pedicels. These flower tubes are yellow at the throat turning to maroon lower down. • Sometimes growing in dense clusters, mustang clover brings great color to its foothill habitat—its bright white, yellow, purple, and magenta epitomize the exuberance of spring in California.

Distribution: The genus *Linanthus* is composed of 41 species in western North America and Chile. *L. montanus* occurs in dry openings in foothill woodlands throughout the central and southern Sierra from 1000–6000'. In our area it won't be found north of the Yuba River. **Names:** *Linanthus* means 'flax flower.' *Montanus* refers to its habitat. **Typical location:** Grassy slopes along Hite's Cove Trail west of Yosemite (1500').

white (or pink) • 5 petals united in tube • annual

Globe Gilia

Gilia capitata

FOOTHILLS, LOW MONTANE

Globe gilia is a typical phlox family member in several ways: the flowers consist of five petals that flare out of the tube to form a shallow bowl, the reproductive parts stick well out of the flower, and the plant has narrow, needle-like leaves adapted to dry environments. However, its species name and common name point to a characteristic that (along with the plant's tall stature) easily distinguishes it from other phlox— the **terminal, spherical head dense with 50–100 small flowers.** • The stem of globe gilia can be as tall as 3'; several narrow, pinnately divided leaves are scattered along its length. The terminal flowerhead is thick with the small white to pale violet flowers. The stamens and style stick well out of the flower; the anthers and stigma are the same delicate color as the petals.

Distribution: *G. capitata* grows in sandy areas throughout the Sierra from 1000–6000'. **Names:** *Gilia* (see p. 188). *Capitata* means 'head' in reference to the terminal flower cluster. **Typical location:** Sandy slopes along Hite's Cove Trail west of Yosemite (1500').

Related Plant: Bridge's gilia (*G. leptalea*; bottom photo), though a close relative of globe gilia, does not have its tall stature nor its head-like cluster of flowers. It does, however, form dense **ground-hugging carpets of gorgeous pink/lavender with suggestions of blue and white** (blue from the anthers and the flower throat; white from the flower tube). It grows on sandy flats throughout the Sierra (and Cascades) from 3000–6500'. *Leptalea* means 'slender.' Annual. Range: Low Montane.

white to lavender • 5 petals united in tube • annual

193

Grand Collomia
Collomia grandiflora

FOOTHILLS, LOW MONTANE, MID TO HIGH MONTANE

Grand collomia is indeed grand—showy for its size and also for its highly unusual color. The single $1/2$–3' stem is topped by a **cluster of large trumpet-like salmon to peach flowers**. The 1–2" slender flower tubes are yellow, flaring out into $1/2$–$3/4$" shallow bowls. The five stamens project out of the bowl; the anthers bear blue pollen, providing a wonderful contrast to the salmon-peach petals. • The stem bears several alternating linear leaves and terminates in a cluster of short, hairy bracts from which project the several flower tubes—there are no pedicels.

• The unusual color of the blossom of this collomia will undoubtedly grab your attention, for it is highly unlikely that any other flowers nearby will be the same hue. It is even more likely to catch your eye because of the dry, somewhat sparse environment it usually inhabits.

Distribution: The *Collomia* genus is composed of 15 species in North and South America. *C. grandiflora* occurs in dry, open places throughout the Sierra from 1500–8000'. It extends in all directions to British Columbia, Colorado, and Arizona. It is naturalized in Europe. **Names:** *Collomia* means 'glue' in reference to the sticky surface of the seeds. *Grandiflora* means 'large-flowered,' though the glorious connotation of 'grand' also applies here! **Typical location:** Dry, sandy slopes along Sagehen Creek in Tahoe area (6200').

salmon • 5 petals united in tube • annual

Tiny Trumpet
Collomia linearis

FOOTHILLS, LOW MONTANE, MID TO HIGH MONTANE

Though a much smaller plant with much smaller flowers than its 'grand' sibling (*C. grandiflora*, p. 194), tiny trumpet is quite striking in its own less conspicuous way. • The slender 4–24" stem bears numerous long (1–2"), linear, rather broad (compared to the flowers), alternating leaves, which are covered with **tiny glands**. At the tip of the stem, just above the leaves, are clusters of leafy bracts out of which rise 7–20 densely packed flower tubes. The ¹/₂–³/₄" slender tubes are much longer than the tiny (¹/₄") pinwheel flower faces. • The **pale pink (or white) petals** provide a vivid contrast to the dark green leaves and bracts just below. The five stamens project slightly out of the throat and bear anthers with sticky white pollen. • Whereas grand collomia demands to be seen, tiny trumpets just invites your attention.

Distribution: *C. linearis* is widespread in open areas throughout the Sierra from 2000–8000'. It extends north to Alaska and shows up in eastern North America as well. **Names:** *Collomia* (see p. 194). *Linearis* refers to the narrowness of the leaves compared to their length (though in comparison to the flowers they appear broad). **Typical location:** Dry flats along trail to Long Lake in Sierra Buttes area (6200').

Related Plant: Staining collomia (*C. tinctoria*; bottom photo) is similar to *C. linearis* but has even smaller pink (or white) flowers with rounded petals. The narrow, glandular leaves, which often extend beyond the small clusters of 2–3 flowers, will stain yellow if you crush them (hence the name *tinctoria*, as in tincture). *C. tinctoria* grows in gravelly areas throughout the Sierra and Cascades from 2000–9000'. Annual. Range: Same.

pink (to white) • 5 petals united in tube
• annual

195

Whisker Brush

Linanthus ciliatus

FOOTHILLS, LOW MONTANE, MID TO HIGH MONTANE

Whisker brush is certainly aptly named, though many of the *Linanthus* species have similar **clumps of 'shaving-brush' leaves spaced at intervals along the stem**. • The flowers of whisker brush entice you to look more closely, for the intricacies of its coloring and design can be fully appreciated only through a magnifying glass. Each ¹/₂" flower tube is white or pink with a yellow throat and flares out into a small (¹/₄") pinwheel flower face. The petals are light to deep pink blending to white at the bases, which then blends to the yellow of the throat. Perhaps the most striking feature of these rainbow petals is the **dark rose-purple spot or triangle** toward their base right at the pink/white junction. • Often forming miniature pink 'forests' (with 3–12" stems) on dry, sandy flats, whisker brush is truly a dazzling member of this remarkable family.

Distribution: *L. ciliatus* is widespread throughout our area and throughout the entire CA-FP below 8000'. **Names:** *Linanthus* (see p. 192). *Ciliatus* means 'fringed' in reference to the hairy-margined bracts and leaves. **Typical location:** Dry, sandy slopes along trail to Paige Meadows from Ward Creek in Tahoe area (6500').

Related Plant: Baby stars (*L. bicolor*; bottom photo) is a similar plant with shaving-brush leaves and small, pink flowers with very long, slender flower tubes. The **pink petals do not have the rose spots**. *L. bicolor* is common in grassy areas throughout the Sierra foothills. *Bicolor* (see p.153). Annual. Range: Foothills, Low Montane.

pink • 5 petals united in tube • annual

Low Polemonium
Polemonium californicum
LOW MONTANE, MID TO HIGH MONTANE

The polemoniums are spectacular and unusual members of the phlox family. They have funnel-shaped flowers (usually blue) whose faces are much larger than the inconspicuous tubes, their leaves are not needle-like but are **narrow ladder-rungs** (opposite pairs), and a few species even grow in wet areas. • Low polemonium grows to only 1' or less. Attached to the lower parts of the hairy, sticky stem are several long petioles bearing 5–12 pairs of opposite leaflets. Each leaf has one terminal leaflet that is fused with the pair of leaflets just below it. • **Many of the ¹/₂" blue (to violet) flowers cluster in the terminal, roundish inflorescence.** The blue petals of each graceful, bell-shaped flower have a yellow throat leading to the white flower tube. The five stamens and one style (with lobed stigma) stick well out of the flower.

Distribution: The *Polemonium* genus is composed of 20 species in North America and Eurasia. *P. californicum* occurs in forest openings throughout the Sierra from 6000–10,000'. It extends north to Washington. **Names:** *Polemonium* is of uncertain origin, though it may have derived from the greek philosopher Polemon. *Californicum* (see p. 59). **Also known as** California Jacob's ladder. The derivation of Jacob's ladder is apparent when you visualize climbing all the way to heaven on those ladder-rung leaflets! **Typical location:** Forest openings along trail up east side of Castle Peak in Tahoe area (7300').

Related Plant: Great polemonium (*P. occidentale*, formerly *P. caeruleum*, bottom photo) bears similar though larger blue flowers, but it is **much taller (to 3')**. It is one of the few members of the phlox family that grows in **very wet areas**, occurring through-out the Sierra from 6000–10,000'. *Occidentale* means 'western.' Perennial. Range: Same.

blue (to violet) • 5 petals united in tube • perennial

Scarlet Gilia

Ipomopsis aggregata

LOW MONTANE, MID TO HIGH MONTANE

Scarlet gilia could just as well be called **scarlet trumpets**, for its 2–3' stem bears many 1–1½" long, bright red, tubular flowers. The petals flare out of the tube with gusto—you can almost hear the trumpet blare! • The red petals are mottled with yellow; occasionally you will find faded pink or even pure white flowers. • A few sparse, needle-lobed leaves, which wither at flowering, branch off the sticky stem.

Distribution: The genus *Ipomopsis* is composed of 30 species in western North America, the southeast United States, and southern South America. *I. aggregata* occurs on dry slopes throughout the Sierra from 4000–10,000'. It extends to British Columbia and the American Rockies. **Names:** *Ipomopsis* means 'striking appearance.' *Aggregata* means 'clustered.' **Typical location:** Sandy flats along Tioga Pass Road in Yosemite (8000').

Related Plant: Ballhead gilia (*I. congesta*; bottom photo) doesn't look much like scarlet gilia: its **small white flowers crowd together in dense spherical balls at the end of prostrate stems.** The hairy leaves look like little mittens. *I. congesta* grows in dry, rocky flats in the Sierra and in the Great Basin to the east from 7000–12,000'. *Congesta* does mean 'congested.' Perennial. Range: Mid to High Montane, Alpine.

red • 5 petals united in tube • perennial

Spreading Phlox
Phlox diffusa

LOW MONTANE, MID TO HIGH MONTANE, ALPINE

P. diffusa is one of the most **common and widespread** of the *Phlox* genus and family, occurring throughout western North America from low montane elevations to well above timberline. • It forms **low and loose mats (though the mats are somewhat tighter at high elevations), its beautiful white, pink, or bluish pinwheel flowers** sometimes completely covering its prickly, needle-like leaves. The mats contour the ground closely, sometimes forming brightly colored mounds draping over rocks. • The rounded petals flare out of a short tube to form a delicate ¹/₂–³/₄" pinwheel. The flowers are sweetly fragrant and bloom quite early, even in the high elevations.

Distribution: *P. diffusa* is widespread in dry, often rocky, areas throughout the Sierra from 4000–12,000'. **Names:** *Phlox* (see p. 190). *Diffusa* means 'spreading' in reference to the mat-like growth form. **Typical location:** Open ground along Round Lake Trail in Sierra Buttes area (6600').

Related Plant: Coville's phlox (*P. condensata*, formerly *P. covillei*) resembles *P. diffusa* with similar white or pink flowers, but as the new name suggests it forms **dense cushion plants rather than loose mats.** *P. condensata* grows in rocky areas throughout the Sierra from 6000–12,000'. Perennial. Range: Same.

white, pink or bluish • 5 petals united in tube • perennial

199

Granite Gilia

Leptodactylon pungens

MID TO HIGH MONTANE, ALPINE

Appearing somewhat similar to spreading phlox (p. 199) with its **dense clusters of white flowers, needle-like leaves**, and rocky environments, granite gilia is nonetheless easily distinguishable from its close relative. • Though the flowers, like spreading phlox, often almost entirely cover the leaves, granite gilia is more of a **mounded shrub** than a low mat. If you look closely at the flower, you will also see that it is more funnel-shaped (less flat) than the phlox and twists in bud. This 'funnel' is often quite closed, for the flower tends to open in late afternoon. • Another highly noticeable difference is with the leaves—just grab a handful of leaves and stem and you'll know why this plant is sometimes called prickly phlox! • The bright white flowers are often tinged with pink.

Distribution: The genus *Leptodactylon* is composed of seven species in western North America. *L. pungens* is widespread in rocky areas throughout the Sierra and the Rockies from 7000–13,000'. **Names:** *Leptodactylon* means 'narrow fringes' in reference to the spiny, needle-like leaves. *Pungens* means 'sharp-pointed.' **Also known as** prickly phlox. **Typical location:** Rocky slopes along Tioga Crest above Saddlebag Lake just east of Yosemite (11,000').

white • 5 petals united in tube • perennial

Sky Pilot
Polemonium eximium
ALPINE

Although several species of the phlox family (especially several members of the *Phlox* genus) grow above timberline, sky pilot is probably the alpine *'piece de resistance'*—it **grows only at or near the summit of the Sierra's highest peaks. • Dense spherical heads of many of these deep-blue (to purple) funnel-shaped flowers** grow at the ends of the 4–12" sticky stems. The stems come from a woody base from which also sprout many petioles thickly crowded with tiny, lobed leaves. The overall effect is something akin to blue bouquets rising above a shrub of mousetails! • Unusual for *Polemonium* is that the stamens and pistil are 'included' (i.e., do not stick out of the flower tube). Not so unusual for this genus is the strong, musky odor of the leaves.

Distribution: *P. eximium* grows in rocky areas of very high elevations (from 10,000–13,000') from just north of Yosemite south. It extends to the southern Sierra, peaking atop Mt. Whitney at above 14,000'. **Names:** *Polemonium* (see p. 197). *Eximium* means 'distinguished.' **Typical location:** Rock outcrops near summit of Mt. Dana in Yosemite (13,000').

Related Plant: Another beautiful blue polemonium of high elevations (though not as high as *P. eximium*) and with **'mousetail' leaves** (though not as dense as *P. eximium*) is showy polemonium (*P. pulcherrimum*; bottom photo). It grows in rocky areas in the central and northern Sierra and north to Alaska from 8000–11,000'. *Pulcherrimum* means 'beautiful' as in 'pulchritude.' Perennial. Range: Mid to High Montane, Alpine.

blue (to purple) • 5 petals united in tube • perennial

201

Gentian Family
(Gentianaceae)

Gentian...that word has a touch of magic for me. Just hearing it brings forth strong, sensual images: of large, deep blue or purple tubular flowers lurking in the grass; of bright, cheery, sky-blue stars sprinkled in a meadow; of tightly wound torpedo-like buds tipped with black-purple satin; of a Swiss liquor so strong that I can still taste the Alps on my tongue 20 years later!

trumpet gentian (*G. kochiana*) of the Swiss Alps

The gentian family is relatively large with approximately 80 genera and some 900 species spreading across the world's temperate and alpine environments. The flowers have five (or four) petals usually united in a tube with one large superior ovary in its center, whose stigma is conspicuously branched or lobed. In some species the tube is large and open, reflexed only at the tips; in others, the tube is smaller and the petals flare out more. In many of the flowers there are delicate fringes between the petal lobes and/or inside the tube and often the insides of the petals are gracefully speckled. Although sky-blue is the most frequent color, you will find purple, fuschia, white, and even yellow.

spring gentian (*G. verna*) of the Swiss Alps

The genus *Gentiana* (with an estimated 300 species worldwide), along with the two genera that botanists have split off *Gentiana* (*Gentianella* and *Gentianopsis*) contain most of the species of the gentian family that you will find in our area and all of the flowers that fit our tubular image of gentians. Note that just about all of these typical gentians occur in the high mountains. Flowers of the genera *Centaurium* and *Swertia* (also in our area) look quite different than our image of a gentian, but do share many of the botanical characteristics of the family.

deer's tongue

Canchalagua

Centaurium venustum

FOOTHILLS

Canchalagua looks as lovely as its name sounds. The half-dollar size, star-shaped flowers have **five intense rose-purple petals** with bright white splotches at the base where they flare out of the red-spotted, narrow tube. Almost as striking as the petals are the **protruding bright yellow anthers, strangely twisted into fleshy corkscrews.** The one delicate style, with branched stigma, is much longer than the stamens but lies flat out of the way until the anthers dry up, at which time it rises to prominence.
• Usually many flowers cluster on the 4–15" stems, and many plants crowd the sunny, grassy fields where they grow, producing a warm purplish glow to the meadow.

Distribution: The genus *Centaurium* is composed of 30 species spread across North America, Eurasia, and Africa. *C. venustum* is fairly common in grasslands and dry scrub below 4000' throughout the CA-FP. It is widespread in areas as diverse as the Mojave Desert and the mountains of northwestern California.
Names: *Centaurium* presumably derives from Centaurus, the mythical centaur who is reputed to have discovered the plant's medicinal properties. *Venustum* means 'charming' or 'handsome'—certainly apt! **Typical location:** Grassy meadows of Buck Meadows along Route 120 heading into Yosemite (3000').

rose-purple • 5 petals united in tube flaring into star • annual

Sierra Gentian
Gentianopsis holopetala
MID TO HIGH MONTANE

You're walking through a grassy meadow somewhere in the Yosemite highcountry. The ground is a bit damp, so you're walking carefully, looking closely where you are putting your feet. Then you notice, among the grass, a slight purple tinge. When you stop to inspect it, you see a small (about 1" long, penny-size in diameter) almost luminous **blue-purple tubular flower seemingly blooming right out of the ground**. You get down on your hands and knees and see that there are dozens of delicate Sierra gentians blooming in the grass, each sitting atop its own slender flower stem and cradle of pointed, black-ribbed, green sepals. • On most of the flowers, the stem is only a few inches tall; sometimes it is longer (up to a foot), but then it is usually only partially erect, most of it lying on the ground. The leaves, too, are nearly on the ground: there may be one or a few very small, narrow stem leaves, but most of the leaves ($1/2$–$1 1/2$" and spoon-shaped) form a basal cluster. • Though members of the gentian family usually have five petals, many (including both Sierra members of the genus *Gentianopsis*) have four.

Distribution: The genus *Gentianopsis* has about 15 species in temperate areas of North America and Eurasia. *G. holopetala* occurs in damp, grassy meadows from 6500–11,000' in the southern and central Sierra (not reaching as far north as Carson Pass). It extends into the White and Inyo mountains east of the Sierra. **Names:** *Gentianopsis* means 'resembling Gentiana.' *Holopetala* means 'whole petal.' **Formerly called** *Gentiana holopetala*. Only fairly recently have botanists split *Gentianopsis* off from the *Gentiana* genus—some books still call Sierra gentian by its former name. **Typical location:** Damp, grassy parts of Tuolumne Meadows in Yosemite (9000').

blue-purple • 4 petals united in tube with flaring tips • annual or perennial

Hiker's Gentian
Gentianopsis simplex
LOW MONTANE, MID TO HIGH MONTANE

Hiker's gentian is one of the two representatives of the genus *Gentianopsis* in our area (see p. 205 for *G. holopetala*). Clearly a gentian with its beautiful blue tubular flower and conspicuous branched stigma, *G. simplex* resembles *G. holopetala* by having only one flower per stem and only four petals. However, the **petals** of hiker's gentian are unusual in that they **are ragged toward the tips and they twist as they flare out from the tube, creating a kind of off-kilter windmill appearance.** • The single flower is perched atop a 4–12" stem with several pairs of narrow, opposite leaves. There is a cluster of spoon-shaped leaves at the base of the stem, but they wither early in the blooming cycle, so you may not find them. The green sepals are narrow and pointed much like those of *G. holopetala* but do not have its dark ribs.

Distribution: *G. simplex* occurs in damp, grassy meadows from 4000–9500' throughout the Sierra. It reaches the Cascades, Klamaths, and the Coast Range of northern California and extends east to Idaho. **Names:** *Gentianopsis* (see p. 205). *Simplex* does mean 'simple,' but its reference is unclear. **Typical location:** Grassy meadows at Luther Pass along Route 89 south of Tahoe (7500').

blue • 4 petals united in tube flaring into windmill • annual

Northern Gentian

Gentianella amarella

LOW MONTANE, MID TO HIGH MONTANE

Although northern gentian has the typical tubular gentian flower, it is unusual for a gentian in several ways: the plant is taller (4–20"); the flower has shorter (less than 1") and narrower (dime-size) tubes barely protruding beyond the long sepals; although sometimes blue, the color usually tends toward the **rose-violet** side of purple; many flowers grow on each plant out of the leaf axils; a dense fringe of long hairs is attached to the inside base of each petal; and frequently you will find **some flowers with four petals and others with five on the same plant.** These last three characteristics are typical of the genus *Gentianella*. • The cluster of spoon-shaped basal leaves withers early in the blooming cycle while the pairs of narrower opposite stem leaves persist.

Distribution: The genus *Gentianella* has approximately 250 species in temperate and alpine environments worldwide except Africa. *G. amarella* is widespread in wet meadows and bogs from 5000–11,000' throughout the Sierra. It extends from Baja to Alaska and occurs in the White and Inyo mountains to the east of the Sierra, on the east coast of America, and in eastern Asia. **Names:** *Gentianella* means 'little Gentiana,' reflecting its having been split off from the genus *Gentiana. Amarella* means 'bitter.' **Also known as** felwort. **Formerly called** *Gentiana amarella.* **Typical location:** Wet meadows along Lyell Canyon trail in Yosemite (9000').

rose-violet • 4 (or 5) petals united in tube with flaring tips • annual

Deer's Tongue
Swertia radiata
MID TO HIGH MONTANE

Just when you thought you were understanding the gentian family and could easily identify a member of it, you encounter deer's tongue. It's hard to believe it's a gentian, for the flowers are not large conspicuous tubes, are not blue, are not solitary or a few to a plant, and do not grow close to the ground! On the contrary, the plant is enormous (**3–6' tall**) **and bears hundreds of greenish-white flowers** in the leaf axils. And to top it off, the four petals open flat to form large (1–2") bowl-like flowers with pairs of pink, hairy nectar glands on each petal! • Despite these dramatic 'irregularities,' deer's tongue does have the radially symmetrical flowers of four united petals and the superior ovary with 2-branched stigma character- istic of the gentian family. • Deer's tongue has many sets of large (4–10") tongue-like leaves in whorls at intervals around its thick, hollow stem. Sometimes the first (and maybe even the second) year of growth will only produce a dense cluster of these leaves (with no flowering stem). Once the huge stem grows and flowers, the plant dies.

Distribution: The genus *Swertia* is composed of about 120 species across temperate North America, Eurasia, and Africa. *S. radiata* occurs from 6800–9500' throughout the Sierra. It grows from Washington to South Dakota and New Mexico. **Names:** *Swertia* is after E. Sweert, 16th-century Dutch herbalist. *Radiata* refers to the radially symmetrical flowers. **Also known as** monument plant. **Formerly called** *Frasera speciosa.* **Typical location:** Dry slopes along dirt road to Wet Meadow Reservoir in Blue Lakes area below Carson Pass (8000').

greenish-white • 4 petals united in cross • peren- nial

208

Explorer's Gentian

Gentiana calycosa

LOW MONTANE, MID TO HIGH MONTANE

When you think of a gentian, you probably think of explorer's gentian, or something very like it. The **five deep blue petals are united into a large (to 2") open tube**. The tips of the petals, marked on the insides with **pale whitish or greenish spots**, flare slightly, creating an inviting vase-shaped flower. There are thread-like fringes between the petal tips. The conspicuous stigma is 2-branched and grows out of a large, stalked ovary. Now this is a gentian! • The plant usually consists of several 6–24" stems sprouting from a root-crown, each stem having a terminal flower and perhaps several more flowers growing out of the upper leaf axils. Each stem bears several pairs of opposite stem leaves, but unlike our other gentians, these stem leaves are broadly ovate (almost round). Explorer's gentian is also one of the few gentians without a cluster of basal leaves. • The plant is an unusually late bloomer, often not reaching full bloom until late August or even September.

Distribution: The genus *Gentiana* is composed of approximately 300 species growing in temperate and alpine environments across North America and Eurasia. *G. calycosa* occurs in wet meadows and seep areas in rocks from 4000–10,500' in the Sierra. It extends to British Columbia and Montana. **Names:** *Gentiana* derives from King Gentius of Illyria. *Calycosa* means 'full calyx.' **Also known as** bog gentian. **Typical location:** Rock ledges near seep springs in Pole Creek Canyon near Squaw Valley (7000').

Related Plant: Alpine gentian (*G. newberryi*; bottom photo) greatly resembles explorer's gentian but has an even larger open tube that often hides in the grass of high mountain meadows or hugs the ground above timberline. It is usually **white with a blue tinge**, though sometimes (especially when hybridizing with *G. calycosa*) it can be pure blue. *G. newberryi* occurs from 7000–12,000' throughout the Sierra and into western Nevada and southern Oregon. John Newberry (see p. 161). Perennial. Range: Mid to High Montane, Alpine.

blue to blue-purple • 5 petals united in large tube • perennial

Pea Family
(Fabaceae)

Outgoing and demonstrative, yet secretive and mysterious—this is the paradox of the pea! These plants grow in showy profusion and have flowers that hold up a banner while holding in a secret. As well, these plants perform a 'magic' somewhat akin to medieval alchemists transforming dross to gold.

red kidney vetch (*Anthyllis vulneraria*) of the Swiss Alps

The five petals of peas are separate and unequal: the upper petal is an upright 'standard'—in many species a large and colorful banner; the lateral two petals (wings) are like a pair of vertical, cradling hands; the remaining two petals form a keel nestled inside the wings. In some species (e.g., lupine) these petal types are easily distinguished; in others (e.g., clover) it takes close examination to locate them.

lupine with upcurving keel

The peas announce and celebrate their presence with a colorful banner, so where's the secretive part? If you pretend to be a bee and land on the wings of a lupine, you will soon discover the pea secret. As the bee's weight pushes the wings down, up pops the keel and out pops its hidden treasure—the long pistil and almost as long stamens covered with brightly colored, sticky pollen. The bee will get jabbed right in the torso with this surprise!

Now what about the alchemy part? Peas are legumes (the Latin name formerly used for the pea family was Leguminosae), which are capable of transforming atmospheric nitrogen to life-giving soil nitrogen. This mysterious ability to create its own fertilizer is the source of the pea's great value in agricultural crop rotation and explains why pea species can often thrive in seemingly barren habitats where very little else has succeeded. Another bit of pea magic lies in the durability of the seeds. Some lupine seeds have demonstrated their viability after decades or even millennia of dormancy. Seeds of *Lupinus arcticus* excavated from frozen lemming burrows 10,000 years old were still viable!

lupine blooming after years of dormancy

211

palmately compound leaf

seedpods of Whitney's locoweed

high meadow of lupine and arnica

Most pea species plants have clusters of flowers in dense racemes, spikes, umbels, or heads. The leaves are usually compound with un-lobed leaflets; the stems sometimes have tendrils and twine.

There are often 10 stamens (sometimes five or fewer) and a superior ovary with one style and one stigma. The fruit is a pod with several to many seeds in two alternating rows.

The pea family is huge with approximately 650 genera and approximately 18,000 species worldwide, many of which are cultivated for food, medicines, and ornamentals. The genera with the most species you are likely to encounter in our area are *Astragalus* (locoweed), *Lathyrus* (wild pea), *Lotus*, *Lupinus* (lupine), and *Trifolium* (clover).

The 'paradoxical peas' are widespread and common in our area (and worldwide), often decorating grasslands, foothill slopes, and mountain meadows with acres of bright colors. You will also find them, though, in splendid isolation on the most hostile, windswept, high mountain ridges. A paradox indeed, these wonderful peas!

field of valley lupine

Douglas Lupine
Lupinus nanus

CENTRAL VALLEY, FOOTHILLS

The lupines are probably the most familiar and most easily recognizable members of the pea family. The dense raceme of usually blue flowers whorling around the stem on short pedicels, the conspicuous banner-wings-keel flower structure, and the palmately compound leaves are all quite obvious and distinctive. • In the California Floristic Province lupine species range from sea level to the highest peaks, but probably their most spectacular displays are in the Central Valley grasslands and the rolling Sierra foothills where they create 'inland seas' of nearly solid blue and paint dazzling multi-colored canvases where they mix with poppy, owl's-clover, goldfield, and other bright spring beauties. • Douglas lupine is in many ways a typical blue-flowered lupine. Branching off the lower part of the $^1/_2$–2' stem (on 1–3" petioles) are hairy, palmately compound leaves (with 5–9 narrow leaflets). The 1–8" raceme bears several whorls of the $^1/_2$" rich blue flowers. The **banners of *L. nanus* are unusual, however, in that they are low and rounded (broader than tall).** Many lupines including Douglas lupine have a blue banner that has a large white splotch in its center that is speckled with black spots.

Distribution: The *Lupinus* genus is composed of approximately 200 species in North and South America. *L. nanus* occurs in open, grassy areas throughout the CA-FP below 4000'. It extends to British Columbia. **Names:** *Lupinus* means 'wolf.' Because lupines (and other peas) are nitrogen-fixing, they can grow on quite barren soil where most other plants can't survive. Apparently the 'namers' of lupine, not realizing that they created their own 'fertilizer,' thought that the soil where some of them grew was barren because the plants were 'wolfing up' the nutrients. *Nanus* means 'dwarf.' David Douglas (see p. 108). **Typical location:** Grassy fields along road up Table Mountain near Oroville (600').

blue • 5 irregular petals (banner, wings, keel) • annual

213

Valley Lupine
Lupinus microcarpus
CENTRAL VALLEY, FOOTHILLS

If you are standing in an open grassy field in the Central Valley or in the foothills and see a blue haze off in the distance hugging the ground, it is most likely lupine and could well be valley lupine, which often **grows in great masses in low elevation open or disturbed areas** (see photo, p. 212). • The flowers of valley lupine are like so many of its genus—blue wings and a blue banner with a large, central, black-dotted, white splotch that turns rosy red with age. Several whorls of these $^1/_2$" flowers occur on the upper part of the $^1/_2$–2', **somewhat hairy stem**. The palmately compound leaves consist of 5–11 narrow leaflets.

Distribution: *L. microcarpus* is abundant in open or disturbed areas throughout the CA-FP below 3000'. It extends from Baja to British Columbia. **Names:** *Lupinus* (see p. 213). *Microcarpus* means 'small-fruited.' **Formerly called** *L. subvexus*. **Typical location:** Open fields atop Table Mountain near Oroville (1500').

Related Plant: Miniature lupine (*L. bicolor*, bottom photo) is another typical lupine that is abundant in low elevation open fields throughout the CA-FP. However, it does have some distinct features: its **flowers are unusually small** ($^1/_4$"), **and the white splotch on the banner is usually triangular**. *Bicolor* (see p. 153). Annual. Range: Same.

blue • 5 irregular petals (banner, wings, keel)
• annual

Succulent Lupine
Lupinus succulentus
CENTRAL VALLEY, FOOTHILLS

Succulent lupine has the typical lupine blue flower with black-spotted white (or yellow) splotch in the center of the banner. As in most other lupines, this splotch turns an intense magenta with age. However, succulent lupine is easy to distinguish from its many siblings. It is a large (to 3' tall) and robust plant with broad, rounded leaflets and a **very thick (to ³/₄" in diameter), fleshy, often hollow stem**. You would probably assume this imposing plant is a perennial, but instead it is a fast-growing, thick-stemmed annual—careful inspection shows that it is not woody.

Distribution: *L. succulentus* occurs in open or disturbed areas in the Central Valley and foothills below 2500'. It extends from northwestern California to Baja. **Names:** *Lupinus* (see p. 213). *Succulentus* means 'succulent' or 'fleshy.' **Also known as** arroyo lupine. **Typical location:** Grassy fields in Jepson Prairie near Dixon (50').

blue • 5 irregular petals (banner, wings, keel) • annual

Spider Lupine

Lupinus benthamii

CENTRAL VALLEY, FOOTHILLS

There are so many species of blue-flowered lupine in the California Floristic Province that it can be quite difficult to know which species you are looking at. Although spider lupine (*L. benthamii*) does have the typical blue flower (with white banner splotch turning magenta with age), its leaves are unique and immediately identify it. As the common name suggests, the **(7–10) leaflets resemble a spider's legs—they are long (2"), widely separated, and extremely narrow.** The plant can grow to $2^{1}/_{2}'$ tall.

Distribution: *L. benthamii* occurs in open, sometimes rocky areas throughout the Sierra foothills (and occasionally in the Central Valley) below 3000'. It grows in the Coast Range of southern California. **Names:** *Lupinus* (see p. 213). George Bentham was a 19th-century English botanist. **Typical location:** Grassy edges of Hite's Cove Trail west of Yosemite (1500').

Related Plant: Whorled lupine (*L. microcarpus* var. *densiflorus*; bottom photo) is another distinctive lupine of open areas in low elevations, but in this case distinctive more for its flowers than its leaves (which consist of 7–11 broad, pointed leaflets). The upper foot or so of the 2–3' stem bears **several dense whorls of white to yellow (rarely rose or purple),** $^{1}/_{2}–^{3}/_{4}"$ **flowers.** *Microcarpus* means 'small-fruited.' *Densiflorus* means 'densely flowered.' Annual. Range: Same.

blue • 5 irregular petals (banner, wings, keel)

• annual

216

Bush Lupine
Lupinus albifrons

CENTRAL VALLEY, FOOTHILLS, LOW MONTANE

One of the most impressive floral displays of early spring is the bush lupine. From a distance, you will see why it is sometimes called silver lupine, for the **tips of the long (to 1') flower spikes are silver**, and the rounded mass of palmately compound leaves are silvery-green. • Closer examination will show the reasons for this silvery appearance: first, almost every part of this plant is covered with fine, silvery-white hairs; second, although most of the many ³/₄" flowers crowded on the flower spikes are the blue-purple typical of lupines, those at the tips of the spikes that are still in bud are a soft, fuzzy white. • The silvery-hairy leaves consist of 6–10 narrow, pointed, widely separate leaflets that can be as long as 1¹/₂". The large, blue-purple flowers have a tightly reflexed banner in the center of which is a yellow (or white), black-flecked patch that turns red-purple with age.

Distribution: *L. albifrons* occurs in open, sandy or rocky places throughout the CA-FP below 5000'. **Names:** *Lupinus* (see p. 213). *Albifrons* means 'white-fronded' (a frond is a large leaf with many divisions). **Also known as** silver lupine. **Typical location:** Sandy slopes along Route 20 east of Marysville (500').

Related Plant: You might mistake beautiful lupine (*L. formosus;* bottom photo) for bush lupine, for it often grows in shrub-like clumps up to 3' tall and has the usual blue (and white) flowers and long, narrow leaflets. However, *L. formosus,* unlike *L. albifrons,* only resembles a shrub, for it is an **herbaceous perennial** (i.e., it does not have woody stems). *L. formosus* grows in open areas throughout the CA-FP below 5000'. *Formosus* means 'beautiful.' Perennial. Range: Same.

blue • 5 irregular petals (banner, wings, keel)
• shrub

Hill Lotus
Lotus humistratus

CENTRAL VALLEY, FOOTHILLS, LOW MONTANE

Whereas lupines are typically blue (sometimes white, yellow, or multicolored) and wild peas (*Lathyrus*) are typically red-purple (sometimes white or yellow), lotuses are usually yellow (sometimes white or pink). Hill lotus is in many ways a typical lotus: the flowers are **yellow (aging red)** with an erect, rounded banner and much smaller wings that are perpendicular to the banner; the leaves are compound with small, elliptical leaflets. However, there are some unusual characteristics of hill lotus that help you distinguish it from the many other lotuses you may encounter in our area. • Most species of lotus have head-like clusters of flowers (see Torrey's lotus, p. 224); *L. humistratus* has **only one flower per leaf axil**. Because the flower is attached directly to the axil (with no pedicel) and it is small ($^1/_4$"), it can sometimes be partially hidden by the leaflets—even as small as they are. These $^1/_4$–$^1/_2$" leaflets are another unusual characteristic of hill lotus: there are usually only four or five, with one at the tip of the petiole, one attached to one side of the petiole, and the other two or three attached to the other side. • The plant sometimes forms mats, and sometimes grows erect to 1' or so. The reddish stem, the leaves, and the narrow, pointed sepals are all covered with stringy, white hairs. If you look closely, you'll see that four of the sepals are behind the banner and only one is under the wings.

Distribution: The *Lotus* genus is composed of about 150 species, mostly in North America. *L. humistratus* is abundant in grasslands and along roads throughout California below 5000'. It extends to Mexico. **Names:** *Lotus* is an old Greek name of uncertain origin. *Humistratus* means 'low layer' in reference to its often low growing nature. **Typical location:** Grassy slopes along Route 20 east of Marysville (500').

yellow • 5 irregular petals (banner, wings, keel) • annual

Tangier Pea
Lathyrus tingitanus
CENTRAL VALLEY, FOOTHILLS

The banner and wings (and hidden keel) characteristic of the peas are quite obvious in the *Lathyrus* (wild pea) genus. In Tangier pea, as in several of the wild pea species, the banner is enormous compared to the wings. • The wild peas differ from the lupines in many ways: the stems are usually sprawling or climbing, the leaf stems end as tendrils or bristles, the leaves are usually pinnately compound (like ladder rungs), and the raceme of flowers is usually on a stem that arises from the leaf axil. Generally the flowers of *Lathyrus* species are far fewer and far looser on the raceme than are the flowers of lupine. • Tangier pea is a **3–8' vine with a flattened stem**. Each leaf consists of a pair of rounded ³/₄–2" leaflets whose stem ends in a slender tendril. This large plant bears only 2–3 flowers, but what extraordinary flowers they are! The large (to 1") banner and the much smaller wings are an **intense maroon to purple to crimson**. Especially when backlit, this flower seems to glow from within with a color so intense it almost hurts!

Distribution: The *Lathyrus* genus has approximately 150 species in temperate North America and Eurasia. *L. tingitanus* is an alien introduced from Europe. It occurs in disturbed areas throughout the CA-FP below 1500'. It is found along the California coast and into Oregon. **Names:** *Lathyrus* means 'stimulating' in reference to the effect of the seeds. *Tingitanus* means 'of Tangiers.' **Typical location:** Along dirt road in Merced area (100').

maroon • 5 irregular petals (banner, wings, keel) • annual

Winter Vetch
Vicia villosa

CENTRAL VALLEY, FOOTHILLS

Vetches, like the wild peas (*Lathyrus*), usually have tendrils that help support the sprawling or climbing stems. Although the banner and wings of the vetches are quite apparent, the flowers of most *Vicia* species are unlike the lupines, wild peas, and lotuses in that they are much longer than wide, the wings are larger than the banner, and the flowers often droop along one side of a dense raceme. • In winter vetch, each raceme (which rises out of a leaf axil) bears **10 or more blue-purple flowers sweeping down off one side of the stem**. The 2–5' vine bears numerous slightly hairy, pinnately compound leaves, each composed of 12–18 narrow leaflets. The leaf stems end in narrow tendrils. With so many flowers densely crowded in each raceme and with the plants often massing together, *V. villosa* puts on quite a purple show!

Distribution: The genus *Vicia* has about 130 species in North America and Eurasia. *V. villosa* is an alien introduced from Europe. It occurs along roadsides and in fields throughout the CA-FP below 3000'. **Names:** *Vicia* is the old Latin name for vetch. *Villosa* means 'soft-hairy' in reference to the soft, white hairs on the stems and leaves. **Typical location:** Open fields near Sacramento (100').

Related Plant: Spring vetch (*V. sativa*; bottom photo) is another alien from Europe but without the long, drooping flowers typical of the vetch. Only **1–3 of the red-purple, large-bannered flowers grow in clusters** on very short pedicels in the leaf axils. The pinnately compound leaves have 4–8 pairs of square-tipped, opposite leaflets. *V. sativa* grows in disturbed areas throughout the CA-FP below 4000'. *Sativa* means 'cultivated.' Annual. Range: Central Valley, Foothills, Low Montane.

blue-purple • 5 irregular petals (banner, wings, keel) • annual

220

Balloon Clover
Trifolium depauperatum
CENTRAL VALLEY, FOOTHILLS

Clovers are one of the most familiar of all flowering plants—you can probably visualize those palmately compound leaves with the proverbial three leaflets (unless you're lucky!) and the flowerheads dense with the many small, white flowers. But perhaps you have never looked closely enough at an individual flower to recognize the banner and wings (and hidden keel) characteristic of the pea family. In clover the individual flower is usually only about ¹/₄", so the banner is tiny and the cupped wings are usually even tinier.

• Balloon clover is a typical clover in many ways, with **three wedge-shaped leaflets and a head of three to many flowers at the end of a slender peduncle**, but these flowers are rather odd. The **pink corolla (with white tips) puffs up into a sac-like structure as the plant goes to fruit.** You have to get on your hands and knees to examine these flowers, for they are small (¹/₈–¹/₄") and hide in the grass on 4–10" stems.

Distribution: The genus *Trifolium* is composed of approximately 300 species mostly in northern temperate areas, but also reaching South America and Africa. *T. depauperatum* occurs in moist areas, including vernal pools, throughout the Central Valley and Sierra foothills below 3000'. It extends to the California coast and to the Cascades and can also be found in South America. **Names:** *Trifolium* means '3-leaved.' *Depauperatum* means 'dwarfed' in reference to the small flowers. **Typical location:** Around margins of vernal pools atop Table Mountain near Oroville (1500').

pink with white tips • 5 irregular petals (banner, wings, keel) • annual

Bearded Clover

Trifolium barbigerum

CENTRAL VALLEY, FOOTHILLS

Bearded clover is a typical clover with its three ovate leaflets, its ½–1" head of small flowers, and its conspicuous spiny stipules (appendages where the petiole branches off the plant stem). However, its flowers are unusual in that they are 2-toned: the **banner is usually a dark red-purple with a white upper half.**
• The plant is ½–1' tall; the leaves and flowerheads are at the ends of long stems. If you look very closely at the calyx, you will see that its narrow lobes are tipped with delicate, feathery bristles.

Distribution: *T. barbigerum* occurs in wet areas, including the margins of vernal pools, throughout the Central Valley and Sierra foothills below 2000'. It extends to western California and Oregon. **Names:** *Trifolium* (see p. 221). *Barbigerum* means 'bearded' in reference to the bristly calyx. **Typical location:** Along margins of vernal pools atop Table Mountain near Oroville (1500').

Related Plant: Tomcat clover (*T. willdenovii*, formerly *T. tridentatum*; bottom photo) is a **very common** clover of the Central Valley and Sierra foothills, often creating **masses of red-purple in damp, grassy fields.** It is sometimes a small plant, but often is robust with stems up to 2'. The three leaflets are very narrow and pointed and they are often serrated. The ½–1½" flowerheads contain many of the red-purple (usually white-tipped) flowers. Carl Willdenow was the director of the Berlin Botanical Garden (1801–12). Annual. Range: Same.

red-purple and white • 5 irregular petals
(banner, wings, keel) • annual

Scotch Broom

Cytisus scoparius

CENTRAL VALLEY, FOOTHILLS

Labeled a 'noxious weed' by botanists (it is an alien from Europe that spreads rapidly and takes over wide areas), Scotch broom is nonetheless a beautiful **shrub with great masses of bright yellow pea flowers.**
• The 6–8' shrub is thick with small, oval leaflets (usually in threes, especially on older branches) but is even thicker with the ³/₄–1", golden yellow flowers that cluster in the leaf axils. • The 1–1¹/₂" fruits (pods) are flat and brown or black and hold 5–12 seeds.

Distribution: The genus *Cytisus* is composed of 33 species native to Europe, western Asia, northern Africa, and the Canary Islands. *C. scoparius* is common in disturbed areas (often along roads) in the Central Valley and Sierra foothills below 3000'. It ranges from the foothills of the Cascades to the southern California coast. **Names:** *Cytisus* is an ancient Greek name of uncertain meaning. *Scoparius* means 'broom-like' presumably in reference to the dense 'plumes' of flowers. **Typical location:** Along Route 80 near Applegate (1500').

Related Plant: Another **shrub (or small tree)** in the pea family is lovely **pink-flowered** redbud (*Cercis occidentalis*; bottom photos). Redbud bears large (1–4"), **heart-shaped leaves** that are glossy bronze when young, and many loose racemes of the delicate pink flowers. The flowers bloom before the leaves appear and often look somewhat frazzled as the wings usually 'flutter' upright with the banner. *C. occidentalis* occurs mostly in ravines and canyons along streambanks throughout the Sierra foothills from 300–4000'. It extends to the mountains of northwestern California and to the Cascades and south to southern California. *Cercis* is an ancient Greek name of uncertain origin. *Occidentalis* means 'western.' Shrub or small tree. Range: Foothills.

yellow • 5 irregular petals (banner, wings, keel)
• shrub

223

Torrey's Lotus
Lotus oblongifolius
FOOTHILLS, LOW MONTANE, MID TO HIGH MONTANE

Although there are many species of lotus in our area, Torrey's lotus is distinct for its 2-toned yellow and white flowers. • The ¹/₂–2' stem of *L. oblongifolius* is either erect or sprawling and bears several pinnately compound leaves, each with 7–11 narrow leaflets. Unlike the *Lathyrus* species (p. 219), the leaf stems of lotus species do not end in tendrils. The flower stems of Torrey's lotus arise from the leaf axils and end in an umbel of several ¹/₂" flowers with **yellow banners and white wings**. Immediately below the flower umbels are 1–3 leaf-like bracts.

Distribution: *L. oblongifolius* occurs in forest openings and wet meadows throughout the CA-FP from 700–8500'. It ranges from Mexico to southern Oregon. **Names:** *Lotus* (see p. 218). *Oblongifolius* means 'oblong-leaved' in reference to the shape of the leaflets. **Also known as** narrow-leaved lotus. **Typical location:** Wet forest openings along trail to Long Lake in Sierra Buttes area (6400').

yellow and white • 5 irregular petals (banner, wings, keel) • perennial

Harlequin Lupine

Lupinus stiversii

FOOTHILLS, LOW MONTANE

If you're at all unclear as to the banner-wings-keel structure of the pea flower, harlequin lupine is a dream come true, for in this spectacular flower the parts are color coded just for you! • The **upright banner is a bright yellow, the wings (the vertical, cupped hands) are an intense pink, and the keel (shaped like a keel of a boat and hidden inside the wings) is white.** If you carefully push the wings down, as would the weight of a straddling bee, the keel and the reproductive parts carefully cradled within it will pop up. You will see that, as in all lupine, there are 10 stamens and one style. Five of the stamens have long filaments with short anthers, and the other five have short filaments with long anthers. • *L. stiversii* grows 4–20" tall, has palmately compound leaves with 7–20 fairly broad leaflets, and has a 1–3" raceme with a dense terminal cluster (not whorls) of the $^1/_2$–$^3/_4$" multicolored flowers.

Distribution: *L. stiversii* occurs in clearings and grassy areas below 4500'. It extends to the mountains of southern California. **Names:** *Lupinus* (see p. 213). Charles Stivers was a collector of California plants. **Typical location:** Along Route 140 paralleling the Merced River west of Yosemite (1800').

yellow, pink, and white • 5 irregular petals (banner, wings, keel)
• annual

Long-stalked Clover

Trifolium longipes

LOW MONTANE, MID TO HIGH MONTANE

Long-stalked clover is very much like what you probably think of when you think clover. Its small white flowers are packed into a rounded 1/2–1" head at the end of a long, slender peduncle (stalk). The leaves are palmately compound with three leaflets, though these leaflets are not the oval you may be envisioning but are **narrow and pointed**. • The 1/2" **flowers are usually a dull white but sometimes are pink-purple or 2-colored.** The calyx lobes are spine-like often with bristly hairs. The flowers droop after they have been pollinated.

Distribution: *T. longipes* is very common in grassy meadows from 3000–9500' throughout the Sierra and Cascades to Washington. It is found east to Montana and Colorado. **Names:** *Trifolium* (see p. 221). *Longipes* means 'long-stalked.' **Typical location:** Grassy meadows along Sagehen Creek in Tahoe (6000').

Related Plant: Shasta clover (*T. kingii*, formerly *T. productum*; bottom photo) is another clover with a dense head of white or pink flowers that grows in mid-elevation meadows (3000–8000'). However, it is easily distinguished by its mop-like head whose **flowers all point downward.** *Kingii* (see p. 109). Perennial. Range: Same.

white (or pink) • 5 irregular petals (banner, wings, keel) • perennial

226

Carpet Clover
Trifolium monanthum

LOW MONTANE, MID TO HIGH MONTANE, ALPINE

Carpet clover, though having the usual banner-wings-keel flowers and the 3-leaflet leaves, is unusual for a clover. Instead of having the typical dense flowerheads, the flowers of carpet clover grow in **few-flowered (1–3) loose clusters**. The **creamy-white**, $^1/_2$" flowers have long, narrow tubes and the keel is often purple-tipped. • As the common name suggests, carpet clover grows low to the ground, often **carpeting wet openings** in forests or meadows with its small ($^1/_8$–$^1/_2$") narrow leaves and creamy flowers.

Distribution: *T. monanthum* occurs in wet openings throughout the Sierra from 5000–12,000'. It extends to the Cascades. **Names:** *Trifolium* (see p. 221). *Monanthum* means 'of the mountains.' **Typical location:** Wet depressions in open flats along trail to Paige Meadows in Tahoe area (6700').

Related Plant: Bowl clover (*T. cyathiferum;* bottom photo) is an even more unusual clover whose tiny white (or yellowish-brown) **flowers cluster within a papery, green-veined, bowl-like bract**. *T. cyathiferum* grows in wet areas throughout the Sierra to British Columbia below 8000'. *Cyathiferum* means 'forming a cup.' Annual. Range: All zones except alpine.

white • 5 irregular petals (banner, wings, keel) • perennial

Broad-leaf Lupine

Lupinus polyphyllus

LOW MONTANE, MID TO HIGH MONTANE

Broad-leaf lupine is an extremely showy plant. It is a typical blue-flowered lupine but **grows to 5' tall with a spike-like inflorescence as tall (3–16") as many entire plants!** • The stout stem bears numerous palmately compound leaves, each on a long (1–18") petiole and each composed of 5–17 broad leaflets. The blue (to violet) flowers are arranged in distinct whorls on the stem. The blue banner often has a white (or yellowish) splotch in its center which usually turns red-purple after pollination. • Because *L. polyphylllus* grows in wet or even boggy areas, usually in 'thickets' with other large and showy plants, its colorful flowers seem even more intense in contrast to the lush vegetation and often bright-flowered species around it.

Distribution: *L. polyphyllus* grows in very wet areas throughout the CA-FP from 4000-8500'. **Names:** *Lupinus* (see p. 213). *Polyphyllus* means 'many-leaved.' **Typical location:** Boggy areas in Paige Meadows in Tahoe area (7000').

Related Plant: Torrey's lupine (*L. lepidus* var. *sellulus*, formerly *L. sellulus*; bottom photo) is a much shorter (4–12"), blue-flowered plant that **grows in the rocks** throughout the Sierra from 4000–10,000'. The **tight and narrow inflorescence rises above nearly basal leaves** and the blue banner of the small flowers has a conspicuous white splotch with black spots. *Lepidus* means 'elegant.' John Torrey was an American chemist and plant taxonomist of the early 1800s. Perennial. Range: Same.

blue • 5 irregular petals (banner, wings, keel)
• perennial

228

White Lupine
Lupinus albicaulis
LOW MONTANE, MID TO HIGH MONTANE

Most lupines are blue (often with white splotches on the banner), so it is unusual to come across a lupine of some other color. In the foothills you might discover the amazing 3-colored harlequin lupine (p. 225); in the higher mountains you might encounter a species or two of white or yellow lupine. • One of the former is the extremely showy *L. albicaulis* with **bright white (sometimes purple) petals whose banners have a rather vague yellowish patch** in the center. The flowers (whether the usual white or the occasional purple) fade brown. • The ¹/₂–3' plant is dense, almost shrub-like, with large (4–18") flower spikes packed densely with the ¹/₂" flowers. Unlike many lupines, the flowers are arranged haphazardly on the stem rather than in distinct whorls. The banner is strongly folded back and the keel is distinctly upcurved. • *L. albicaulis* is quite leafy; each palmately compound leaf is composed of 5–10 narrow, somewhat silky-haired leaflets.

Distribution: *L. albicaulis* occurs on dry slopes throughout the Sierra from 2000–8500'. It extends to Washington. **Names:** *Lupinus* (see p. 213). *Albicaulis* means 'white-stemmed.' **Also known as** pine lupine. **Typical location:** Dry slopes along trail to Charity Valley south of the Tahoe area (7500').

Related Plant: One of the few **yellow** lupines of the higher mountains, yellow lupine (*L. arbustus* ssp. *calcaratus*; bottom photo) grows on dry sagebrush slopes mostly on the eastern side of the Sierra but extends into the eastern edge of our area from 5000–9500'. It grows in the Tahoe area on sagebrush flats along Sagehen Creek (6200'). *Arbustus* means 'like a small tree.' *Calcaratus* means 'spurred' in reference to the distinct calyx spur. Perennial. Range: Same.

white • 5 irregular petals (banner, wings, keel)
• perennial

Brewer's Lupine
Lupinus breweri

LOW MONTANE, MID TO HIGH MONTANE, ALPINE

Brewer's lupine is an exquisite blue- to violet-flowered representative of the *Lupinus* genus, which has at least 30 species (and numerous varieties) present in our area. Although its flower is typical of lupines, it is unusual in being a **dwarfed, matted, or tufted** plant. • *L. breweri* grows nearly flat on the ground: its woody stem is prostrate or barely erect, and the plant does not exceed 8" tall. There are many of the silvery-hairy leaves growing on 1–2" petioles coming off the stem. • The **inflorescence is tiny (1–2" tall) but usually thick with flowers**. The blue (to violet) banner has a white (sometimes yellow) splotch in its center; the keel is straight and glabrous. • Though a small plant, Brewer's lupine can be quite showy because it often grows in dense mats, covering large areas of otherwise bare ground.

Distribution: *L. breweri* is common on dry flats throughout the Sierra from 4000–12,500'. It extends to southern Oregon. **Names:** *Lupinus* (see p. 213). *Breweri* (see p. 86) has several species of California plants named after him. **Typical location:** Dry, bare slopes along Mt. Rose Trail in Tahoe area (9500').

blue (to violet) • 5 irregular petals (banner, wings, keel) • perennial

Whitney's Locoweed
Astragalus whitneyi
MID TO HIGH MONTANE, ALPINE

When it is in bloom, Whitney's locoweed appears to be quite a typical though dwarfed member of the pea family. The 4–16" stem is usually prostrate, so the plant sprawls across its rocky or gravelly habitat. The leaves are pinnately compound, each leaf consisting of 5–21 tiny (¹/₈–³/₄") leaflets in opposite pairs (with one terminal). From some of the leaf axils rise pedicels lifting a few of the cream (or pink or purple) ¹/₄–¹/₂" flowers above the leaves. The banner and wings have faint, darker veins. • So far, all is more or less as expected in a pea—flowers that have a banner and wings (and hidden keel) and leaves that are compound. But when this locoweed goes to fruit— wow! The peapod is extraordinary: a ¹/₂–1¹/₂" **yellow-green, papery, inflated 'bladder' mottled with reddish-brown splotches!** Late in fall you may find and shake dried pods that haven't yet opened. The 'death-rattle' of the seeds within is the final macabre locoweed touch.

Distribution: The genus *Astragalus* is huge, with over 2000 species worldwide. Almost 400 of these species occur in North America with almost 100 in the CA-FP. Many of the species, including *A. whitneyi*, intergrade and have numerous varieties. *A. whitneyi* (in at least one variety) occurs throughout the Sierra in rocky or gravelly places from 6000–12,000'. It extends to Washington and east to Idaho. **Names:** The common name locoweed refers to its toxicity (silenium), which causes animals that eat it to go 'crazy.' *Astragalus* means 'ankle-bone' or 'dice,' apparently in reference to the rattling seeds. J.D. Whitney was the 19th-century geologist for whom Mt. Whitney was named. **Typical location:** Rocky, exposed ridges near Silver Peak in Tahoe area (8200').

white (pink or purple) • 5 irregular petals (banner, wings, keel)
• perennial

Buttercup Family
(Ranunculaceae)

Variable, profuse, odd, showy, memorable, toxic...all of these words come to mind when one thinks of the buttercup family. Only a few of its species have the typical five regular petals and five green sepals; most species diverge at least somewhat (and often wildly) from this norm. That 5-petaled yellow buttercup you put to your chin to see if you like butter is much more the exception than the rule in this bizarre family!

In many species the petals are variable in number, sometimes ranging from five to as many as 20 on neighboring flowers. In some species (e.g., *Caltha, Anemone, Clematis*), these 'petals' are actually sepals; in others (e.g.,

pasqueflower (*Anemone occidentalis*)

Aconitum, Delphinium) the wildly showy parts are the sepals and the petals are much smaller and less conspicuous. Some species have many true petals, some none, some two, some four, some five, some can't seem to make up their mind how many to have!

alpine anemone (*Pulsatilla alpina*) of the the Swiss Alps   larkspur

233

One thing you can count on in the buttercup family, besides variability, is that the flowers will have a cluster of many stamens and usually many pistils as well. This old family resembles the pine trees in reproductive strategy, in that it has many males to produce a lot of pollen and many females to receive it!

Though that sweet, yellow buttercup (*Ranunculus* species) may linger in your mind, don't eat it! Some species of that genus and many species of other buttercup genera (e.g., *Aquilegia, Actae, Caltha, Delphinium*) are very **toxic**.

pasqueflower in seed

The buttercup family contains approximately 60 genera and approximately 1700 species worldwide, especially in northern temperate and tropical mountainous areas. In our area the genera with the most species or with the showiest species you are likely to encounter include *Aconitum* (monkshood—the only species but remarkable for its very showy and dramatic flower), *Anemone*, *Aquilegia* (columbine—only two species but also showy), *Delphinium* (larkspur—more than 10 species), *Ranunculus* (buttercup—more than 15 species), and *Thalictrum* (meadow rue).

The buttercups include some of our showiest and most intriguing flowers. Many buttercups are cultivated as ornamentals and many more are loved and treasured in the wild.

hybrid columbine

234

Royal Larkspur
Delphinium variegatum
CENTRAL VALLEY, FOOTHILLS

Royal larkspur is a stunning member of the buttercup family: the color of the large (1¹/₂") flowers is one of the **deepest, richest blue-purples** you will ever see. The 1–3' stem lifts the dense inflorescence well above its surroundings: in the peak of their bloom the spectacular flowers dance on center stage against a backdrop of lush green grass. • Several narrowly divided leaves come off the lower part of the stem at intervals on 1–2" petioles, but they tend to wither early. • As in all larkspurs, the showy parts of the flower are actually sepals: an upper sepal ending in a long, backward-projecting spur, two lateral sepals, and two lower sepals pointing down. The four small petals, cradling the dense cluster of reproductive parts, project out of the center of the flower—the upper two angling upward, the lower two on edge. • In royal larkspur the **upper two petals are narrow and whitish; the lower two are usually blue-purple and form a rounded dome covered with white hairs.**

Distribution: The genus *Delphinium* is composed of approximately 250 species in northern temperate areas. *D. variegatum* occurs in grasslands and open woodlands in the Central Valley and Sierra foothills below 3000'. It extends to the California coastal ranges. **Names:** *Delphinium* means 'dolphin' in reference to the shape of the flower in bud. *Variegatum* means 'variegated.' **Typical location:** Foothill grasslands along Route 49 near Chinese Camp (1500').

blue-purple • 5 irregular petal-like sepals • perennial

Sacramento Valley Buttercup

Ranunculus canus

CENTRAL VALLEY, FOOTHILLS, LOW MONTANE

Buttercups of the *Ranunculus* genus are the closest thing to 'normal' in the bizarre buttercup family. Most *Ranunculus* species have five regular petals and five smaller sepals (usually yellowish-green) underneath, unlike many other buttercup family genera whose flowers have all sorts of petals and sepals that vary in numbers and shapes. • However, just to stay true to its strange and unpredictable family, Sacramento Valley buttercup is atypical of its genus because its **flowers are crowded with many (5–17) overlapping petals. The five sepals underneath the petals are yellow-green and sharply reflexed.** The many yellow stamens surround a central cluster of greenish pistils. • The ¹/₂–2' stem is stout and hairy. The upper stem leaves are long and narrow and clasp the stem. From the upper leaf axils rise the long (4–8") pedicels that bear the bright, shiny, 1" wide, yellow flowers. The lower stem leaves are deeply 3-lobed and are toothed or deeply cut on the edges. • The seeds are disk-like and shiny black with a short, straight beak with a small hook at the tip.

Distribution: The genus *Ranunculus* is composed of approximately 250 species worldwide. *R. canus* occurs in grassland and forest openings throughout the Central Valley and Sierra foothills below 6000'. It extends from southern Oregon to Baja. It often intergrades with *R. californicus*. **Names:** *Ranunculus* means 'little frog' in reference to the wet habitats of most species. *Canus* means 'hairy' in reference to the white-hairy stems. **Typical location:** Grassy fields near creek along Route 140 near Planada (170').

yellow • 5–17 separate petals • perennial

Western Buttercup

Ranunculus occidentalis

FOOTHILLS, LOW MONTANE

Western buttercup is a usual *Ranunculus* in most ways: its petals are broad, rounded, shiny and yellow; its dense cluster of stamens and pistils are yellow and green, respectively; its leaves are deeply lobed; and it grows in damp meadows and forest openings. • True to its family peculiarity, *R. occidentalis* does have an oddity, however: though **most of its flowers have five petals, some have six.** • The ¹/₂–2' stem has few branches and bears several of the lobed leaves and the ¹/₂–1" flowers. The fruits have short, hooked beaks.

Distribution: *R. occidentalis* occurs in damp meadows, sagebrush scrub, and forest openings throughout the Sierra from 300–7000'. It extends to Alaska. **Names:** *Ranunculus* (see p. 236). *Occidentalis* means 'western.' **Typical location:** Damp, grassy meadows along Sagehen Creek in Tahoe area (6200').

Related Plant: Aquatic buttercup (*R. aquatilis*; bottom photo) is a very unusual member of its genus. Whereas the flowers of most *Ranunculus* are yellow, those of aquatic buttercup are white; whereas most *Ranunculus* grow in wet ground, aquatic buttercup grows in water. It has two types of leaves: 'water leaves,' which are submerged and are divided into thread-like filaments; and 'sun leaves,' which emerge above the water and are broad. The small (¹/₂") **flowers sometimes float on the water's surface and sometimes stick up above it,** and I have frequently seen them actually blooming underwater! *R. aquatilis* occurs in water throughout the CA-FP below 9500'. It extends from Alaska to Mexico. *Aquatilis* refers to the very wet habitat of this species. Perennial. Range: Foothills, Low Montane, Mid to High Montane.

yellow • 5 (or 6) separate petals
• perennial

Waterfall Buttercup
Kumlienia hystricula

FOOTHILLS, LOW MONTANE

Waterfall buttercup is quite an anomaly even for a member of the peculiar buttercup family. It was formerly classified in the *Ranunculus* genus, but in many ways it **looks much more like a marsh marigold** (see p. 242) **than a buttercup**. Botanists have now moved it to its own genus, which only contains two species. • Like the marsh marigold, the leaves of waterfall buttercup are round or kidney-shaped and scalloped or shallowly lobed. The 3–10" stem bears one, or sometimes two or three, of the 1/2–3/4" flowers, which have **five or six, or sometimes more, white, ray-like, petaloid sepals**. These sepals are usually rounded with small, pointed tips, but sometimes they may be notched or even shallowly lobed at the tips. In the center of the flower is a dense cluster of stamens and pistils; the fruits form a head-like cluster and have hooked beaks. • However, unlike *Caltha*, *Kumlienia* does have petals—5–12 of them! But if what look like petals are actually sepals, where are the petals? It turns out that they are the small, yellow, or green, gland-like structures that angle up and away from the sepals on tiny stalks. At first glance you might think they are part of the cluster of reproductive parts, for they look more like slightly larger, rectangular stamens than petals.

Distribution: The genus *Kumlienia* has only two species, both of which are in western North America. It occurs in wet places, especially along streams, throughout the Sierra from 1000–7000'. **Names:** T.L. Kumlien was a 19th-century Swedish naturalist. *Hystricula* means 'porcupine' probably in reference to the beaked fruits. **Typical location:** Creek edges along Hite's Cove Trail just west of Yosemite (1500').

white • 5 (6) separate petal-like sepals • perennial

238

Western Rue-anemone
Isopyrum occidentale
FOOTHILLS, LOW MONTANE

Western rue-anemone is one of the most graceful and delicate of all the species in the buttercup family, both for its **fragile-looking, lobed leaves** (very much like those of meadow rue, p. 246), and for its **pale white (to pink-purple) flowers.** • **The 3–10" stems are slender and gray-black**, contrasting with the light green leaves, which are divided into many small, wedge-shaped leaflets. The stems bear several short pedicels, each bearing one beautiful $^1/_2$–$^3/_4$" flower. The five (sometimes four, sometimes six) petal-like sepals surround a central cluster of many yellow stamens and a few (or many) green pistils. The fruits have a thin, pointed snout.
• Western rue-anemone is all the more special for its early blooming. In late March or April when most flowers in the foothills hit peak bloom, you will probably

find only its delicate leaves and clusters of seedpods. Though these will tell you the plant is a member of the buttercup family, you will be left to wonder about the flower you missed! *Isopyrum* blooms in February while most of the flowers around it are still in seed.

Distribution: The genus *Isopyrum* is composed of approximately 30 species in temperate North America and Eurasia. *I. occidentale* occurs uncommonly on shaded slopes throughout the Sierra from 1000–5000'. It extends to central western California. **Names:** *Isopyrum* is the ancient Greek name that refers to the grain-like fruit. *Occidentale* means 'of the west.' **Typical location:** Shady slopes along Independence Trail (1200').

white (to pink-purple) • 5 (4–6) separate petal-like sepals • perennial

Red Larkspur
Delphinium nudicaule
FOOTHILLS, LOW MONTANE

When you spot a patch of bright red flowers on the side of that rocky cliff up ahead, you may have to look more than once before you realize it's a larkspur. *D. nudicaule* does have the general shape of a typical larkspur in its flower, bud, and leaves, but it lacks the royal delphinium blue. The **showy sepals and smaller, less conspicuous petals of red larkspur are all the same intense red-orange**. • Several of the flowers arch out from the stem on 1/2–3" pedicels. • Most of the leaves occur on long (to 6" or so) petioles from the lower part of the 1/2–2' stem. They are palmately lobed (usually with five lobes) with each lobe shallowly lobed again or toothed.

Distribution: *D. nudicaule* occurs on wooded, rocky slopes through-out the northern and central Sierra below 6500'. It extends to the Cascades of Oregon. **Names:** *Delphinium* (see p. 235). *Nudicaule* means 'naked stem' in reference to most of the leaves coming off the lower part of the stem. **Also known as** canon larkspur. **Typical location:** Rocky cliff-edges of Table Mountain near Oroville (1500').

Related Plant: Slender larkspur (*D. gracilentum*; bottom photo) is a more typical larkspur of low and medium elevations, because its spurred flowers are the **usual dark blue-purple**. Its name is quite appropriate: its **thin, delicate stem and loosely arranged flowers give it a graceful and slender look**. *D. gracilentum* occurs in forests throughout the Sierra from 500–8000'. Perennial. Range: Same plus Mid to High Montane.

red • 5 irregular petal-like sepals • perennial

Water-plantain Buttercup

Ranunculus alismaefolius

LOW MONTANE, MID TO HIGH MONTANE, ALPINE

Water-plantain buttercup creates spectacular displays when its large (¹/₂–1"), bright yellow flowers **can almost completely cover boggy meadows in the early spring**. At higher elevations in the spring, when night temperatures often drop below freezing, one can frequently find water-plantain buttercup and marsh marigold (p. 242) in full bloom above ice-covered leaves. • This showy buttercup has numerous long, narrow, undivided leaves, most of which are basal. The 2–20" stems are sometimes decumbent, so the several yellow flowers can be either close to the ground, or a foot or two above it. This plant is highly variable: **often the flowers are small (¹/₂" wide) with five petals; sometimes they are much bigger (over 1" wide) with as many as 15 petals**. Regardless of their number, the shiny petals glisten in the sun. The sepals under the petals are small and yellowish-green and are often reflexed. The anthers are yellow; the pistils are greenish.

Distribution: *R. alismaefolius* occurs in very wet areas (or areas that are wet in early spring) throughout the Sierra from 4000–12,000'. It extends to British Columbia. **Names:** *Ranunculus* (see p. 236). *Alismaefolius* means 'leaf like *Alisma*' and refers to the leaves of a species of *Alisma* in the water-plantain family. **Typical location:** Boggy meadows near Grass Lake in Sierra Buttes/Lake Basin area (6300').

yellow • 5–15 separate petals • perennial

Marsh Marigold
Caltha leptosepala

LOW MONTANE, MID TO HIGH MONTANE

When you see the dense cluster of reproductive parts, you've already narrowed down the family to just a few possibilities. When you count the regular 'petals' of several neighboring flowers and come up with numbers ranging from 7–10, you're pretty certain you have a member of the buttercup family. • Marsh marigold has very **distinctive, large (1–3" wide), basal leaves: they are round or kidney-shaped and fleshy-green.** Each plant has at least one 4–12" stem, each of which bears only one flower at its tip. The ray-like 'petals' vary in number (5–10 or sometimes more) and are actually sepals because there are no sepals underneath them. • The **many stamens and pistils clumped in the center of the flower are a beautiful yellow-green.** When the flower goes to seed, it is almost as interesting as when it is in bloom because the cluster of 3–8 beaked fruits is a bright yellow-green and can be up to ³/₄" long. Marsh marigold is one of the earliest spring bloomers in wet mountain meadows, and often covers large areas of icy bogs with its bright blooms.

Distribution: The genus *Caltha* has 10 species in temperate North America and Eurasia. *G. leptosepala* occurs in marshy places throughout the Sierra from 4000–10,500'. It extends to Alaska. **Names:** *Caltha* means 'bowl-shaped' in reference to the flower. *Leptosepala* means 'thin-sepaled' and refers to the ray-like sepals. **Formerly called** *C. howellii.* **Typical location:** Boggy meadows along Glacier Point Road in Yosemite (7500').

white • 5–11 separate petal-like sepals
• perennial

242

Monkshood
Aconitum columbianum

LOW MONTANE, MID TO HIGH MONTANE

Monkshood is among those plants that gives the buttercup family its peculiar character. At first glance it's difficult to differentiate between the petals and sepals or find the reproductive parts. In profile, the flowers resemble fat, blue-purple ducks! • Monkshood is a very striking plant: its **stout stem may reach 6'**, and the loose inflorescence alone may be 1–2' of this! Many of the large (1–2"), **deep blue-purple flowers** branch off the stem on ascending pedicels. The large (to 8") **maple-like leaves** are deeply 3–5 lobed. • A close look at this fascinating flower begins to reveal its secrets. There are no regular green sepals under the blue-purple 'petals,' so these petals must actually be the sepals. The **upper sepal forms the 'hood'** (or duck's head), the two lateral sepals form the swollen 'body,' and the two lower sepals are narrow 'feet' that point down. If you look inside the body and the hood, you will find a tight cluster of yellowish-green reproductive parts and two small blue or whitish petals. Needless to say, it's not the petals in this flower that attract the pollinators! • Monkshood is **very poisonous** to livestock and to humans. A European species of monkshood is the 'wolfbane' of werewolf lore.

Distribution: The *Aconitum* genus is composed of approximately 100 species in temperate North America and Eurasia. *A. columbianum* occurs in wet areas (often in willow thickets) throughout the Sierra from 4000–8700'. It extends to British Columbia. **Names:** *Aconitum* is the ancient Greek name for a 'monk's hood.' *Columbianum* means 'Columbian,' a name linked historically to western North America. **Typical location:** Damp creekbanks near Grass Lake in Sierra Buttes/Lakes Basin area (6400').

blue-purple • 5 irregular petal-like sepals • perennial

243

Glaucous Larkspur
Delphinium glaucum
LOW MONTANE, MID TO HIGH MONTANE

At first glance you might confuse glaucous larkspur with monkshood (p. 243). They are both very tall plants (to 6' or so) with large, maple-like leaves and many large (1–2"), oddly shaped, deep blue-purple flowers. In fact, both these species are members of the butter-cup family, and thus share more than these immediately obvious characteristics. In both plants, the five irregular, deep-blue 'petals' are actually the sepals, which surround the small petals and the dense cluster of reproductive parts. However, in larkspur there are four petals, and in monkshood there are only two. Of course the more noticeable difference between the two genera, as the names suggest, is the spur in the former and the hood in the latter. • In glaucous larkspur the sepals are all sharp-pointed, the $^1/_2$–$^3/_4$" **nectar spur is straight with a slight down-curve at the tip**, the upper petals are narrow and notched, and the lower petals are folded together and not notched. The petals are usually blue-purple but are sometimes whitish. • Glaucous larkspur can paint a wide swathe of blue-purple on a hillside because each stem may bear more than 50 flowers, and frequently many plants grow together in a dense 'forest.'

Distribution: *D. glaucum* occurs along streams and in wet thickets throughout the Sierra from 5000–10,000'. It extends to Alaska. **Names:** *Delphinium* (see p. 235). *Glaucum* means 'glaucous' in reference to the whitish powdery film covering the lower part of the stem. **Typical location:** Seep areas along trail to Winnemucca Lake in Carson Pass area (8800').

blue-purple • 5 irregular petal-like sepals • perennial

Drummond's Anemone

Anemone drummondii

LOW MONTANE, MID TO HIGH MONTANE

Drummond's anemone is among those members of the buttercup family with no real petals. Instead, it has a variable number (5–8) of white, ray-like sepals radiating out from the dense cluster of yellow stamens and pistils. • You might want to make a special effort to see this gorgeous flower early and late in its blooming season because it has different treasures to offer at each time. It is one of the earliest flowers to blossom in its high, rocky habitat, so you may have to cross some snow-fields and do some wet-rock scrambling to see it in full bloom. • Each 1–1¹/₂" flower seems to blossom right out of the rocky

ground, for it sits on a short (4–10") stem and rises only slightly above its **soft, deeply divided, blue-green leaves**. The 5–8 sepals are bright white, forming a flat pinwheel, which contrasts deliciously with the thick cluster of exuberant, yellow stamens and pistils. Early in the bloom the **undersides of the still-crinkly sepals are heavily tinted with a luscious blue-purple**. Lying flat on the rocks (or perhaps the snow) near a cluster of these freshly bloomed flowers and looking at them from underneath reveals a collage of blues, whites, and yellows all intermingling to create a memorable picture. • Later in the season the flowers are equally interesting, for the fruits form an intricate woolly, spherical head.

Distribution: The genus *Anemone* is composed of approximately 100 species worldwide. *A. drummondii* occurs in rocky areas in the central and northern Sierra from 5000–10,500'. It extends to Alaska. **Names:** *Anemone* means 'shaken by the wind' in reference to its wind-tousled fruits. Thomas Drummond was a Scottish naturalist who made an ill-fated collecting trip to America in the mid-1800s. **Typical location:** Base of rock cliffs at head of Pole Creek in Tahoe area (7200').

white • 5–8 petal-like sepals • perennial

Fendler's Meadow Rue

Thalictrum fendleri

LOW MONTANE, MID TO HIGH MONTANE

In a family of odd flowers, meadow rue certainly does not disappoint! A tall, delicate, and graceful plant (2–5'), Fendler's meadow rue is also puzzling. The **nodding, tassel-like flowers** quivering in the breeze are actually a cluster of many (15–30) delicate, yellowish-brown stamens hanging from a whitish 'cap.' You are not surprised, being buttercup-wise, to find that this 'cap' is the sepals—there are no petals. You might be more surprised, however, coming across a flower with only the hanging stamens—the sepals often fall off early in the blooming. • Of course, despite your pleasure in identifying this meadow rue as a buttercup, a nagging question arises: where are the pistils? The mystery is solved when you come across another plant of *T. fendleri* and find that instead of dangling stamens, its flowers consist of erect, swollen, whitish stigmas. Now here's a foolproof method of preventing self-pollination—separate male and female plants! • The leaves of Fendler's meadow rue add to its grace: they are 3-lobed into broad, rounded segments and are uncommonly thin and fragile. The lobes and stamens rustle invitingly in the slightest breeze.

Distribution: The genus *Thalictrum* has about 80 species in North America and Eurasia. *T. fendleri* occurs in moist forest openings throughout the Sierra from 4000–10,000'. It extends from Washington to northern Mexico. **Names:** *Thalictrum* is the ancient Greek name. Augustus Fendler was an American tradesman-turned-plant collector who participated in a plant expedition to New Mexico in the 1840s. **Typical location:** Thickets near streams along Pohono trail in Yosemite (7100').

whitish (sepals and stigmas) and yellowish (stamens) • 5 (4) petal-like sepals (dropping off early) • perennial

Crimson Columbine
Aquilegia formosa
LOW MONTANE, MID TO HIGH MONTANE

If you've been exploring the buttercup family in this book and/or in the field, you probably have encountered a wide variety of petal and sepal arrangements: petal-like sepals and no petals (e.g., *Anemone, Caltha, Thalictrum*); petal-like sepals and much smaller, inconspicuous petals (e.g., *Aconitum, Delphinium*); and the typical arrangement of petals above and sepals beneath (e.g., *Ranunculus*). The columbines offer yet another variation, with their showy, but different, petals and petal-like sepals. • In crimson columbine the **five petals are long (1–1¹/₂") tubes ending in amber, backward-projecting nectar spurs**. These odd petals are usually yellow at the mouth, turning to red or orange most of the length of the tube. The five red or orange sepals flare out among the tubular petals. • As spectacular as the petals and sepals are the **mass of protruding ¹/₂–³/₄" stamens tipped with yellow anthers**. The 1–4' stem bears only a few of these striking flowers, which nod gracefully on long, arching pedicels until they are pollinated, at which point they rise back up to an upright position. The broad leaves are 3-lobed. • Gimson columbine can provide hours of fascinating entertainment: hummingbirds reach deep into the spurs for the nectar treat, and many bees resort to biting holes in the spurs and thus steal the nectar without picking up or depositing pollen on the reproductive parts of the flower.

Distribution: The genus *Aquilegia* is composed of approximately 70 species in temperate North America and Eurasia. *A. formosa* occurs in moist places and forest openings throughout the Sierra from 3000—9500'. It extends from Alaska to Baja. **Names:** *Aquilegia* means 'eagle,' which may refer to the 'claw-like' nectar spurs. *Formosa* means 'beautiful' or 'graceful.' **Typical location:** Damp fringes of forest in Paige Meadows in Tahoe area (7000').

red (orange) • 5 irregular petals • perennial

Alpine Columbine
Aquilegia pubescens
MID TO HIGH MONTANE, ALPINE

Alpine columbine is a gorgeous plant, especially remarkable for its rather austere habitat. Its very large flowers (2" wide with nectar spurs even longer) seem almost too large and showy for the rocky environment near and above timberline. • Although easily recognized as a columbine, this flower has some striking differences from crimson columbine (p. 247), its lower elevation relative. Alpine columbine is a much shorter plant with more flowers, the flowers are erect instead of nodding, and the **petals and sepals are creamy white (often pink-tinged).** • It reflects a great amount of ultraviolet light because of its whiteness, and thus attracts long-tongued moths, among other insects, which sample its nectar and pollinate it in the process. Although alpine columbine and crimson columbine grow in different habitats at different elevations and are visited by different pollinators, there are a few places in Yosemite at 9500–10,000' where the miraculous happens—these two columbines hybridize (bottom photo). The hybridization may occur because of indiscriminate bees that bite the nectar spurs of both plants and brush the reproductive parts in the process. The result of this hybridization is a large, glorious pink and white columbine at some angle between erect and nodding. These ephemeral marvels are well worth the strenuous hike to see them.

Distribution: *A. pubescens* occurs in rocky areas from Yosemite south from 9000–12,000'.
Names: *Aquilegia* (see p. 247). *Pubescens* means 'hairy.' **Also known as** Coville's columbine.
Typical location: Rocky talus below Dana Plateau near eastern border of Yosemite (11,000'). Look for the hybrid just north of the Dana Plateau on the slope east of Saddlebag Lake (10,000').

white • 5 irregular petals • perennial

Alpine Buttercup
Ranunculus eschscholtzii

MID TO HIGH MONTANE, ALPINE

Alpine buttercup is a stunning plant, especially when found in the rocky terrain above timberline. **Huddling among the rocks on a windswept ridge or peering out from the shelter of a rock overhang**, these **large (to 1" wide), shiny yellow flowers** seem even larger and brighter as you feel the chill of the howling alpine wind. • Usually these 2–10" · plants cluster together, and the large flowers rise above the tufted, 3-lobed, blue-green leaves. • *R. eschscholtzii* has typical clusters of yellow stamens and greenish pistils. Although it usually has only five petals, it can have six or more petals.

Distribution: *R. eschscholtzii* occurs in rocky areas throughout the Sierra from 8000–13,000'. It extends to Alaska. **Names:** *Ranunculus* (see p. 236). *Eschscholtzii* (see p. 95). **Typical location:** Under rock overhangs near summit of Mt. Rose in Tahoe area (10,750').

yellow • 5 separate petals • perennial

Purslane Family
(Portulacaceae)

The flowers of the purslane family are variable but not irregular, unpredictable but not bizarre. This family does not have the dense clusters of reproductive parts or the strange-shaped petal-like sepals of the buttercup family. It has regular petals all alike, but it does sometimes have unusual (and variable) numbers of petals (and stamens and stigmas). On some species, the flowers have five petals; on others, the flowers have 3–7 petals; on a few others there may be as many as 18 petals or as few as four! Often there is one stamen opposite each petal, but sometimes the number of stamens is unrelated to the number of petals. There are usually two or three stigmas but there can be as many as eight.

lewisia with 7 petals

So, does anything besides variability remain constant in this family? Yes...well, kind of. A defining characteristic of purslanes is its number of sepals. If you find a flower with only two sepals—green and fleshy—overlapping to form a sort of vase for the flower tube, you can be fairly certain it's a member of the purslane family. Of course, just to stay faithful to its variable nature, this family does have a few species that have more than two sepals (as many as eight) and in some species the sepals aren't even green but are colored like the petals.

The leaves of purslane species are also variable but are almost always fleshy. If you are out in late summer or fall, you may discover another fairly consistent characteristic of this family: spilling out of the split seedpod might be a few or many shiny black seeds (see photo p. 257).

typical 2 sepals

bitterroot

Purslane flowers are usually white and rather small, but some are larger, some are pink or red, and some are even pink-striped. Flowers of a few genera, especially *Lewisia*, are prized as ornamentals.

The purslane family is small, with only about 20 genera and approximately 400 species in North and South America, Australia, and southern Africa. The genera with the most species or the most noticeable species you are likely to encounter in our area include *Calandrinia, Calyptridium* (pussypaws), *Claytonia, Lewisia,* and *Montia.* You will find purslanes from the Central Valley and foothills to the highest peaks. Some species of pussypaws cover almost this entire range all by themselves!

Although a small family with, for the most part, small flowers, some purslane species are among our most distinctive and treasured flowers.

pussypaws

252

Miner's Lettuce

Claytonia perfoliata

CENTRAL VALLEY, FOOTHILLS, LOW MONTANE

Though recognizable as a purslane by its two overlapping sepals, the most noticeable and distinct feature of miner's lettuce is the remarkable **round, fleshy leaf completely surrounding the stem immediately below the sprig of small flowers**. Actually two opposite stem leaves that have fused, this large (up to almost 4" in diameter), succulent leaf forms a platform for the slender raceme bearing numerous (5–40) tiny ($^1/_8$–$^1/_4$"), nodding, white or pinkish flowers.
• The 1–16" stem also bears numerous elliptic, fleshy, tasty, basal leaves that give miner's lettuce its name. • Miner's lettuce is extremely variable with several subspecies, but all of its forms have the distinctive 'platform' leaf, though its shape may vary from round to squarish and it may not always surround the stem completely.

Distribution: The genus *Claytonia* has 28 species in North and Central America and eastern Asia. *C. perfoliata* is common in shady or disturbed sites throughout the CA-FP below 6000'. It extends to British Columbia and can be found in Central America. **Names:** John Clayton was a botanist of colonial America. *Perfoliata* means 'perfoliate' (i.e., 'through leaf') in reference to the leaf surrounding the stem. **Formerly called** *Montia perfoliata*. **Typical location:** Grassy edges of the dirt road paralleling the Merced River and Route 140 west of Yosemite (1700').

white (or pinkish) • 5 separate petals • annual

Red Maid
Calandrinia ciliata
CENTRAL VALLEY, FOOTHILLS, LOW MONTANE

Though the flowers of red maid are small (usually less than 1/2" wide), in bright sun they can light up a meadow or field with their **shiny red or crimson-purple petals and bright orange anthers**. However, if you visit this field on a cloudy day, you may look for the flowers in vain because they open only in bright sun and are scarcely noticeable when closed. • The plant is low-growing with several spreading 4–20" stems, each bearing 1/2–3" narrow, fleshy leaves and several small flowers. You probably won't find more than one flower per stem in bloom at a time, however, for these dazzlers bloom only for a few hours before wilting. • The five separate petals form a shallow bowl; although they are usually shiny red or red-purple, you will find some pure-white flowers. Under the petals are the two overlapping sepals typical of the purslanes. The anthers are bright orange, contrasting deliciously with the red-purple (or white) petals. There are usually more than five stamens, but they can vary from as few as three to as many as 15. The shiny black seeds were prized by the Indians as a food source; as in many of the purslanes, the leaves are tasty.

Distribution: The genus *Calandrinia* is composed of about 150 species in the western U.S., Central and South America, and Australia. *C. ciliata* is common in meadows and fields throughout the CA-FP below 6000'. It extends to New Mexico and is found in Central and South America. **Names:** J.L. Calandrini was an 18th-century Swiss botanist. *Ciliata* means 'fringed' in reference to the fine hairs on the edges of the sepals. **Typical location:** Grassy edges of Hite's Cove Trail just west of Yosemite (1500').

red (crimson-purple) • 5 separate petals • annual

254

Bitterroot
Lewisia rediviva

FOOTHILLS, LOW MONTANE, MID TO HIGH MONTANE

Although it is the state flower of Montana and is widespread through the mountains of the American West, bitterroot is not at all common in our area. If you are lucky enough to come across bitterroot your first reaction will probably be like mine—WOW! The flowers are **huge (2–3" across), the petals are numerous (10–19) and gorgeous (a soft, almost translucent white to pink),** and the leaves are showy (succulent and finger-like in a dense basal cluster). To top it off, usually several flowers bloom together in a low tuft, and they are one of the first flowers to bloom in spring. Often occurring on barren-looking rock ledges or flats, these amazing flowers almost seem too large and too spectacular to have grown out of the ground. To add to the mystique, bitterroot flowers close at night, opening again only in the warmth of the sun. • The variable number of petals and fleshy plant parts of bitterroot are typical of the purslanes. However, it does not have the usual 'cup' of two fleshy, green sepals; rather it has a variable number (6–8) of petal-like sepals. Complementing the pastel pink (or white) of the petals is the dense cluster of 6–8 creamy, worm-like stigmas and 30–50 stamens with pink anthers. • Meriwether Lewis of the Lewis and Clark Expedition, for whom the genus *Lewisia* is named, discovered to his chagrin that the roots of *L. rediviva* were not as tasty as the flowers were beautiful—hence the common name 'bitterroot.'

Distribution: The genus *Lewisia* has 20 species in western North America. *L. rediviva* occurs throughout the Sierra from 200–9000'. It extends from the California coastal ranges to the Rocky Mountains. **Names:** This genus and several species of other genera (e.g., p. 158) were named in honor of Meriwether Lewis. *Rediviva* means 'brought to life' in reference to its medicinal qualities.
Typical location: Rocky flats atop Table Mountain near Oroville (1500').

pink (or white) • 10–19 separate petals
• perennial

255

Three-leaf Lewisia
Lewisia triphylla
LOW MONTANE, MID TO HIGH MONTANE

Three-leaf lewisia is in many ways a typical purslane. Like many purslanes, *L. triphylla* has **small white to pinkish flowers with two overlapping, green sepals**, and it has fleshy leaves. Its name (common and Latin), however, suggests a feature that sets it apart both from other members of the purslane family and from other species of *Lewisia*. Its **slender 1–4" stem is naked except for one set of fleshy, linear leaves coming out of the same spot on the stem**; sometimes this set consists of three whorled leaves, but often it consists of only a pair of opposite leaves. Usually the leaves are vertical on the stem, looking like narrow wings about to flap. • The ¹/₂" flower has a variable number (5–9) of separate petals, which are usually white with pink veins or pink tinting. The 3–5 stamens bear colorful reddish-brown anthers. Because the flowers usually grow in clusters and the stems are so short, you will often find dense patches of these bright flowers.

Distribution: *L. triphylla* occurs in damp areas in meadows or on bare ground throughout the Sierra from 5000–11,000'. It extends to the Coast Range of northern California and to the Cascades. **Names:** *Lewisia* (see p. 255). *Triphylla* means '3-leaved,' though perhaps it should be names bi/tri-phylla! **Typical location:** Damp bare ground along trail to Paige Meadows in Tahoe area (6800').

white (to pinkish) • 5–9 separate petals • perennial

Nevada Lewisia

Lewisia nevadensis

LOW MONTANE, MID TO HIGH MONTANE, ALPINE

With its variable number of separate white (to pinkish) petals, its two overlapping sepals, and its fleshy leaves, you can be quite certain Nevada lewisia is a member of the purslane family. • Its white (to faintly pink) flowers put on quite a show because although **each 1–4" stem typically bears only one flower at its tip**, each plant has several to many stems, so you will often find many large ($^3/_4$–$1^1/_4$") flowers blooming together above the loose rosette of fleshy, basal leaves. • The **6–10 petals overlap to form a shallow bowl** at whose center is a cluster of 6–15 stamens with yellow anthers and 3–6 whitish stigmas. The fruits contain many tiny, shiny, black seeds (bottom photo).

Distribution: *L. nevadensis* occurs in moist meadows and forest openings throughout the Sierra from 4500–12,000'. It extends to the Coast Range of northern California and to the Cascades of Washington. **Names:** *Lewisia* (see p. 255). *Nevadensis* means 'of the Sierra Nevada.' **Typical location:** Damp meadows near Gaylor Lakes in Yosemite (10,000').

white • 6–10 separate petals • perennial

257

Toad Lily

Montia chamissoi

LOW MONTANE, MID TO HIGH MONTANE

Toad lily is an especially lovely, delicate member of the purslane family. Its 1–12" stem bears **several pairs of opposite, egg-shaped leaves** and 2–8 small (less than ¹/₂") flowers. The **five separate petals, forming a shallow bowl above the two overlapping sepals, are white (or pinkish) with green veins**. Adding to this pastel treasure are the pale pink anthers at the tips of the five stamens. Early in the blooming, before the stamens rise, these anthers may be confused for pink spots on the petals. The stigma adds further to the color late in the blooming as it opens into three showy, red lobes. • You will often find many toad lilies growing together close to the ground, because the plants send out stolons (above-ground runners) that root at intervals and send up plant shoots.

Distribution: The genus *Montia* is composed of 12 species in America, Australia, and Siberia. *M. chamissoi* occurs in wet meadows throughout the Sierra from 4000–11,000'. It extends to Alaska and east to the north-central U.S. **Names:** Giuseppe Monti was an 18th-century Italian botanist. Adelbert von Chamisso was the Prussian poet and self-taught botanist who accompanied J.F. Eschscholtz on a Russian expedition in search of the Northwest Passage. **Formerly called** *Claytonia chamissoi.* **Typical location:** Edges of wet Paige Meadows in Tahoe area (7000').

Related Plant: Narrow-leaved montia (*M. linearis;* bottom photo) is a small (2–8") plant with slender, reddish stems; small, linear leaves; and small (¹/₄–¹/₂") white (or pale pink) flowers. A **cluster of 5–12 of the flowers branch (often nod) off one side of the thread-like stem.** The two green sepals form an almost closed urn from which the tiny flowers emerge. *M. linearis* occurs in moist, grassy meadows throughout the central and northern Sierra below 7500'. *Linearis* (see p. 195). Annual. Range: Same.

white (to pinkish) • 5 separate petals • perennial

Pussypaws
Calyptridium umbellatum
LOW MONTANE, MID TO HIGH MONTANE, ALPINE

Pussypaws is one of the most familiar and charming of Sierra flowering plants. You will find its **elegantly symmetrical rosette of narrowly spoon-shaped leaves** and its spherical clusters of papery flowers on dry soil all through the Sierra—from rocky or sandy flats to dry forest openings, from low montane elevations to the highest peaks. • Pussypaws is highly variable, depending on its elevation. At lower elevations its flower stem may reach 1' or even 2'; at higher elevations they rarely exceed 9" and may be as short as 1–2". At lower elevations the flowers tend to be creamy white; at higher elevations they are often pink-tinged or even a deep rose-pink. • Although pussypaws does have the two sepals typical of purslanes, this feature is very hard to identify because the sepals and the four petals are difficult to distinguish (or count, for that matter) because they are all papery and tightly clustered together. Many of these papery flowers are packed together in each soft, spherical head, which does (in appearance and texture) rather resemble kittens' paws. The fruits bear many tiny, black, shiny seeds. • Pussypaws is a 'weather indicator': the **flower stems lie flat on the ground until it is heated up, then they slowly rise (sometimes to an almost erect position)**, lifting the flowers away from their hot earth bed.

Distribution: The genus *Calyptridium* has eight species in western America. *C. umbellatum* is common on dry sandy or rocky soils throughout the Sierra from 2500–12,000' (a remarkably wide elevational range). It extends to the coastal ranges of central and northern California, to the Cascades, and into the Great Basin. **Names:** *Calyptridium* means 'cap' in reference to the uniting of the petals, when the flower is in fruit, into a cap-like structure that falls off as one unit. *Umbellatum* means 'umbel' in reference to the soft, spherical flowerheads. **Typical location:** Dry volcanic slopes of Sonora Peak in Sonora Pass area (10,000').

pink (or creamy white) • 4 separate petals in tight spherical cluster • perennial

Composite (Sunflower) Family
(Asteraceae)

The composite (or sunflower) family is one of the largest and most familiar families worldwide and in the California Floristic Province: it contains approximately 1300 genera and approximately 21,000 species worldwide, with over 200 genera represented in the California Floristic Province!

The old name for the family (Compositae) was very descriptive because the 'flowers' of this family are actually composites of many flowers, each with petal-like parts and reproductive parts. There are three main types of head-like inflorescences in this family: 1) sunflower-like with both ray-like flowers and a central 'button' of disk flowers, 2) dandelion-like with only ray flowers, and 3) thistle-like with only disk flowers.

Coulter's daisy with ray and disk flowers

If you closely examine a ray of a sunflower or daisy, for example, you will notice that it has a thread-like structure attached to its base that sticks up above the ray. This is a pistil. With a petal and a reproductive part, that ray, then, is indeed a separate flower. So a daisy with, say, 30 ray 'petals' actually consists of 30 separate ray flowers clustered together into a flower 'commune.' And that's not all! Closely inspect the center of the daisy and you will notice it is composed of many tiny 5-petaled tubes, each with a projecting pistil and, partway down the tube, 4–5 stamens fused into the tube.

Stephanomeria (*Stephanomeria lactucina*) with only ray flowers

dusty maiden (*Chaenactis douglasii*) with only disk flowers

This innocent-looking daisy, then, actually consists of 30 ray flowers and maybe 50–100 disk flowers. Any of these separate ray or disk flowers might have trouble attracting a pollinator, but the collective of many such flowers certainly doesn't!

This family has developed relatively recently in the evolution of flowering plants—its reproductive strategy is sophisticated and highly entwined with insect pollinators.

alpine daisy

Another characteristic typical of many composites is the pappus—the furry, white hairs attached to the seeds, which serve as 'parachutes' to distribute the seeds far from the parent plant.

The individual flowers (rays and disks) have highly modified sepals (pappus); under the flowerhead are many narrow sepal-like bracts called phyllaries.

salsify (*Tragopogon dubius*) seeds

Of the many familiar genera in the composite family you are likely to encounter in our area, those with the most species you may see include *Arnica, Artemisia* (sagebrush), *Aster, Cirsium* (thistle), *Erigeron* (daisy), *Hemizona* (tarweed), *Lessingia, Madia* (tarweed), and *Senecio* (groundsel).

From the solid masses of tidy tips (p. 263) in the Central Valley and the dazzling carpets of goldfield (p. 264) in the foothills to the small clusters of blue alpine daisy and alpine gold (p. 281) atop the highest Sierra peaks, flowers of the composite family are a major part of our flora, amazing us with their sheer numbers and lifting our spirits with their bright cheer.

tidy tips   daisy and pollinator

Tidy Tips
Layia fremontii
CENTRAL VALLEY, FOOTHILLS

Tidy tips is a classic composite flower with both petal-like ray flowers (3–15) and a central cluster of many (4–100) disk flowers. It would be difficult to imagine a more appropriate name for this flower than tidy tips. **Each bright yellow ray flower is neatly white-tipped**, so tidily tipped that each flower appears to have a nearly perfectly circular yellow sun at its center tinged by fringes of white.

• Each 2–16" stem bears numerous small, pinnately lobed leaves and one large (1–1½"), terminal 'flower' (technically, of course, this 'flower' actually consists of many separate ray and disk flowers). The white tips of each of the ray flowers is cut into three lobes. • Tidy tips is a striking, cheery flower, all the more dramatic because it usually grows in large, showy masses. A grassy field filled with tidy tips glows like a thousand suns against a backdrop of fleecy, white clouds.

Distribution: The genus *Layia* is composed of 14 species, all of which are in western North America. *L. fremontii* occurs in grassy fields throughout the Central Valley and Sierra foothills below 2000'. It extends to the Coast Range of northern California. **Names:** George Lay was a 19th-century English plant collector. *Fremontii* (see p. 49). **Typical location:** Grassy fields along Route 99 north of Marysville (50').

yellow (white-tipped) • many ray and disk flowers • annual

Goldfield
Lasthenia californica
CENTRAL VALLEY, FOOTHILLS

'Fields of gold'... just hearing those words stirs old longings and timeless dreams of Eldorado, Shangri La, and Christmas presents under the tree. On a hot sunny day in April the Sierra foothills seem bathed in gold. The gentle slope you're standing on is a solid field of gold...of poppy (p. 95), fiddleneck, and goldfield that melt into you and burn away the dross and take you happily to the golden center. Here's a treasure you can count on, like presents always waiting under the tree because every spring they will return to warm you once again. • It seems appropriate, somehow, that goldfield is a composite because in composites each 'flower' is actually a treasure chest of scores of flowers. In goldfield **6–13 golden-yellow rays (often with tinges of orange at their base) surround a myriad of like-colored tubular disk flowers.** The 4–16" stem (sometimes simple, sometimes branched) bears a few pairs of light green, narrow, opposite leaves and one or several of the ¹/₂–1" flowerhead. The stem and leaves are generally somewhat hairy.

Distribution: The genus *Lasthenia* has 17 species in western North America and Chile. *L. californica* is abundant in grassy fields and slopes throughout the CA-FP below 3000'. It extends from southern Oregon to Mexico. **Names:** Lasthenia was a pupil of Plato—perhaps these flowers now have something to teach us! *Californica* (see p. 85). **Formerly called** *L. chrysostoma*. **Typical location:** Grassy slopes along Hite's Cove Trail west of Yosemite (1500').

golden yellow • many ray and disk flowers • annual

Common Tarweed
Madia elegans

CENTRAL VALLEY, FOOTHILLS

Though its common name tarweed doesn't seem to hold much promise, the Latin species name *elegans* seems more hopeful. And indeed, this large (1–1¹/₂") flower is a striking beauty with **5–20 bright yellow rays often splotched red at the base, and many (25–50) intense purple disk flowers clustered in the center.** • So why the rather unflattering name tarweed? Brush against this plant and you'll find out: the 1–3' stem and the narrow, alternating leaves are covered with glandular hairs, which will leave a sticky, black 'tar' on contact. On a hot day, tarweed can leave a heavy, 'sticky' fragrance in the air as well. • In mid-day you may be surprised to find the flowers curled shut, but they'll open again in late afternoon and stay open all night.

Distribution: The genus *Madia* is composed of 21 species in western North America and southwestern South America. *M. elegans* (highly variable with several subspecies) occurs in grassy fields throughout the CA-FP below 3000'. It extends from Oregon to Baja. **Names:** *Madia* is a Chilean name of uncertain meaning. *Elegans* (see p. 69). **Typical location:** Grassy slopes along Hite's Cove Trail west of Yosemite (1500').

yellow • many ray and disk flowers • annual

Blennosperma

Blennosperma nanum

CENTRAL VALLEY, FOOTHILLS

Blennosperma is a big name for a little flower: the $^1/_4$–$^1/_2$" yellow 'flower' sits atop a rather succulent 2–8" stem. The small leaves are linear and pinnately lobed. At first glance you might think this early-spring bloomer is a smaller goldfield (p. 264), but a more careful look will reveal several noticeable differences: in blennosperma the rays are narrower and more separated and a **paler yellow**, the rays are a **dark red-purple on the back**, and the pollen is bright white, often creating white blotches on the disk. • Although blennosperma sometimes occurs in open grassy fields, it usually grows in wet areas—sometimes in the highly specialized vernal pool environment.

Distribution: The genus *Blennosperma* has only three species in California and Chile. *B. nanum* occurs in wet, open areas throughout the Central Valley and Sierra foothills below 3000'. It extends to the California coastal ranges and to the Channel Islands. **Names:** *Blennosperma* means 'slimy seed.' *Nanum* means 'dwarf.' **Also known as** yellow carpet. **Typical location:** Fringes of vernal pools atop Table Mountain near Oroville (1500').

Related Plant: Woolly marbles (*Psilocarphus brevissimus*; bottom photo) is another composite that frequents drying vernal pools and other formerly wet environments. You might not think it is a composite, however, until you realize that the 'furry white marbles' are disk flowers—it has none of the showier ray

flowers you associate with composites like daisies and sunflowers. *P. brevissimus* (usually only an inch tall) grows in dense mats in drying vernal pools throughout the CA-FP below 6500'. *Psilocarphus* means 'slender chaff.' *Brevissimus* means 'very short.' Annual. Range: Same plus Low Montane.

yellow • many ray and disk flowers • annual

California Thistle

Cirsium occidentale var. *californicum*

CENTRAL VALLEY, FOOTHILLS, LOW MONTANE

Despite not having any of the showy ray flowers characteristic of so many of the composites, California thistle is nonetheless a spectacular collection of flowers. Its **large (1–3") flowerhead is packed with scores of beautiful, thread-like, pink to rose disk flowers.** The bracts under the flowers are cobwebby at the base. • As with most thistles, the plant is tall (2–4') and rough with coarse, spiny leaves. It commonly grows in disturbed areas.

Distribution: The genus *Cirsium* is composed of approximately 200 species in North America and Eurasia. *C. occidentale* var. *californica* occurs in disturbed areas throughout the Sierra below 6500'. It extends to the Coast Range of southern California. **Names:** *Cirsium* means 'swollen' in reference to thistles' reputed medicinal qualities. *Occidentale* means 'western.' *Californicum* (see p. 59). **Formerly called** *C. californicum.* **Typical location:** Rocky slopes along Hite's Cove Trail west of Yosemite (1500').

Related Plant: Brass buttons (*Cotula coronopifolia*; bottom photo) is another showy composite with only disk flowers. Though much smaller than the thistle ($^{1}/_{4}$–$^{1}/_{2}$" flowerheads on a 8–16" stem), these **bright yellow buttons** are quite attractive and showy. An alien found mostly along the California coast, it can also be found around vernal pools in the Jepson Prairie Preserve near Dixon (50'). *Cotula* means 'small cup.' *Coronopifolia* means 'crown-leaf.' Perennial. Range: Central Valley.

pink • many disk flowers • biennial

267

Common Senecio

Senecio vulgaris

CENTRAL VALLEY, FOOTHILLS, LOW MONTANE

Almost all *Senecios* have yellow (or orange) flowers. Although some *Senecio* species have a few ray flowers, *S. vulgaris* is one of the many with only disk flowers. The 4–20" stem bears many of the discoid flowerheads. • The yellow disk flowers emerge only slightly above the long, green phyllaries; as is typical (and identifying) of *Senecio* species, these **phyllaries are pointed and black-tipped.** • Scattered along the stem are several rough, pinnately lobed leaves. The stem is filled with milky sap. • When the flowers go to seed, they have dandelion-like parachutes, as is typical of composites.

Distribution: The genus *Senecio* is composed of approximately 1500 species worldwide. *S. vulgaris* is common in disturbed areas throughout California below 5000'. It is an alien introduced from Eurasia. **Names:** *Senecio* (from the same root as 'senile') means 'old man' in reference to the white pappus (hairs or scales) that carry the seeds on the wind. *Vulgaris* (see p. 176). **Also known as** common butterweed. **Typical location:** Grassy fields of the Jepson Prairie Preserve near Dixon (50').

Related Plant: Pineapple weed (*Chamomilla suaveolens*; bottom photo) is another alien composite with only disk flowers common to disturbed sites in lower elevations throughout the CA-FP. The ¹/₄–¹/₂" **yellow, conical flowerheads are nestled in the soft, fragrant leaves** much like pineapples on a bed of lettuce. *Chamomilla* is of unknown derivation. *Suaveolens* means 'sweet scented.' Annual. Range: Central Valley, Foothills.

yellow • many disk flowers • annual

268

Sierra Lessingia

Lessingia leptoclada

FOOTHILLS, LOW MONTANE

Lessingia is a beautiful, though somewhat puzzling, composite that brings a gentle touch of lavender to waning summer and early fall in low to mid elevations in the Sierra. Growing at the tips of the sticky, much-branched stems are the **delicate ¹/₂" pale to deep lavender flowerheads**. Each head appears to consist of several flaring ray flowers, but a close look reveals something different: no ray flowers at all, but rather 6–25 disk flowers, some of which are quite odd. The flowers around the periphery of the flowerhead have **flaring lobes** that give them the appearance of ray flowers! • Under the flowers, the phyllaries form a long, cylindrical cup; some of the phyllaries curl out, creating a somewhat messy appearance reminiscent of the phyllaries of asters.
• The leaves are mostly basal; the few stem leaves are very small and narrow.

Distribution: The genus *Lessingia* has 14 species in the American West. *L. leptoclada* occurs in open meadows throughout the Sierra from 1200–6000'. **Names:** C.F. Lessing was a 19th-century German specialist in composites. *Leptocladon* means 'thin-stemmed' or 'thin-branched.' **Typical location:** Grassy meadows in Yosemite Valley (4000').

blue-lavender • many disk flowers (some of which resemble ray flowers) • annual

Pearly Everlasting
Anaphalis margaritacea

FOOTHILLS, LOW MONTANE, MID TO HIGH MONTANE

Pearly everlasting and rosy pussytoes (see Related Plant) are closely related composites—they both have only disk flowers and both have flowerheads 'cradled' by overlapping tiers of papery bracts. • In pearly everlasting, many of the small flowerheads are clustered at the tip of the ¹/₂–3' stem. The disk flowers are yellow; the surrounding bracts are white. The common name is wonderfully appropriate because the **pearly white bracts retain their color even when they dry. • In rosy pussytoes, the disk flowers are white and the surrounding papery bracts are rosy-red.** The 4–16" stem bears clusters of the flowerheads and numerous felt-covered, linear leaves.

Distribution: The genus *Anaphalis* has approximately 100 species in North America and Asia. *A. margaritacea* grows in woods and disturbed places from 2000–9500'. It extends north to Alaska and can also be found on the East Coast and in Eurasia. **Names:** *Anaphalis* is an old Greek name of uncertain meaning. *Margaritacea* means 'pearly.' **Typical location:** Wooded edges of Pole Creek in Tahoe area (6300').

Related Plant: Rosy pussytoes/rosy everlasting (*Antennaria rosea*; bottom photo) grows in meadows and on rock ridges throughout the Sierra (and north to Alaska) from 4000–11,500'. *Antennaria* refers to the swollen tips of the pappus, which somewhat resembles a butterfly's antenna. Perennial. Range: Low Montane, Mid to High Montane, Alpine.

white (bracts) with yellow disk flowers • many disk flowers • perennial

Mule Ears
Wyethia mollis
LOW MONTANE, MID TO HIGH MONTANE

Mule ears is one of the **most common and showy** composites of mid elevations in our area. Its bright yellow flowerhead of many disk flowers and 5–11 ray flowers is very large (up to 4" or so across), it grows in **huge masses sometimes almost covering entire hillsides**, and its leaves are enormous (up to 1¹/₂' long and 3–4" wide) and softly hairy. • Whenever you see a hillside of mule ears, you can be pretty certain that hillside is volcanic: mule ears have very long roots ideally suited to reach the water that has seeped deep into the porous volcanic soil. You will usually find the huge leaves growing vertically—this, along with the dense hairs, helps reduce evaporation.

Distribution: The genus *Wyethia* has seven species in our area, though only *W. mollis* occurs above low montane elevations. *W. mollis* grows on open slopes (mostly volcanic) in the central and northern Sierra from 4000–10,500'. It extends to southeast Oregon and western Nevada. **Names:** Nathaniel Wyeth was a 19th-century American explorer. *Mollis* means 'soft' in reference to the downy leaves. **Typical location:** Open volcanic hillsides in Sherwood Forest in Tahoe area (6700').

Related Plant: Balsamroot (*Balsamorhiza sagittata*; bottom photo) **often grows with mule ears and closely resembles it**. Its yellow flowerheads are smaller and brighter than mule ears, it blooms earlier (it is one of the first bloomers of mid-elevation slopes), and its **leaves are shinier, arrow-shaped, and more parallel to the ground**. *B. sagittata* occurs on open slopes throughout the Sierra (and to British Columbia) from 4500–8500'. *Balsamorhiza* means 'balsamroot' and refers to the sticky sap. *Sagittata* means 'arrow-shaped' in reference to the leaves. Perennial. Range: Same.

yellow • many ray and disk flowers • perennial

271

Leafy-headed Aster

Aster foliaceus

LOW MONTANE, MID TO HIGH MONTANE

Leafy-headed aster is one of the most beautiful of the composites for its delicious contrast of intense colors—the **rays are violet to purple and the conspicuous disk flowers are a bright yellow/orange.** • The common name and species name of *A. foliaceus* point to the characteristic that makes this species easy to distinguish from the many other asters and their close relatives, the daisies, which you are likely to find in our area: **there are many green, leafy bracts that stick out perpendicular to the stem directly beneath the flowerhead.** • Like the daisies, the asters typically have numerous ray flowers (which are not yellow) and disk flowers with pappus (i.e., the white hairs, scales, or bristles attached to the seeds). The rays can be bluish, pinkish, purplish, red, or white, but unlike many of the other composites, the rays are not yellow. • It can be difficult to distinguish asters from daisies. Often asters are fall-bloomers but the most reliable difference is in the phyllaries. Asters tend to have 'messy' phyllaries, arranged in three or four overlapping rows (like shingles) and reflexing (bending out) at the tips, whereas daisies (*Erigeron*) usually have their phyllaries arranged in 1–2 neat rows with tips erect. • The leaves of *A. foliaceus* are large (2–6"), broad, and clasping the ¹/₂–3' stem.

Distribution: The genus *Aster* is composed of about 250 species in North America, Eurasia, and Africa. *A. foliaceus* occurs in open woods and meadows throughout the Sierra from 5000–8000'. It extends to Alaska. **Names:** *Aster* means 'star' in reference to the flaring rays. *Foliaceus* means 'leafy.' **Typical location:** Moist meadows around Benson Lake in Yosemite (7000').

blue-lavender • many ray and disk flowers • perennial

Bigelow's Sneezeweed
Helenium bigelovii
LOW MONTANE, MID TO HIGH MONTANE

There are so many genera and species of composites with yellow ray flowers and a central 'button' of yellow, orange, or brown disk flowers that you might just throw up your hands in resignation and call them all DYCs ('damn yellow composites' or, if you're in a cheerier mood, perhaps 'delightful yellow challenges'). There are, however, noticeable differences between some of these many DYCs that help you distinguish and identify.
• Both Bigelow's sneezeweed and California coneflower (see Related Plant) are easily recognizable because they both have very unusual and conspicuous flowerheads. In sneezeweed, **the head of disk flowers is a large (1–1¹/₂") globe from the bottom of which flare out 14–20 yellow ray flowers** in a momentous 'sneeze.' The globe of disk flowers is usually yellow in bloom, drying a dark brown or purple. The 1–3' stem bears narrow leaves that clasp and run down the stem a ways before insertion.

Distribution: The genus *Helenium* has approximately 35 species in North and South America. *H. bigelovii* occurs in wet meadows throughout the Sierra from 3000–10,000'. It extends to the Cascades and the coastal ranges. **Names:** *Helenium* is after Helen of Troy—perhaps this is the flower that launched a thousand ships! J. Bigelow was a plant collector on the Mexican Boundary Survey of the 1850s. Sneezeweed is apparently in reference to the use of this plant (dried and powdered) by pioneers to induce sneezing as a way of relieving congestion. **Also known as** snakeweed. **Typical location:** Along Merced River in Yosemite Valley (4000').

Related Plant: California coneflower (*Rudbeckia californica*; bottom photo) occurs in meadows throughout the Sierra (e.g., Crane flat in Yosemite) from 5000–8000'. The **head of greenish-yellow disk flowers is a tall (1–2"), narrow cylinder rising above the 8–21 long (to 2"), yellow rays that often droop.** The 2–6' stem bears long (to 1'), broad leaves. The Rudbeckias were two Swedish botany professors of the 17th and 18th centuries. *Californica* (see p. 85). Perennial. Range: Same.

yellow • many ray and disk flowers
• perennial

273

Wandering Daisy

Erigeron peregrinus

LOW MONTANE, MID TO HIGH MONTANE

The daisies (*Erigeron*) are one of the most familiar of the composites—you can probably visualize quite easily that large flowerhead with showy ray and disk flowers so characteristic of the daisy. However, it is not always easy to tell the difference between daisies and asters (see p. 272 for an explanation of these differences). • Wandering daisy is a frequent and cheery resident of high mountain meadows. Its **bright yellow disk flowers are surrounded by many (30–100) narrow, overlapping rays of a delicate, pale purple**. Although usually there is only one large (to 2" across) flowerhead per stem, there can be as many as four per plant, and frequently many plants grow together—so you will often find beautiful clusters of these flowers gracing Sierra meadows. • The long (to 8"), relatively narrow leaves are mostly basal but also are spaced occasionally along the 4–20" stem.

Distribution: The genus *Erigeron* has about 375 species worldwide. *E. peregrinus* occurs in mountain meadows throughout the Sierra from 4000–10,000'. It extends north to Alaska and east to Colorado and also occurs in eastern Asia. **Names:** *Erigeron* means 'early old age.' *Peregrinus* means 'exotic' or 'foreign' or 'wanderer.' **Also known as** mountain daisy. **Typical location:** Along Tuolumne River below Tuolumne Meadows in Yosemite (8500').

Related Plant: Coulter's daisy (*E. coulteri*; bottom photo) is another very showy daisy with **many (45–140) narrow rays that are bright white and clearly (though barely) separated** (i.e., not overlapping). The ³/4" flowerhead is atop a ¹/2–2' stem that also bears more or less clasping, ovate leaves. *E. coulteri* occurs in wet meadows through-out the Sierra from 6000–10,000'. *Coulteri* (see p. 98). Perennial. Range: Same.

purple • many ray and disk flowers • perennial

274

Heartleaf Arnica
Arnica cordifolia
LOW MONTANE, MID TO HIGH MONTANE

In the highly populated world of composite species with yellow ray and disk flowers, the arnicas stand out, both for their beauty and their easy recognizability. Their flowerheads are large and showy and their **leaves are** unique to this 'world'—**broad and in opposite pairs**. There is something deeply satisfying about the symmetry and elegance of these bright-flowered beauties.
• Heartleaf arnica is especially pleasing to the eye, with its 2–4 pairs of **large (2–4"), dark green, heart-shaped leaves** and 1–5 bright yellow flowerheads poised gracefully at the end of long pedicels. The 6–15 rays are broad and pointed and overlap slightly at their base. Coming across this ¹/₂–2' plant lighting up the shade of its forest habitat is always a surprise and a delight.

Distribution: The genus *Arnica* is composed of approximately 27 species in North America and Eurasia. *A. cordifolia* occurs in forest openings throughout the central and northern Sierra from 4000–10,000'. It extends west to the northern California coast and east to Wyoming. **Names:** *Arnica* means 'lamb's skin' in reference to the soft-hairy leaves. *Cordifolia* means 'heart-shaped leaves.' **Typical location:** Woods along Shirley Creek in Tahoe area (6500').

Related Plant: Soft arnica (*A. mollis*; bottom photo), as the name suggests, has **sticky, softly hairy leaves** (3–5 opposite pairs) and stems. It often grows in great masses in meadows throughout the Sierra (and north to Canada) from 8000–10,000'. *Mollis* (see p. 271). Perennial. Range: Mid to High Montane.

yellow • many ray and disk flowers • perennial

Drummond's Thistle

Cirsium scariosum

LOW MONTANE, MID TO HIGH MONTANE, ALPINE

Even without the showy ray flowers of many composites, the thistles are quite dramatic and interesting plants. They usually have tall stems with rugged, prickly leaves and large heads of colorful, spiny disk flowers. • Drummond's thistle is unusual for a thistle in a couple of ways: although the stem can be over 3' tall, **most plants are stemless with the flowerheads nestled right in the rosette of spiny, basal leaves;** and the disk flowers in the 1–2" wide flowerheads are usually a **creamy white (sometimes pale purple).** • Because of the color of the flowers and because the flowerheads are usually almost flat on the ground, this thistle is easy to overlook, but it deserves a close look because despite its rather rough appearance its flowers are really quite delicately beautiful.

Distribution: *C. scariosum* (in its various forms) is widespread in meadows throughout the Sierra from 3000–11,000'. It extends from British Columbia to Baja. **Names:** *Cirsium* (see p. 267). *Scariosum* means 'scarious' (i.e., membranous and translucent) in reference to the phyllaries. **Also known as** dwarf thistle. **Formerly called** *C. drummondii.* **Typical location:** Grassy clearings along Sagehen Creek in Tahoe area (6200').

Related Plant: Anderson's thistle (*C. andersonii*; bottom photo) is a more typical thistle with **stems as tall as 3' and cylindrical flowerheads of rose-red disk flowers.** The leaves are spiny and deeply divided. *C. andersonii* grows in dryish openings throughout the Sierra (and Cascades) from 5000–10,000'. Nils Andersson was a 19th-century Swedish botanist who collected plants in California. Perennial. Range: Low Montane, Mid to High Montane.

creamy white (sometimes purplish) • many disk flowers • perennial or biennial

Yarrow
Achillea millefolium

LOW MONTANE, MID TO HIGH MONTANE, ALPINE

Most composites that have both ray flowers and disk flowers have a central 'button' of scores of tubular disk flowers surrounded by numerous radiating, narrow ray flowers. Yarrow is an odd exception to this norm. • Yarrow doesn't even look like a composite: its **many flowerheads are very small (¹/₄") and occur in flat-topped clusters, and its ray flowers are tiny and round rather than ray-like.** Only a few (3–8) of these white or pink ray flowers surround the tiny central cluster of 15–40 buff-colored disk flowers. • The leaves are quite distinctive as well—very deeply divided (fern-like) and strongly aromatic. The 1–4' stem is densely covered with white, woolly hairs.

Distribution: The genus *Achillea* is composed of approximately 85 species in North America, Eurasia, and northern Africa. *A. millefolium* is highly variable and widespread throughout the CA-FP from 3000' to (in a smaller form) above timberline. It is circumboreal, ranging widely in the Northern Hemisphere. **Names:** *Achillea* is after the legendary Greek hero, Achilles, who presumably used yarrow to cure some of his soldiers' wounds. *Millefolium* (and the common name milfoil) means 'thousand-leaved' in reference to the much-divided, fern-like leaves. **Also known as** milfoil. **Formerly called** *A. lanulosum.* **Typical location:** Grassy meadows in Yosemite Valley (4000').

white (or pink) • few ray flowers and many disk flowers • perennial

Orange Mountain Dandelion

Agoseris aurantiaca

LOW MONTANE, MID TO HIGH MONTANE, ALPINE

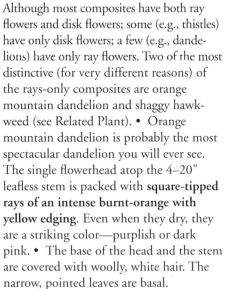

Although most composites have both ray flowers and disk flowers; some (e.g., thistles) have only disk flowers; a few (e.g., dandelions) have only ray flowers. Two of the most distinctive (for very different reasons) of the rays-only composites are orange mountain dandelion and shaggy hawkweed (see Related Plant). • Orange mountain dandelion is probably the most spectacular dandelion you will ever see. The single flowerhead atop the 4–20" leafless stem is packed with **square-tipped rays of an intense burnt-orange with yellow edging**. Even when they dry, they are a striking color—purplish or dark pink. • The base of the head and the stem are covered with woolly, white hair. The narrow, pointed leaves are basal.

Distribution: The genus *Agoseris* has 10 species in North America. *A. aurantiaca* occurs uncommonly in meadows throughout the Sierra from 6000–11,500'. It extends all the way to Alaska. **Names:** *Agoseris* is the old Greek name for chicory. *Aurantiaca* means 'orange-red.' **Typical location:** Dry, grassy meadows along Pole Creek in Tahoe area (6600').

Related Plant: Shaggy hawkweed (*Hieracium horridum*, bottom photo) has small, rather inconspicuous **yellow flowers (rays only)**; its distinctive characteristic is its remarkably hairy leaves, which feel soothingly soft to the touch. *H. horridum* grows in rocky places throughout the Sierra (and into Oregon) from 5000–11,000'. *Hieracium* means 'hawk.' *Horridum* means 'prickly.' Perennial. Range: Same.

orange • many ray flowers • perennial

Western Eupatorium
Ageratina occidentalis
MID TO HIGH MONTANE, ALPINE

Eupatorium is proof that a composite doesn't have to have ray flowers to be gorgeous and showy. This ¹/₂–2 ¹/₂' woody perennial bears many **dense clusters of pink (or white or bluish) flowerheads of long-protruding disk flowers.** Usually many plants grow together in dense masses, **cascading down rock ledges and cliffs**—the splashes of color and sweet fragrance put on quite a show! • The leaves are triangular and toothed and if you happen to crush them, the resulting odor might encourage you to walk more carefully next time! • I've developed quite a special affection for eupatorium because it is a late-bloomer, bringing its charms to the rocks in fall when most other flowers have already gone to seed.

Distribution: The genus *Ageratina* is composed of four species in western North America and Mexico. *A. occidentalis* occurs in rocky areas throughout the Sierra from 6500–11,000'. It extends to Washington. **Names:** *Ageratina* is Latin for 'resembling Ageratum.' *Occidentalis* means 'western.' **Formerly called** *Eupatorium occidentale.* **Typical location:** Rock ledges along head of Pole Creek in Tahoe area (7200').

pink (or white or bluish) • many disk flowers • perennial

Silky Raillardella
Raillardella argentea
MID TO HIGH MONTANE, ALPINE

Silky raillardella is another of the composites with only disk flowers (for others, see pp. 266-70, 276, and 279). Its common names and Latin species name point to its most distinctive feature—its **basal leaves are covered with fine, silky, silvery hairs** that reflect an amazing amount of dazzling sunlight in the thin air of these high altitudes. • Like most alpine plants, silky raillardella is **dwarfed**. Each 1–7" peduncle rising above the basal leaves bears one cylindrical flowerhead, which holds 7–25 bright yellow disk flowers. The 2-parted yellow stigmas project gracefully out of the flower tubes.

Distribution: The genus *Raillardella* is composed of only three species in California, Nevada, and Oregon. *R. argentea* occurs in open, gravelly areas throughout the Sierra from 9000–12,000'. It extends north to Oregon and east to western Nevada. **Names:** *Raillardella* is of uncertain meaning. *Argentea* means 'silvery' in reference to the leaves. **Also known as** silver mat. **Typical location:** Rocky flats near Gaylor Lakes in Yosemite (10,000').

yellow • many disk flowers • perennial

Dwarf Alpine Daisy

Erigeron pygmaeus

MID TO HIGH MONTANE, ALPINE

Some of the most beautiful of the composites grow in the harshest environments on open windswept ridges high above timberline. What makes these flowers so striking is the size of the flowerheads in relation to the height of the plant. Most alpine plants adapt to the sweeping winds and intense solar radiation of these elevations by dwarfing—rarely do these plants exceed 1' tall and more frequently rise only a few inches above the ground. Because their flowerheads are often the same size as those of their much taller low elevation relatives, the flowerheads on many of these alpine 'dwarfs' appear enormous. • Dwarf alpine daisy **is only 1–3" tall and the glorious flowerheads of blue-lavender rays and bright yellow disks can be up to** ³/₄**" across!** At this flower width-to-stem height ratio, just imagine how big a flower a 6' plant of low elevation would have! • Dwarf alpine daisy is hairy and sticky with mostly basal leaves. The 15–35 blue rays provide a vivid contrast to the long-protruding, yellow disk flowers.

Distribution: *E. pygmaeus* grows on rocky ridges in the southern part of our area from 10,000' to the summits of the highest peaks. It extends into the high mountains of western and central Nevada. **Names:** *Erigeron* (see p. 274). *Pygmaeus* means 'pygmy.' **Typical location:** Rocky flats on summit of Freel Peak at south end of Tahoe area (11,000').

Related Plant: Alpine gold (*Hulsea algida*; bottom photo) is another stunning composite of **very high elevations** (10,000' to the summits of the highest peaks). It grows to about 16"; its **head of 25–60 bright yellow ray flowers and many, many disk flowers can be as large as 1" across.** The entire plant is sticky and aromatic. G.W. Hulse was a 19th-century U.S. army surgeon and botanist. *Algida* means 'of the cold.' Perennial. Range: Same.

blue-lavender • many ray and disk flowers
• perennial

Glossary

alien: not native, introduced from another place (see mouse-ear chickweed, p. 103)

annual: living only one year, having to start over each year from seed

anther: the pollen-producing tip of the male sex part of the flower

auricle: a small appendage at the base of a leaf blade or a sepal (see baby blue-eyes p. 123)

banner: the upper petal of a pea flower (see pea family, pp. 211–31)

basal leaf: leaves located at the base of a plant (see foothill saxifrage, p. 112)

bracts: leaf-like structures performing different function than a leaf does (see purple owl's-clover, p. 148)

CA-FP: California Floristic Province

calyx: collective term for the sepals

composite flower: consisting of many separate flowers in a tight head (see composite family, pp. 261–81)

cushion plant: a plant of the alpine zone with densely-packed, ground hugging leaves (see Coville's phlox, p. 199)

disk flower: in the composite family the small, tubular flowers comprising the 'button' in the center of the flowerhead; some composites only have disk flowers (see brass buttons, p. 267)

endemic: confined to a certain region, e.g., a Sierra endemic is found only in the Sierra (see glassy onion, p. 70)

fellfield: type of tundra that is 35–50% bare rock with cushion plants, mosses, and lichens between.

filament: the stalk of the male part of a flower which bears the anther at its tip

5-merous: with plant parts (i.e., petals, sepals, anthers) occurring in 5's

green root-parasite: having some green leaves for photosynthesis but also parasitizing other plants

inferior ovary: an ovary situated below the petals (see bellflower family, pp. 181–85)

inflorescence: the cluster of flowers on a plant

keel: the lower two petals cradling the reproductive parts in pea flowers, somewhat resembling the keel of a boat (see pea family, pp. 211–31)

leaf axil: where the leaf stalk joins the plant stem

palmate: usually describing a leaf having divisions or lobes radiating from a central point (see Douglas lupine, p. 213)

panicle: when the pedicels (individual flower stalks) are attached to a branched plant stem (see brook saxifrage, p. 118)

pedicel: the stalk of an individual flower

peduncle: the stalk of an entire inflorescence

pendent: drooping or hanging from a point of attachment above (see globe lily, p. 50)

perfoliate: a leaf transsected by its stem, so the leaf completely surrounds the stem (see miner's lettuce, p. 253)

perennial: living for more than one year; usually the above-ground part of the plant withers, but the rootstalk remains for many years to sprout new stems

petaloid: resembling a petal, usually referring to a sepal that is colorful like a petal (see lily family, pp. 47–61)

phyllary: one of the narrow, green bracts forming the cup of the flowerhead in the composite family (see composite family, pp. 261–81)

pinnate: usually describing a leaf having a main central axis with secondary branches, resembling rungs of a ladder (see low polemonium, p. 197)

pistil: the female sex part of the flower, including the ovary, style, and stigma

raceme: when the pedicels (individual flower stalks) are attached to an unbranched plant stem

ray flowers: the wide-flaring flowers (rays) of members of the composite family (see orange mountian dandelion, p. 278)

rosette: a crowded whorl of basal leaves (see Pacific sedum, p. 137)

sepal: the usually green part of the flower beneath the petals, forming the outer protective layer in the bud

silicle: a small, round silique (see lacepod, p. 81)

silique: a long, thin seedpod with a central partition of the mustard family (see field mustard, p. 83)

stamen: the male sex part of the flower, including the filament and the anther

staminode: a sterile stamen, i.e., the stamen has no anther (see scarlet penstemon, p. 160)

stigma: the pollen-receiving tip of the female sex part

style: the thin stalk connecting the ovary and the stigma of the female sex part

subshrub: a plant with the lower stems woody the upper stems and twigs not woody and lying back seasonally

succulent: usually describing a leaf that is fleshy, thick, and juicy (see stonecrop family, pp. 135–41)

superior ovary: an ovary that is situated above the petals (see mustard family, pp. 79–91)

tendril: a slender, coiling appendage on a stem which is used for climbing and support (see tangier pea, p. 219)

tepal: one of the petals or sepals in flowers whose sepals look just like the petals (see amaryllis family, pp. 63–77)

umbel: where all the pedicels (the individual flower stalks) radiate from the same point on the plant stem (see amaryllis family, pp. 63–77)

wings: the two lateral petals in flowers of the pea family, usually cradling the keel

whorled: three or more similar structures (leaves, bracts, etc.) encircling a stem (see tiger lily, p. 57)

References

Bailey, L.H. *How Plants Get Their Names.* New York, NY: Dover Publishing, 1963.

Barbour, M., and J. Major, eds. *Terrestrial Vegetation of California.* New York, NY: Wiley and Sons, 1977.

Blackwell, L. *Wildflowers of the Tahoe Sierra.* Edmonton, AB: Lone Pine Publishing, 1997.

Borror, D. *Dictionary of Word Roots and Combining Forms.* Palo Alto, CA: Mayfield Publishing, 1971.

Botti, S. and A. Mendershausen. *Wildflowers of the Hite's Cove Trail.* Fresno, CA: Pioneer Publishing, 1985.

Carville, J. *Lingering in Tahoe's Wild Gardens.* Chicago Park, CA: Mt. Gypsy Press, 1989.

Crittenson, M. and D. Telfer. *Wildflowers of the West.* Millbrae, CA: Celestial Arts, 1975.

Fauver, T. *Wildflower Walking in Lakes Basin.* Orinda, CA: Fauver and Steinbach, 1992.

Hickman, J., ed. *The Jepson Manual of Higher Plants in California.* Berkeley, CA: University of California Press, 1993.

Horn, E. *Wildflowers 1: The Cascades.* Beaverton, OR: Touchstone Press, 1972.

Morgenson, D. *Yosemite Wildflower Trails.* Yosemite, CA: YNHA, 1975.

Munz, P. *California Spring Wildflowers.* Berkeley, CA: University of California Press, 1961.

Munz, P. *California Mountain Wildflowers.* Berkeley, CA: University of California Press, 1963.

Munz, P. *A California Flora.* Berkeley, CA: University of California Press, 1968.

Niehaus, T. *Pacific States Wildflowers.* Boston, MA: Houghton Mifflin, 1976.

Nilsson, K. *A Wildflower by any other Name.* Yosemite, CA: Yosemite Assoc., 1994.

Pojar, T. and A MacKinnon. *Plants of the Pacific Northwest Coast.* Lone Pine Publishing, Edmonton, Alberta, 1994.

Sawyer, J. and T. Keeler-Wolf. *A Manual of California Vegetation.* Sacramento, CA: CNPS, 1995.

Smith, G. *A Flora of the Tahoe Basin.* San Francisco, CA: USF, 1984.

Spellenberg, R. *The Audubon Society Field Guide to North American Wildflowers: Western Region.* New York, NY: Alfred Knopf, 1979.

Weeden, N. *A Sierra Nevada Flora.* Berkeley, CA: Wilderness Press, 1996.

Selected articles from *FREMONTIA: A Journal of the California Native Plant Society:*

Keator, G. "Differentiating California's Brodiaeas," 14(4), Jan. 87, 20–24.

Koptur, S. "Extrafloral Nectaries in California Plants," 24(2), April 96, 23–26.

McDonald, H. "The Genus Calochortus in California: part II," 25(1), Jan. 97, 20–25.

Mills, J. and J. Kummerow. "Root Parasitism in Indian Paintbrush," 16(3), Oct. 88, 12–14.

Norwick, S. "Vernal Pools and other Seasonal Bodies of Standing Water," 19(3), July 91, 8–19.

Preston, R. "Theme and Variations on the Rock Cress," 19(1), Jan. 91, 19–21.

Ross, E. "Insect/Plant Relationship: A Photographic Essay," 24(2), April 96, 3–22.

Thorp, R. and J. Leong. "Native Bee Pollinators of Vernal Pool Plants," 23(2), April 95, 3–7.

Index

Scientific Names

Common Names

287

About the Author

Laird R. Blackwell, who received his Ph.D. from Stanford University, has lived and studied in the Sierra Nevada for over 20 years. He lives at Lake Tahoe, where he is professor and Chairman of Humanities at Sierra Nevada College, teaching courses in field ecology, literature, psychology, and mythology. His first wildflower book, *Wildflowers of the Tahoe Sierra*, was published in spring 1997. In this, his most recent book, he covers a much wider area from the Central Valley to the crest of the Sierra. Laird and his wife Melinda share a passion for teaching, wildflowers, and the mountain wilds.